Nursing Malpractice

Sidestepping Legal Minefields

NURSING MALPRACTICE

Sidestepping Legal Minefields

Ann Helm, RN, MS, JD, Executive Clinical Editor
Consultant — Medical Malpractice
Faculty, Oregon Health Sciences University
Lieutenant Colonel, United States Air Force Reserves,
Judge Advocate General Department
Portland

LIPPINCOTT WILLIAMS & WILKINS
A **Wolters Kluwer** Company
Philadelphia • Baltimore • New York • London
Buenos Aires • Hong Kong • Sydney • Tokyo

Staff

Publisher
Judith A. Schilling McCann,
RN, MSN

Editorial Director
H. Nancy Holmes

Clinical Director
Joan M. Robinson, RN, MSN

Senior Art Director
Arlene Putterman

Clinical Editor
Jana L. Sciarra, RN, MSN, CRNP
(clinical project manager)

Editors
Jennifer P. Kowalak (senior
associate editor), Kate Jackson,
Jacqueline E. Mills

Copy Editors
Kimberly Bilotta,
Heather Ditch, Amy Furman,
Pamela Wingrod

**Digital Composition
Services**
Diane Paluba (manager),
Joyce Rossi Biletz (senior
desktop assistant),
Donna S. Morris

Manufacturing
Patricia K. Dorshaw (senior
manager), Beth Janae Orr
(book production coordinator)

Editorial Assistants
Danielle J. Barsky,
Beverly Lane, Linda Ruhf

Librarian
Catherine M. Heslin

Indexer
Ellen S. Brennan

Cover
Larry Didona

NM – D N O
04 03 02   10 9 8 7 6 5 4 3 2 1

**Library of Congress
Cataloging-in-Publication Data**

Nursing malpractice : sidestepping legal minefields.
    p. ; cm.
    Includes index.
    1. Nurses—Malpractice—United States.
    2.Nursng—Law and legislation—United States.
    I. Lippincott Williams & Wilkins.
    [DNLM: 1. Legislation, Nursing—United
States—Legal Cases. 2. Malpractice—legislation &
jurisprudence— United States—Legal Cases.
WY 44 AA1 N974 2003]
KF2915.N83N877 2003
344.73'0414—dc21
ISBN 1-58255-207-X (pbk. : alk. paper)   2002011858

Contents

	Contributors and consultants	vii
	Foreword	ix
One	**Nursing practice and the law**	1
Two	**Medication errors**	34
Three	**Failure to communicate information**	49
Four	**Failure to document information**	66
Five	**Failure to perform a proper assessment**	88
Six	**Failure to protect**	106
Seven	**Failure to perform reasonable patient care**	123
Eight	**Breach of confidentiality**	141
Nine	**Criminal actions**	160
Ten	**Advocacy, ethics, and legal duties**	173
Eleven	**Legal risks of understaffing**	188
Twelve	**Surviving a lawsuit**	203
	Glossary	216
	Court case citation index	232
	General index	236

Contributors and consultants

Ginny Wacker Guido, RN, MSN, FAAN, JD
Associate Dean and Director,
Graduate Studies
University of North Dakota, College
of Nursing
Grand Forks

Barbara E. Hirsch, BA, BSN, JD
Director, Legal Affairs and Risk
Management
Washington Adventist Hospital
Takoma Park, Md.

Carol Holmes, RN, BSN, JD, PC
Attorney
Lake Orion, Mich.

Deborah Lessard, RN, BSN, JD
Principle
Lessard Law Office
Mechanicsburg, Pa.

Linda MacDonald Glenn, JD, LLM candidate
Adjunct Professor
University of Vermont School of
Nursing
Burlington

Janet E. Michael, RN, MS, JD
Nurse Attorney in Private Practice
Law Office of Janet E. Michael
Portland, Maine

Linda F. Rosen, RN, MA, JD
Attorney at Law
M. Mark Mendel, Ltd.
Philadelphia

Jacqueline Walus-Wigle, RN, JD, CPHQ
Compliance, Regulatory and
External Affairs Director
University of California San Diego
Health Plan Services

LaTonia Denise Wright, RN, BSN, JD
Attorney and Healthcare
Consultant
Law Office of LaTonia Denise
Wright, RN, LLC
Cincinnati

If you've never been sued for nursing malpractice, the information in *Nursing Malpractice: Sidestepping Legal Minefields* alone can help you ensure that your name never appears as a defendant on a malpractice complaint. If you *are* sued, the material in this invaluable nursing manual can guide you methodically through that process with some degree of quietude — and with expert guidance for your practice in the future.

Profit over patients. You've heard this slogan — and seen headlines such as these: *Nursing mistakes kill, injure thousands — Cost-cutting exacts toll on patients, hospital staffs.* The numbers are astounding. In its 1999 landmark report on medical errors in the United States, the Institute of Medicine estimated that as many as 98,000 deaths occur every year as a result of preventable medical errors. In September 2000, the Chicago Tribune cited "at least 1,720 hospital patients accidentally killed and 9,584 others injured since 1995 from the actions or inactions of registered nurses across the country."*

But that's not *you.* You're a *good* nurse, right?

Until one morning when the Risk Management Office notifies you that you're being sued for nursing malpractice! You struggle to remember the patient. Was it a "near miss"? Was there even a "bad" outcome? You want to stop everything. Find the chart *now.* You're preoccupied with trying to recall every detail of your care to that patient.

Or, you vividly *do* recall that patient, the infant, and her death. But how can *you* be responsible for understaffing that night? For the physician's refusal to come in for the delivery? For a vacuum extractor that malfunctioned?

Your world has turned upside down. Will the hospital back you up — or support the physician? Will you still have a job or can they fire you? What will your colleagues think? Your family? Will anyone trust you alone with a patient again? Will you lose your license? How can you continue to do your job today, tomorrow, without being obsessed with worry and second-guessing your actions?

When did every step of nursing become like walking alone through a minefield?

Nursing Malpractice: Sidestepping Legal Minefields steers you nimbly through that minefield. It shows you where danger lies and tells you how to chart your path.

The unique approach in this indispensable book brings the lessons home. Chapters open with two actual, recent nursing malpractice lawsuits; you read all about the charges, the nurse's defense, and the outcome. Then you learn about the le-

*Michael J. Berens, *Chicago Tribune,* September 11, 2000

gal points at issue in each case, how the nurse could have evaded the lawsuit, and the specific ways *you* can keep from committing the same errors in your practice. To further illustrate key and related points, chapters highlight many additional precedent-setting court cases involving nurses around the country.

Attention-getting graphic icons draw your eye to expert opinions on specific legal points, additional related court cases, and case lessons to take to heart. The glossary defines the legal terms you see written in ***bold italic*** type in the chapters. You'll also find a general index and an index of the court case citations.

Why are nurses sued? For all the reasons *Nursing Malpractice* explains in detail — medication errors and omissions; failure to monitor the patient, to document all nursing actions, to communicate timely and clearly with physicians and other providers; misuse of equipment; failure to educate the patient and family; and failure to provide a safe environment, including misuse of chemical and physical restraints and breaches in patient confidentiality and privacy — to list just a few.

If you *are* sued, how can you prove you didn't commit malpractice? What do courts consider the appropriate standard of nursing care?

Nursing Malpractice: Sidestepping Legal Minefields gathers the court cases that define your legal risks; quotes the opinions of legal experts; and applies the case lessons to your practice. It shows you legally how to meet the best standards of patient care — and how to prove that you

did. What's more, it shows you how to legally advocate for your patient — and yourself — as a nurse.

Once you're educated to the risks that lead to nursing malpractice lawsuits, you're armed with a detector to cross that minefield. You'll have renewed confidence in your nursing practice and can clearly focus on what you love best: providing high quality care to all your patients.

Ann Helm, RN, BSN, MS, JD
Consultant — Medical Malpractice
Faculty, Oregon Health Sciences
    University
Lt. Col, U.S. Air Force Reserves,
    Judge Advocate General
    Department
Portland

Chapter One ●●●●●●●●●●●●●●●●●●●●●●●●

NURSING PRACTICE AND THE LAW

NO LEGAL ISSUE sparks as much anxiety among nurses as malpractice liability. Malpractice litigation can be emotionally harrowing, professionally devastating, and financially disastrous. Unfortunately, more and more nurses are being named in lawsuits, and this trend shows no sign of changing. Several reasons exist for this phenomenon:
● Patients are increasingly knowledgeable about health care, and their expectations are higher.
● To help contain costs, the health care system is increasingly replacing nurses with technicians or aides, whom the nurses typically supervise. The nurses are then responsible for their own actions as well as those these subordinates.
● Nurses are increasingly autonomous in their practice, making them more liable for errors and increasing their likelihood of being sued.
● The courts are expanding the definition of *liability*, holding all types of professionals to higher standards of accountability.

Losing a malpractice lawsuit can jeopardize your career. Prospective employers and insurance companies will inquire whether you've been found liable for nursing malpractice, or if you've ever been a *defendant* in a lawsuit. If you have, you may find job hunting more difficult. (See *National Practitioner Data Bank,* pages 2 and 3.) You'll also pay a higher premium for *professional liability insurance*, and some insurance companies may refuse to insure you.

What's more, a judgment against you may involve a large amount of money. According to the American Nurses Association (ANA), the average award in a claim against a nurse is $145,000. The highest judgment against a nurse was $5 million, awarded after a nurse failed to read a medication label and administered 10 times the ordered dose of lidocaine.

Fortunately, you can limit your vulnerability to malpractice litigation. The most important strategy is to give your patients the best possible nursing care, according to the highest professional *standards*. Standards of care consist of the limitations set out in every state's

1

National Practitioner Data Bank

The National Practitioner Data Bank, which began operation in 1990, stores malpractice data on a national scale. The data bank collects information about physicians, dentists, nurses, and other health care practitioners who have paid malpractice judgments, entered into settlements, or had adverse actions taken against their licenses or privileges to practice. The information collected is available for review by potential employers. (The information isn't available to the general public at this time.) The data bank was created under the Health Care Quality Improvement Act of 1986 and the Medicare and Medicaid Patient and Program Protection Act of 1987.

Reporting requirements

All hospitals and health care facilities, professional health care societies, state licensure boards, and insurance companies are required to report the following information about nurses to the data bank:

- malpractice payments made by a nurse (including judgments, arbitration decisions, and out-of-court settlements)
- actions taken against a nurse's clinical privileges
- adverse licensure actions, including revocations, suspensions, reprimands, censure, or probation.

Failure to report a nurse's malpractice payment of any amount — no matter how small — carries a $10,000 fine. However, the fact that a suit has been filed isn't, by itself, reportable; only the making of any size payment is. Adverse clinical privilege actions against nurses may be reported at the discretion of the reviewing health care agency.

Federal agencies

Under the law, federal agencies aren't required to report to the National Practitioner Data Bank. However, the Department of Defense, Drug Enforcement Administration, and Department of Health and Human Services have voluntarily agreed to observe the regulations.

Availability of information

The information in the data bank isn't available to the general public nor is it available to attorneys except in a very specific context. If a practitioner is sued and it's determined that the employer didn't check the data bank, the plaintiff's attorney can send verification that the employing institution didn't check, along with the charges currently pending. If a similar case is in the data bank, notification will be sent to the plaintiff's attorney. State licensing boards, hospitals, professional societies, and health care facilities involved in peer review may access the data bank. Nurses and other health care practitioners have access to records that pertain to themselves.

All hospitals and other clinical settings must check the data bank when a nurse applies for clinical privileges. The hospital must request information on the nurse again every 2 years. The courts will pre-

National Practitioner Data Bank *(continued)*

sume that the hospital is aware of any information the data bank contains on any nurse or other practitioner in its employ. If knowledge of the information contained in the data bank would have resulted in denial of clinical privileges, the hospital could be held liable for negligence in hiring a practitioner involved in a malpractice lawsuit.

Information in the data bank

Reports made to the data bank will include the following information:

- practitioner's full name, home address, date of birth, professional schools attended and graduation dates, place of employment, Social Security number, and license number and state
- name, title, and phone number of the official submitting the report

- relationship of the reporting person to the practitioner
- dates of judgment or settlement or amount paid
- description of judgment, settlement, or action.

Disputing a report

If a report about you is submitted to the data bank, you'll receive a copy for your review. If you believe the report is in error, ask the official submitting the report to correct it. The official making the report must submit corrections to the data bank.

If you fail to get satisfaction from the reporting official, you'll need to follow a detailed procedure for disputing the report. This must be done within 60 days of the initial processing of the report. Ultimately, you may request review from the Secretary of Health and Human Services.

---

nurse practice act, policies and procedures established by the health care facility where you work, standards adapted by the ANA, and standards of clinical specialty nursing organizations. Every nurse should be familiar with the nurse practice act of her state and other standards applicable to her practice.

You can further protect yourself by becoming familiar with malpractice law. This chapter describes malpractice issues, defines key legal terms, and explains legal doctrines that may be used as a defense during a malpractice lawsuit. You'll find extensive information on

steps to take to avoid malpractice suits and advice on how to shop for professional liability insurance.

Understanding malpractice law

Our legal system's view of malpractice evolved from the premise that everyone is responsible, or liable, for the consequences of his own actions. Malpractice law deals with a professional's liability for negligent acts, omissions, and intentional harms. (See *Understanding tort law,* pages 4 and 5.)

NURSING LIABILITY

Educational and licensing requirements for nurses increased after World War II as nursing tasks became more complex, leading to specialization. These changes meant that nurses began to make independent judgments. Although this increased responsibility provides a more rewarding working environment, it also makes nurses more liable for errors and increases their likelihood of being sued.

Causes of lawsuits against nurses

Patient falls and medication errors are the two most common causes of lawsuits against nurses. Other problems that prompt lawsuits include:
- operating room errors, such as sponges or instruments being left

---

Understanding tort law

Most lawsuits against nurses fall into the tort category. If you're ever a defendant in a lawsuit, understanding the distinctions in this broad category may prove important.

A ***tort*** is a civil wrong or injury resulting from a breach of a legal duty that exists by virtue of society's expectations regarding interpersonal conduct or by the assumption of a duty inherent in a professional relationship (as opposed to a legal duty that exists by virtue of a contractual relationship). More generally, you may define a tort as "any action or omission that harms somebody." Malpractice refers to a tort committed by a professional acting in his professional capacity.

Unintentional vs. intentional torts

The law broadly divides torts into two categories — unintentional and intentional. An *unintentional tort* is a civil wrong resulting from the defendant's negligence. If someone sues you for negligence, he must prove four things in order to win:
- You owed him a specific duty. (In nursing malpractice cases, this duty is equivalent to the standard of care.)
- You breached this duty.
- The plaintiff was harmed. (The harm can be physical, mental, emotional, or financial.)
- Your breach of duty caused the harm.

An *intentional tort* is a deliberate invasion of someone's legal right. In a malpractice case involving an intentional tort, the plaintiff doesn't need to prove that you owed him a duty. The duty at issue (for example, not to touch people without their permission) is defined by law, and you're presumed to owe him this duty. The plaintiff must still prove that you breached this duty and that this breach caused him harm. These lawsuits are usually based on a theory of lack of informed consent.

Understanding tort law *(continued)*

TORT CLAIM	ACTIONS THAT LEAD TO CLAIM

Unintentional tort

Negligence	• Leaving foreign objects inside a patient after surgery • Failing to observe a patient as the physician ordered • Failing to obtain informed consent before a treatment or procedure • Failing to report a change in a patient's vital signs or status • Failing to report a staff member's negligence that you witnessed • Failing to provide for a patient's safety • Failing to provide the patient with appropriate teaching before discharge

Intentional tort

Assault	• Threatening a patient
Battery	• Assisting in nonemergency surgery performed without the consent of the patient • Forcing a patient to ambulate against his wishes • Forcing a patient to submit to injections • Striking a patient
False imprisonment	• Confining a patient in a psychiatric unit without a physician's order • Refusing to let a patient return home
Invasion of privacy	• Releasing private information about a patient to third parties, including family members, without consent • Allowing unauthorized persons to read a patient's medical records • Allowing unauthorized persons to observe a procedure • Taking pictures of the patient without his consent
Slander	• Making false statements about a patient to a third person, which causes damage to the patient's reputation

inside the patient because of unperformed or inaccurate needle and sponge counts
• communication breakdowns between nurses and physicians or between one nursing shift and the next
• inadequate observation of patients leading to misdiagnoses or injuries.

In addition, nurses who work in special practice areas may be especially vulnerable to lawsuits. (See *Liability in specialty practice settings.*)

Negligence vs. malpractice

The court's view of nursing liability has changed significantly over the years. At one time, nurses were charged only with **negligence**. Now, however, courts in several states, including Wyoming, Louisiana, and Rhode Island, have recognized nursing negligence as a form of malpractice.

Negligence is the failure to exercise the degree of care that a person of ordinary prudence would exercise under the same circumstances. A claim of negligence requires that there be a **duty** owed by one person to another, that the duty be breached, and that the breach of duty result in injury. Malpractice is a more restricted, specialized kind of negligence, defined as a violation of professional duty, a failure to meet **standards of care**, or a failure to use the skills and knowledge of other professionals in similar circumstances.

The distinction shows that the courts are beginning to recognize nursing as a legitimate profession. This emerging professional status may affect the **statute of limita-**

tions applicable in a particular case. The statute defines the time period in which a suit may be filed. Many states have statutes of limitations for medical malpractice claims that are shorter than those for other negligence actions.

Criminal negligence

Although negligence is usually a civil matter, courts are increasingly considering criminal charges against nurses for negligence when their acts or omissions are grossly negligent or indicate wanton disregard of a patient's well-being. For example, three nurses (Linda Fitchett, Barbara Golz, and Kathleen King [1997]) eventually pled guilty to criminally negligent homicide after a 1-day-old baby in their care died in a hospital near Denver. Because of a medication error, the baby had received 10 times the appropriate I.M. dose of penicillin and had received it I.V. A grand jury ruled against a lesser charge.

MALPRACTICE DEFENSES

Over the years, the law has developed special **doctrines**, or theories, to apply to cases involving subordinate-superior relationships. These doctrines may be used in a nurse's defense during a lawsuit. Exactly how much protection they offer, however, depends on the circumstances of the case and the development of the law in the nurse's state or province.

Respondeat superior

One of the most important malpractice defenses is the doctrine of **respondeat superior** (Latin for "let

Liability in specialty practice settings

Although errors can be made in virtually any practice setting, nurses who work in certain settings are more vulnerable to malpractice charges because their errors usually prove more costly for patients. Also, the courts may expect a higher standard from a nurse who practices a specialty.

Obstetric nursing

Cases involving obstetric errors have at least two plaintiffs: mother and infant. Because the courts recognize a legal duty owed to the unborn, an obstetric nurse may also be charged with violating the rights of a fetus. Monetary damages tend to be large because of the permanent or long-term injuries that can occur to newborns. An obstetric nurse may be held liable for:

- negligence through participation in transfusion of incompatible blood, especially in relation to Rh factor incompatibility
- failure to attend to or monitor the mother or fetus during labor and delivery
- failure to recognize labor symptoms and to provide adequate support and care
- failure to monitor contractions and fetal heart rate, particularly in obstetric units that have internal monitoring capabilities
- failure to recognize high-risk labor patients who show signs of preeclampsia or other labor complications
- failure to warn parents of the risks of diagnostic tests — or the

consequences of refusing such tests — if the failure contributes to maternal or fetal injury
- abandonment of a patient in active labor
- failure to exercise independent judgment such as knowingly carrying out medical orders that will harm the patient
- failure to ensure that a patient has given informed consent for various procedures or treatments, including physical examinations, administration of a potent medication, type of delivery method, sterilization, and postdelivery surgical procedures.

Other common sources of malpractice suits filed against obstetric nurses include failure to attend to an infant in distress, failure to monitor equipment, use of defective equipment, failure to monitor oxygen levels, and failure to recognize and report neonate jaundice during the immediate postnatal period.

In some states, parents can file a *wrongful birth* lawsuit if a nurse failed to advise them of contraceptive methods or the methods' potential for failure, potential genetic defects, the availability of amniocentesis to detect defects, or the option of abortion to prevent birth of a defective child. A child with a genetic defect can file a wrongful birth lawsuit if a nurse failed to inform the parents of amniocentesis and the option of abortion. Failure to provide adequate genetic counseling and prenatal testing when the

(continued)

Liability in specialty practice settings *(continued)*

mother has a history of Down syndrome can also result in a wrongful birth or wrongful life lawsuit.

Critical care nursing

Compared to nurses in other units, critical care nurses spend proportionately more of their time in direct contact with their patients, thus increasing the opportunity for error and the number of potential lawsuits. Because of the many invasive and potentially harmful procedures performed in this setting, critical care nurses are especially vulnerable to charges of negligence or battery. If they perform expanded-role duties and procedures, they may be accused of practicing medicine without a license.

Additional tort claims that may be leveled against critical care nurses include:

- abandonment — the unilateral severance of a professional relationship with a patient without adequate notice and while the patient still needs attention. A critical care nurse who fails in her duty to observe the patient closely for any subtle changes in condition is vulnerable to this charge.
- invasion of privacy, intentional infliction of emotional distress, or battery — such cases usually involve a patient who was placed on or removed from a life-support system
- failure to obtain informed consent — this is more likely to occur in a critical care setting because of the inherent pressure and

urgency for immediate treatment. Critical care nurses who deny a competent patient the right to refuse treatment — even if lack of treatment results in the patient's death — expose themselves to charges of various intentional torts.

Emergency department nursing

Many of the day-to-day practices of emergency department (ED) nurses fall into a legal gray area because the law's definition of a true emergency is open to interpretation; for instance, health care workers who treat a patient for what they regard as a true emergency may be liable for battery or failure to obtain informed consent if the court ultimately concludes that the situation wasn't a true emergency.

One of the most common charges filed against ED nurses is failure to assess a patient's condition and report it to the physician. Inadequate triage may be considered negligence.

All too often, the use of high-tech equipment combined with a hectic daily pace increases the potential for lawsuits.

Other tort claims made against ED nurses may involve:

- failure to instruct a patient adequately before discharge
- discounting complaints of pain from a patient who is mentally impaired by alcohol, medication, or injury

---

Liability in specialty practice settings *(continued)*

- failure to obtain informed consent, giving rise to claims of battery, false imprisonment, and invasion of privacy.

Psychiatric nursing

Malpractice cases involving psychiatric care usually involve failure to obtain informed consent. A nurse may wrongly assume she doesn't need informed consent, especially if the patient's condition interferes with his awareness or understanding of the proposed treatment or procedure. Violation of a patient's right to refuse treatment may stem from the mistaken belief that all mentally ill patients are incompetent. (The right to refuse treatment isn't absolute, however, and can be abrogated if medications or treatments are required to prevent serious harm to the patient or others. Generally, a nurse doesn't make this decision.)

A nurse who reveals personal information about a patient to someone not directly involved in the patient's care is vulnerable to malpractice charges. Violation of a patient's right to privacy and confidentiality is a common complaint in lawsuits against psychiatric health care workers, probably because of the stigma still associated with seeking care for mental illness.

Malpractice allegations may also stem from failing to protect a patient from inflicting foreseeable harm to himself or others. If a nurse fails to report information given by the patient, even in confidence, that could have prevented the harm, she may be held liable for violating her duty to assess and report his condition.

Suits against nurses alleging failure to monitor (involving violence or sexual assault by other patients or employees) are also on the rise in the psychiatric setting.

---

the master answer"), also called the theory of vicarious liability. This doctrine holds that when an employee is found negligent, the employer must accept responsibility if the employee was acting within the scope of his employment. The doctrine applies to all occupations, not just health care — a utility company, for instance, is liable for injuries that result if one of its on-duty truck drivers negligently hits a pedestrian.

To the extent that a nurse is working as the health care facility's functionary, she can claim some protection under this theory. This doctrine is attractive to *plaintiffs* as well as employees because facilities usually have much more money available to pay claims than nurses do (a reality facetiously known as the "deep pocket" doctrine).

Consider, for example, *Nelson v. Trinity Medical Center* (1988). A nurse delayed placing a woman who was in labor on a continuous fetal heart rate monitor, despite **standing orders** to do so. The child was born severely brain-damaged, a condition that might have been prevented if the monitor had been operating to alert the physician and if a cesarean delivery had been performed. It was the hospital, not the nurse, who was found liable for the actions of its employee. (The physician settled out of court before the trial.) The parents were awarded $5.5 million.

In another case, *Crowe v. Provost* (1963), a mother returned with her child to her pediatrician's office one afternoon after having been there earlier that morning. She said her child was convulsing. The physician was at lunch, so the office nurse briefly examined the child. The nurse then called the physician, told him that she didn't feel the child's condition had changed since he had examined her, and advised that he need not rush back. After the nurse left the office, the child vomited violently, stopped breathing, and died before the receptionist could contact the physician. The mother filed negligence charges against the nurse. At the trial, the court found the nurse's negligence was indeed the **proximate cause** of the child's death. However, the physician was also liable, according to the doctrine of respondeat superior, because the nurse was working as the physician's employee.

Borrowed servant

A concept closely related to respondeat superior is the **borrowed-servant** or **captain-of-the-ship doctrine**. It's still applied in malpractice lawsuits, but not as often as in the past. The borrowed-servant doctrine might apply if you, as an employee of a health care facility, commit a negligent act while under the direction or control of someone other than your supervisor such as a physician in the operating room. Because the physician is an **independent contractor** and you're responsible to him during surgery, you're considered his borrowed servant at the time. If you're sued for malpractice, his liability is vicarious, meaning that even though the physician didn't direct you negligently, he's responsible because he was in control.

Many states have moved away from strict application of the borrowed-servant doctrine. One reason for this shift is that operating room procedures are becoming so complex that they're beyond the direct control of any one person, thus making it too difficult for courts to determine responsibility under the borrowed-servant doctrine.

Res ipsa loquitur

The Latin phrase **res ipsa loquitur** literally means, "The thing speaks for itself." *Res ipsa loquitur* is a rule of evidence designed to equalize the plaintiff's and the defendant's positions in court, when otherwise the plaintiff could be at a disadvantage in proving his case — a disadvantage not of his own making. Essentially, the rule of *res ipsa loquitur* allows a plaintiff to prove negligence with **circumstantial evidence** when the defendant has the primary, and sometimes the only, knowledge of what happened to cause the plaintiff's injury. (*Res ipsa loquitur* doesn't apply when a plaintiff simply fails to prove his case.)

Res ipsa loquitur derives from a 19th-century English case, *Byrne v.*

Boadle (1863). In this case, the injured person had been struck by a flour barrel that fell from a second-floor window of a warehouse. In the ensuing lawsuit, the plaintiff wasn't able to show which warehouse employee had been negligent in allowing the barrel to fall. The court applied the concept of *res ipsa loquitur* to the warehouse owners, who were found liable in the absence of proof that the employees weren't responsible for the plaintiff's injury.

APPLYING *RES IPSA LOQUITUR*

In most medical malpractice cases, the plaintiff has the responsibility for proving every element of his case against the defendant; until he does, the court presumes that the defendant met the applicable standard of care. However, when a court applies the *res ipsa loquitur* rule, the burden of proof shifts from the plaintiff to the defendant. The defendant must prove that the injury was caused by something other than his negligence.

For the *res ipsa loquitur* rule to apply against a nurse, three circumstances must be met:

● The act that caused the plaintiff's injury was exclusively in the nurse's control.

● The injury wouldn't have happened in the absence of the defendant nurse's negligence.

● No negligence on the plaintiff's part contributed to his injury.

The *res ipsa loquitur* rule was invoked in *Chin v. St. Barnabas Medical Center* (1998). A New Jersey Appellate Court ruled that when an unconscious surgical patient suffered an injury unrelated to the scope of the surgery, those who had custody of the patient must prove their nonculpability to avoid liability. The burden of proof shifts to the defendants. The patient entered the hospital for a hysteroscopy. The procedure was performed using a scope with catheters for introducing fluid into the uterus and for draining the fluid, which was removed by a gas exhaust line. Gas was introduced into the patient's abdominal cavity and circulatory system with fatal results due to loosening and misconnection of one of the scope lines. The Court found in the plaintiff's favor because Ms. Chin was unconscious and blameless at the time of her injury.

INCIDENTS ASSOCIATED WITH *RES IPSA LOQUITUR*

Perhaps the most common incident associated with the *res ipsa loquitur* rule is the foreign-object case, in which a sponge, needle, pin, or other object is left inside the patient after surgery. Cases of retained surgical sponges or foreign bodies usually settle out of court or result in jury verdicts ranging from $50,000 to $200,000, depending on the duration of the foreign body's presence, infections, and the extent of surgery required to remove the item. Courts have also been willing to invoke the rule when injuries occur involving body parts completely unrelated to the plaintiff's surgery.

Consider the Wisconsin malpractice case, *Beaudoin v. Watertown Memorial Hospital* (1966). A patient suffered second-degree burns on the buttocks during vaginal surgery. She brought suit, claiming negligence. The court applied the *res ipsa loquitur* rule on the basis that injury to an area unrelated to surgery automatically results from failure to exercise due care.

FOR AND AGAINST *RES IPSA LOQUITUR*

Critics of the *res ipsa loquitur* rule call it "the rule of sympathy" and believe the courts have been too lenient in allowing plaintiffs to use it. **Health care professionals** usually contend that the rule puts them at an unfair disadvantage during a malpractice defense. They feel that, by assigning them the burden of proof, the court singles them out for more negligence liability than other types of defendants. Also, invoking the rule usually eliminates the plaintiff's responsibility to introduce expert testimony.

Supporters of the rule feel that it draws attention to the fact that a plaintiff's unusual or rare injury is, in itself, sufficient to cause suspicion that the defendant was negligent.

STATE INTERPRETATIONS

In some states, courts can't apply the *res ipsa loquitur* rule. Most states, however, do allow courts to apply some form of it. For example, neither Michigan nor South Carolina uses the rule by name, but both permit circumstantial evidence of negligence, which is, in effect, the same concept. (See *Challenging a malpractice suit.*)

Understanding statute of limitations

A statute of limitations specifies a particular number of years within which one person can sue another. For malpractice lawsuits, the statute of limitations is specified in each state's medical malpractice law. These limits vary widely from state to state, and it's important to know the limits in your state. Contact the attorney, lobbyist, or legislative committee members of your state nurses' association for information about the statute of limitations in your state. Statutes of limitations also vary widely from jurisdiction to jurisdiction in Canada, and even within a jurisdiction.

PURPOSE OF STATUTES OF LIMITATIONS

Statutes of limitations are useful because as time passes, evidence vanishes, witnesses' memories fail, and witnesses die. A time limit for bringing a lawsuit ensures that enough relevant evidence exists for a judge or jury to decide a case fairly.

Statutes of limitations for general negligence usually give a person 3 years to sue another for damages. Defendants may invoke these limits as a defense in general personal-injury lawsuits. However, in response to pressure from medical and insurance groups, states established shorter statutes of limitations for professions that require independent judgments and frequent risks. The statute of limitations of medical malpractice laws, for example, usually give the patient 2 years or less to sue for damages.

DETERMINING WHICH STATUTE APPLIES

In many states, only physicians and dentists are expressly subject to medical malpractice statute of limi-

Challenging a malpractice suit

If your attorney can establish one of the following malpractice defenses, the court will either dismiss the allegations or reduce the damages for which you're liable.

DEFENSE	RATIONALE
False allegations	Does the plaintiff have legally sufficient proof that your actions caused his injuries? If he doesn't, the court may rule that the allegations against you are false and dismiss the case.
Contributory negligence	Did the plaintiff, through carelessness, contribute to his injury? If he did, some states permit the court to charge the plaintiff with failing to meet the standards of a reasonably prudent patient. Such a ruling may prevent the plaintiff from recovering any damages. A few states permit the court to apportion liability, which prevents the plaintiff from recovering some, but not all, of the damages he claims.
Comparative negligence	Has more than one defendant been named in the lawsuit? In some states, the court may apportion liability according to the negligence of the defendants involved, with the total damages divided up among them in proportion to the fault of each.
Assumption of risk	Did the plaintiff understand the risk involved in the treatment, procedure, or action that allegedly caused his injury? Did he give proper informed consent and so voluntarily expose himself to that risk? If so, the court may rule that the plaintiff assumed the risk, knowingly disregarded the danger, and therefore relieved you of liability.

tations. These states view the nurse as someone carrying out orders and not making independent, risk-taking judgments.

If a nurse alleges a patient's claim is invalid because he didn't file suit until after the statute of limitations had expired, the court must determine which applies: the statute of limitations for state medical malpractice law or the statute of limitations for general personal-injury lawsuits. (The malpractice law's statute of limitations is usually shorter.) The court bases its decision on two considerations:

● How much statute of limitations protection the court believes the defendant nurse's job warrants. If her job forces her to make many independent patient care judgments, the court may apply a strict, or short, statute of limitations. A short time limit offers more protection for the nurse because the patient has less time to seek damages.

● The type of negligent act the plaintiff patient claims the nurse committed. An injured patient may sue a nurse for any single, or for several, of the charges that constitute negligence or malpractice. The patient's attorney determines which charge has the best chance of winning the most damages for his client and structures his case accordingly. Then, if a statute of limitations is used as part of the nurse's defense, the court will decide which statute of limitations applies in relation to the plaintiff's charges.

In an Alaska case, *Pedersen v. Zielski* (1991), the plaintiff argued that a 6-year statute of limitations for controlled claims applied to a health care provider's negligence because the physician had a contract to provide care to him. The Alaska court held that the 2-year statute of limitations was applicable because the plaintiff's claims arose in **tort** or personal injury law, not in contract law.

APPLYING THE STATUTE OF LIMITATIONS

Suppose a patient files suit long after the statute of limitations has expired. Don't think your worries are over. Remember, the patient's attorney knows about the statute of limitations, and he's filing suit anyway. That means he believes the court may set aside the statute of limitations.

Normally, the statute begins to run on the date the plaintiff's injury

occurred — but what if the plaintiff didn't know he was injured or didn't find out he had grounds for a suit until after the normal limitation period expires? Determining when the applicable statute actually begins to run has become the pivotal question whenever a defense attorney invokes the statute of limitations.

Legislatures and the courts, which are continually struggling with this question, have devised a series of rules to help decide, in individual malpractice cases, when a statute should properly begin to run. A court can apply these rules when a plaintiff patient's attorney requests that it do so to extend the applicable statute of limitations beyond the limit written in the law. In that event, the nurse's use of a statute of limitations as a defense is invalidated and the plaintiff patient is still allowed to sue.

Occurrence rule

Under the **occurrence rule**, the statute of limitations begins to run on the day a patient's injury occurs. The occurrence rule generally leads to the shortest time limit. In several states, the courts have interpreted the occurrence rule strictly, so that even badly injured patients have been prevented from bringing suit after the applicable statute of limitations had expired.

Termination-of-treatment rule

The courts may apply the **termination-of-treatment rule** when a patient's injury results from a series of treatments extended over time, rather than from a single treatment. The termination-of-treatment rule states that the statute of limitations begins on the date of the last treatment. In devising this rule, the courts reasoned that for the patient, a series of treatments could obscure just how and when the injury occurred.

The Supreme Court of Virginia applied this rule in *Justice v. Natvig* (1989). In this case, a patient filed a lawsuit 8 years after an allegedly negligent operation. The patient had continued to receive treatment during this interval. The defendant physicians argued that the statute of limitations had lapsed. The court ruled, however, that the statute did not begin to run until the treatment had ended, so the patient's lawsuit was allowed.

Constructive continuing treatment rule

The ***constructive-continuing-treatment rule*** is essentially the same as the termination-of-treatment rule, but it applies even after the patient leaves a nurse's or a physician's care. For example, suppose a patient you cared for is injured later, in someone else's care, and sues. Under the constructive-continuing-treatment rule, if the subsequent health care providers relied on decisions you made earlier in caring for the patient, the court may extend the statute of limitations in malpractice cases.

Discovery rule

Under the ***discovery rule***, the statute of limitations begins to run when a patient discovers the injury. This may take place many years after the injury occurred. The discovery rule considerably extends the time a patient has to file a malpractice lawsuit. The discovery rule is most commonly applied in foreign object and sterilization cases.

When a nurse or a surgeon leaves a scalpel, sponge, or clamp inside a patient, the patient might not discover the error until long after his surgery. Under the discovery rule, the applicable statute of limitations wouldn't begin to run until the patient found out about the error. A court's decision to apply the discovery rule in foreign object cases depends on whether it believes that the patient could have discovered the error earlier. If evidence indicates the patient should have recognized that something was wrong (for example, if he had chronic pain for months after the surgery but didn't take legal action until long afterward), the court could apply the termination-of-treatment rule instead. Time limits for applying the discovery rule in foreign-object cases vary from state to state. Missouri allows the longest period — up to 10 years after discovery of injury. California has the shortest period — 1 year from discovery of injury.

In lawsuits involving tubal ligations or vasectomies, the courts have sometimes allowed the discovery rule to apply when a subsequent pregnancy occurs. In these cases, the courts' reasoning is that a patient can't discover the negligence until the procedure proves unsuccessful, no matter how long after the surgery this proof appears.

Because the discovery rule is so generous to plaintiffs, some states, notably Texas, have restricted its application. A number of states have adopted separate statutes of limitations, one for readily detected injuries and one for injuries discovered later. Other states permit statutes of limitations extensions only in foreign-object cases.

Proof of fraud

In most states, courts will extend the limitation period indefinitely if a plaintiff patient can prove that a nurse or physician used *fraud* or falsehood to conceal from the patient information about his injury or its cause. In most cases, the law says that the concealment must be an overt act, not just the omission of an act. The most flagrant frauds involve concealing facts to prevent an inquiry, elude an investigation, or mislead a patient. (See *Extending the statute of limitations*.)

Consider, for example, *Garcia v. Presbyterian Hospital Center* (1979). In this case, the patient who sued was operated on for cancer of the prostate gland twice in 1972 and once again in 1973. He had repeatedly asked his physician and attending nurses why the third operation was needed, but he hadn't received any explanation. Some time later, he learned that the third operation had resulted from retention of a catheter in his body during the second operation. The court held that the applicable statute of limitations didn't prevent the patient from bringing suit.

Minor or mentally incompetent patients

In most states, laws give special consideration to *minors* and *mentally incompetent patients* because they lack the legal capacity to sue. Some states postpone applying the statute of limitations to an injured minor until he reaches the age of majority — age 18 or 21, depending on the state. Some states have specific rules about how statutes of limitations apply to minors. However, the parents or guardian may file a suit on a child's behalf when he's still a minor.

Cases involving mentally incompetent patients who file after the statute of limitations has expired usually follow the discovery rule or a special law. Most of these special laws state that a statute of limitations doesn't begin until the patient recovers from his mental incompetence.

USING THE STATUTE OF LIMITATIONS DEFENSE

When a defendant nurse and her attorney use a statute of limitations as a defense, they're making, in legal terms, an *affirmative defense*. The defendant must prove that the statute of limitations has run out. If the court decides the statutory time limit has expired, the plaintiff patient's case is dismissed.

For example, in *Claypool v. Levin* (1997), the statute of limitations covering malpractice actions was determined to begin running when a plaintiff obtained *actual notice* (oral or written) or *constructive notice* (through self-discovery) of injury and its cause. The fact that there is more than one possible cause doesn't toll (or pause) the statute. Thus, a patient can't argue that the statute is tolled because he sought legal advice that indicated he had no viable claim.

Extending the statute of limitations

If a plaintiff patient can prove that a nurse or physician willfully deceived him, the court may lengthen the statute of limitations for filing a lawsuit.

Painful overtreatment

Consider the case of *Lopez v. Swyer* (1971). Mary Lopez, age 32, underwent a radical mastectomy after discovering a lump in her breast. Several physicians prescribed postsurgical radiation treatments, which were performed by a radiologist.

These treatments occurred 6 times per week for more than 1 month and left painful radiation burns over most of her body. When Mrs. Lopez asked why the complications were so severe, her physician assured her that the burns weren't unusual. They never suggested that the treatments could have been too numerous or too long.

Mrs. Lopez's condition worsened. Over the next several years she was hospitalized 15 times, including twice for reconstructive surgery made necessary by the radiation treatment. She didn't file a malpractice suit until she heard a consulting physician tell other physicians, gathered near her hospital bed, that she was a victim of negligence.

Extra time for the plaintiff

A lower court dismissed the suit because the 2-year statute of limitations for malpractice had expired. An appeals court ruled that the statute of limitations didn't begin to run until Mrs. Lopez learned that her physicians had concealed the truth from her. This effectively lengthened the statute of limitations by nearly 10 years. The appeals court ruling allowed Mrs. Lopez to bring the facts of her case before a jury.

RETAINING MEDICAL RECORDS

Because a patient may file a malpractice suit years after he claims his injury occurred, accurate *medical records* should be kept on file for years. In the event of a malpractice suit, the entire medical record will be gathered, including such information as X-ray films and fetal monitoring strips. The complexity of malpractice cases requires you to recall specific clinical facts and procedures. Complete *documentation* of your care is usually found only in the records. These records provide your best defense. Without them, you're legally vulnerable.

Few states have laws setting precise time periods for the required maintenance of medical records, but many legal experts urge hospitals and other health care facilities to maintain medical record files long after patients are discharged. New Jersey, for example, requires hospitals to keep medical records for 7 years.

Some states have adopted the Uniform Business Records Act. This act calls for keeping records for no less than 3 years. Some states allow microfilm copies of medical records to be admitted as evidence in malpractice cases, but other states insist that only the original records can be used in court.

In *Keene v. Brigham and Women's Hospital* (2001), a plaintiff brought suit for severe and permanent brain damage that occurred on the first day of life. A judge found that, as a result of the hospital's failure to maintain crucial parts of the medical record, the plaintiff was unable to identify any of the nurses or physicians responsible for his care at that time and, therefore, couldn't seek redress against any of the negligent parties. The case proceeded to the judge to set damages, and the award was $6.7 million with interest. An appeal is expected.

Avoiding malpractice liability

You can take steps to avoid tort liability by using caution and common sense, and by maintaining heightened awareness of your legal responsibilities. Follow the guidelines described below.

KNOW YOUR OWN STRENGTHS AND WEAKNESSES

Don't accept responsibilities for which you aren't prepared. For example, if it has been some time since you have worked in pediatrics, accepting an assignment to a pediatric unit without orientation only increases your chances of making an error. If you do make an error, claiming that you weren't familiar with the unit's procedures won't protect you against liability.

As a professional, you should not accept a position if you can't perform as a ***reasonably prudent nurse*** would in that setting. Courts may, however, be more lenient when dealing with nurses who work in emergency settings, such as a fire or flood. However, simply being told "We need you here today" doesn't constitute an emergency.

Evaluate your assignment

You may be assigned to work on a specialized unit, which is reasonable as long as you're assigned duties you can perform competently and as long as an experienced nurse on the unit assumes responsibility for the specialized duties. Assigning you to perform total patient care on a specialized unit is unsafe if you don't have the skills to plan and deliver that care.

For example, if you're assigned to coronary care, you could monitor the I.V. lines, take vital signs, and report your observations to the coronary care nurse. She'll check the monitors, administer the medications, and make decisions. This arrangement fragments the patient's care, however, so it isn't appropriate as a permanent solution to a staffing problem.

DELEGATE CAREFULLY

Exercise great care as a supervisor when delegating duties because you may be held responsible for subordinates, and you can be sued for negligent supervision for the acts of your subordinates. Inspect all equipment and machinery regularly, and make sure subordinates use them competently and safely. Report incompetent health care personnel to superiors through the facility's chain of command.

CARRY OUT ORDERS CAUTIOUSLY

Never treat any patient without orders from his physician. Don't prescribe or *dispense* any medication without authorization. In most cases, only physicians and pharmacists may legally perform these functions.

Don't carry out any order from a physician if you have doubts about its accuracy or appropriateness. Follow your facility's policy for clarifying ambiguous orders. Document your efforts to clarify the order, and whether the order was carried out.

If after you carry out an order the treatment is adversely affecting the patient, discontinue it and contact his physician. Document all of your efforts to contact the physician and the results of those efforts. Report all unfavorable signs and symptoms to the patient's physician. Resume treatment only after you have discussed the situation with the physician and clarified the orders. Document your actions.

Keep in mind that a physician can change his orders at any time, including while you're off duty. A patient may know something about his prescribed care that no one has told you. If a patient protests a procedure, medication dosage, or medication route — saying that it's different from "the usual," or that it has been changed — give him the benefit of the doubt. Question the

physician's orders, following your facility's policy.

If you're an inexperienced nurse, you should take steps to clarify all standing orders. Contact the prescribing physician for guidance, or tell your supervisor you're uncertain about following the order and let her decide whether to delegate the responsibility to a more experienced nurse.

ADMINISTER MEDICATIONS CAREFULLY

Medication errors are the most common, and potentially the most dangerous, of nursing errors. Mistakes in dosage, patient identification, or drug selection by nurses have lead to vision loss, brain damage, cardiac arrest, and death.

In *Estate of Stanislaw Walicez, deceased v. Dr. Gandhi Gutta, MD, and Alexian Brothers Hospital* (2001), heparin was administered to the wrong patient. A 47-year-old construction worker was admitted to the emergency department with multiple fractures and abdominal bleeding after falling at a construction site. He was placed in a room recently vacated by a cardiac patient. An I.V. bag containing heparin was delivered to the room for the cardiac patient, who had already been transferred. Either the physician or a hospital employee (nurse) mistakenly administered the I.V. bag contents to the construction worker, resulting in massive brain hemorrhage and death. A jury cited the physician and the hospital and awarded the family $6.5 million. During jury deliberations, the physician had entered into an agreement that capped his personal liability at $800,000, so presumably the hospital paid the remainder of the verdict.

MAINTAIN RAPPORT WITH THE PATIENT

Trial attorneys have a saying: "If you don't want to be sued, don't be rude." Failing to communicate with patients is the cause of many legal problems.

Always remain calm when a patient or his family becomes difficult. Patients must be told the truth about adverse outcomes, but this information should be communicated with discretion and sensitivity. (See *Who's looking for litigation?*.)

DON'T OFFER OPINIONS

Avoid offering your opinion when a patient asks you what you think is the matter with him. If you do, you could be accused of making a medical diagnosis, which is *practicing medicine without a license*. Don't volunteer information about possible treatments for the patient's condition or about possible choices of physicians, either.

Avoid making any statement that could be perceived by the patient as an admission of fault or error. Don't criticize other nurses or health care practitioners, or the care they provide, if the patient can hear you. Don't discuss with the patient or visitors which members of the health care team are covered by malpractice insurance.

Be careful not to discuss a patient's care or personal business with anyone, except when doing so is consistent with proper nursing care.

READ BEFORE YOU SIGN

Never sign your name as a *witness* without fully understanding what you're signing as well as the legal significance of your signature. When you sign as a witness, you're usually certifying only that you saw the person, known to you by a certain name, place his signature on the document. You aren't necessarily certifying the presence or absence of duress, undue influence, fraud, or error. When you witness consent forms in a nursing capacity, however, your signature attests to:
- authenticity
- voluntariness
- capacity.

If you're called to testify about the signing, don't underestimate the importance of your testimony. A court looking into charges of fraud or undue influence used in executing a document will usually give great weight to a nurse's perception. You may be asked about the patient's physical and mental condition at the time of the signing, and the court may ask you to describe his interactions with his family, his attorney, and others.

DOCUMENT CARE ACCURATELY

From a legal standpoint, documented care is as important as the actual care. If a procedure wasn't documented, the courts assume it wasn't performed. Documentation of observations, decisions, and actions is considered more reliable evidence

Who's looking for litigation?

Patients who are more likely to file lawsuits against nurses share certain personality traits and behaviors. What's more, nurses who are more likely to be named as defendants also have certain common characteristics. However, keep in mind that all nurses are vulnerable to a suit if they simply make a mistake.

Beware of these patients

Although not all people displaying the behaviors listed below will file a lawsuit, a little extra caution in your dealings with them won't hurt. Providing professional and competent care to such patients will lessen their tendency to sue.

A patient who is likely to file a lawsuit may:
- persistently criticize all aspects of the nursing care provided
- purposefully not follow the care plan
- overreact to any perceived slight or negative comment, real or imagined
- unjustifiably depend on nurses for all aspects of care and refuse to accept any responsibility for his own care
- openly express hostility to nurses and other health care personnel

- project his anxiety or anger onto the nursing staff, attributing blame for all negative events to health care providers
- have filed lawsuits previously.

Nurses at risk

Nurses who are more likely to be named as defendants in a lawsuit display certain characteristic behaviors. If you recognize any of these attributes within yourself, changing your behavior will reduce your risk of liability.

A nurse who is likely to be a defendant in a lawsuit may:
- be insensitive to the patient's complaints or fail to take them seriously
- fail to identify and meet the patient's emotional and physical needs
- refuse to recognize the limits of her nursing skills and personal competency
- lack sufficient education for the tasks and responsibilities associated with a specific practice setting
- display an authoritarian and inflexible attitude when providing care
- inappropriately delegate responsibilities to subordinates.

than oral testimony. The patient's chart, when taken into the jury room, is a nurse's "best evidence" of the care given. The chart should follow the "FACT" rule: be *f*actual, *a*ccurate, *c*omplete, and *t*imely.

Use ***incident reports*** to identify and report any accidents, errors, or injuries to a patient. Instead of placing incident reports in the patient's chart, give them directly to the facility's ***risk manager***. A long period may elapse between an incident and subsequent court proceedings, and this documentation may be the only proof of what actually happened.

Never correct or revise a patient's medical record after the fact. The case of *Freeman et al. v. Cresthaven Nursing Residence et al.* (2001) illustrates the liability a health care facility may incur when nurses or other employees alter or destroy patient records. In this case, a patient at Cresthaven Nursing Residence fell and broke her femur. She was transferred to a local hospital, where she died 16 days later. Several nurses at the residence later testified that, on the day the patient died, the Assistant Director of Nursing (DON) called them to "update" the patient's chart. One of these nurses said she merely recopied earlier notes at the behest of the Assistant DON and made no changes in content; however, this nurse's time sheet showed that her entries were made on a day that she wasn't working in the patient's wing. Another nurse had written her notes on a day that, according to her time sheet, she didn't work. Also, there were entries made in the patient's chart for days when she was actually at the hospital. The jury found for the patient's family and awarded them $9 million.

The case of *Sweet v. Sisters of Providence Hospital* (1994) held that a **rebuttable presumption** of negligence arises if a health care facility's records are unavailable to a plaintiff, and the plaintiff can demonstrate that the missing records are necessary to prove his negligence claim. This greatly facilitates the plaintiff's lawsuit.

Document the use of restraints

Restraints must be applied correctly and checked according to the health care facility's policy and procedure. Documentation must be exact about the reason, the amount, and the type of restraint used, and the status of the restrained patient. An omission or failure to monitor a restrained patient may result in a malpractice claim.

EXERCISE CAUTION WHEN ASSISTING IN PROCEDURES

Don't assist with a surgical procedure unless you're satisfied the patient has given proper *informed consent*. Never force a patient to accept treatment he has expressly refused. Don't use equipment you aren't familiar with, aren't trained to use, or that seems to be functioning improperly. If you're an operating room nurse, always check and double-check that all surgical equipment, such as sponges or instruments, are accounted for after an operation is completed.

TAKE STEPS TO PREVENT PATIENT FALLS

Patient falls are a common area of nursing liability. Patients who are elderly, infirm, sedated, or mentally incapacitated are the most likely to fall. Although falls may occur frequently, they're hardly benign and may result in seriously debilitating injuries, including amputation or a permanent vegetative state.

COMPLY WITH LAWS ABOUT ADVANCE DIRECTIVES

The Patient's Self-Determination Act, a federal law, requires that every patient, on admission to a health care facility, be given information concerning *advance directives — living wills* and *durable power of attorney*. Follow the facility's policy and procedure for providing the required information. Don't, as one of the patient's health care providers, witness a living will or a durable power of attorney. You should also be aware of state laws concerning living wills and advance directives.

FOLLOW FACILITY POLICIES AND PROCEDURES

You have a responsibility to be familiar with the policies and procedures of the facility where you work. If the policies and procedures are sound, and you follow them carefully, they can protect you against a malpractice claim. The court in *Roach v. Springfield Clinic* (1993) held that "hospital policies are admissible as standards of care for the treatment of patients within that hospital."

The medication procedure may involve checking all medication cards against a central Kardex. If you do this and the Kardex is in error, you may not be liable for a resulting medication error because you followed all appropriate procedures and acted responsibly. The person who made the original error, however, would be liable. If you didn't follow the procedure, however, you might also be liable because

you didn't do your part to prevent the error.

Inexperienced nurses may be high liability risks. A registered nurse must be able to recognize her limitations and admit to them, if the safety of the patient is at issue. If the nurse doesn't know how to perform a nursing function or doesn't understand the reason for a particular treatment, it's her duty to obtain assistance that's timely and appropriate.

Keep policies and procedures up to date

As nursing changes, so should the facility's policies and procedures. As a professional, you're responsible for maintaining up-to-date procedures. For instance, do you have written policies on dealing with emergency situations? "We've always done it this way" isn't an adequate substitute for a clearly written, officially accepted policy.

If administrators are reluctant to make policy changes based on one nurse's suggestion, join with colleagues to present the legal implications.

PROVIDE A SAFE ENVIRONMENT

When providing care, you should not use faulty equipment. If you find that a piece of equipment isn't working properly, clearly mark it as defective and unusable and follow your facility's procedure for obtaining repair. Even after repairs are done, don't use the repaired equipment until technicians demonstrate that the equipment is operating properly. Document the steps you took to handle problems with faulty equipment to show that you followed the facility's policy and procedures.

Also, be sure to use equipment safely, according to the instructions from the manufacturer. Any deviations in use can result in negligence charges if a lawsuit is filed.

Liability insurance

Your expanded health care role makes having professional liability insurance essential. In any work setting, you're at risk for malpractice suits. The risk increases if you work in a specialized setting, such as the intensive care unit, or as an advance practice nurse.

Some nurses believe that purchasing professional liability insurance makes them a more attractive target for compensation claims and increases their chances of being sued. They also believe that, as employees of a health care facility, they're protected by *respondeat superior* and the facility's insurance policy. These beliefs, given the legal risks in modern society, are dangerously naïve. You simply can't afford to be without insurance. Your liability policy can cover legal expenses to defend against a complaint filed against you. This may cover out-of-court expenses, such as depositions. Check with your malpractice carrier for details about expanding your insurance coverage. (See *Choosing liability insurance.*)

UNDERSTANDING INSURANCE COVERAGE
When you buy professional liability insurance, you're protected, under contract, for a designated period from the financial consequences of certain professional errors. The type of insurance policy you buy determines the amount the insurance company will pay if the judgment goes against you in a lawsuit. You may, for instance, purchase a policy designated with "single limits" or "double limits." In a single-limits policy, you buy protection in set dollar increments; for example, $100,000, $300,000, or $1 million. The stipulated amount will shield you if a judgment, arising out of a single nursing malpractice occurrence, goes against you.

In the double-limits policy, you buy protection in a combination package, such as $100,000/$300,000, $300,000/$500,000, or $1 million/$3 million. The smaller sum is what your insurance company will make available to protect you from any one injury arising out of a single nursing malpractice occurrence. The larger sum is the maximum amount that will be paid for all claims under that policy in a given year. Although the single-limits policy will also protect you against injuries to more than one patient, the double-limits policy makes considerably more money available to protect you if you're involved in multiple lawsuits.

Occurrence and claims-made policies
Professional liability insurance may cover either the time the malpractice occurred (***occurrence policy***) or when a lawsuit is filed (***claims-made policy***). An occurrence policy protects you against any incidents occurring during a policy period, regardless of when the patient files a claim against you — even after the policy has expired.

Choosing liability insurance

To find the professional liability coverage that fits your needs, compare the features of a number of policies. Understanding insurance policy basics will enable you to shop more aggressively and intelligently for the coverage you need. You should work with an insurance agent who is experienced in this type of insurance. If you already have professional liability insurance, the information below may help you evaluate your coverage.

Type of coverage

Ask your insurance agent about the type of coverage the policy provides. A *claims-made* policy covers only claims made during the policy's coverage period, whereas an *occurrence* policy covers any negligent act committed during the policy period — even if the patient doesn't file a suit until after the policy has expired. Keep in mind that an occurrence policy provides more coverage than a claims-made policy.

Coverage limits

All malpractice insurance policies cover professional liability. Some also cover personal liability, disciplinary defense actions, medical payments, assault-related bodily injury, and all property damage.

The amount of coverage varies, as does your premium. Remember that professional liability coverage is limited to acts and practice settings specified in the policy. Make sure your policy covers your nursing role, whether you're a student, graduate nurse, or working nurse with advanced education and specialized skills.

Options

Check whether the policy will provide coverage for the following incidents:

- negligence on the part of employees under your supervision
- misuse of equipment
- errors in reporting or recording care
- failure to properly teach patients
- errors in administering medication
- mistakes made while providing care in an emergency outside your employment setting.

Be sure to ask whether the policy provides protection if your employer (the hospital) sues you.

Definition of terms

Definition of terms can vary from policy to policy. If your policy includes any restrictive definitions, you won't be covered for actions outside those guidelines. For the best protection, seek the broadest definitions possible and ask the agent for examples of actions the company hasn't covered.

Duration of coverage

Insurance is an annual contract that can be renewed or canceled each year. The policy usually specifies how it can be canceled — in writing by either you or the insurance company. Some contracts require a 30-day notice for cancellation. If the

(continued)

Choosing liability insurance *(continued)*

company is canceling the policy, you'll probably be given at least 10 days' notice.

Exclusions

Ask your agent about exclusions — areas not covered by the insurance policy. For example, "this policy doesn't apply to injury arising out of performance of the insured of a criminal act" or "this policy doesn't apply to nurse anesthetists."

Other insurance clauses

All professional liability insurance policies contain "other insurance" clauses that address payment obligations when a nurse is covered by more than one insurance policy, such as the employer's policy and the nurse's personal liability policy:

- The *pro rata* clause states that two or more policies in effect at the same time will pay any claims in accordance with a proportion established in the individual policies.
- The *in excess* clause states that the primary policy will pay all fees and damages up to its limits, at which point the second policy will pay any additional fees or damages up to its limits.
- The *escape clause* relieves an insurance company of all liability for fees or damages if another insurance policy is in effect at the same time; in effect, the clause states that the other company is responsible for all liability.

If you're covered by more than one policy, be alert for "other insurance" clauses and avoid purchasing a policy with an escape clause for liability.

Additional tips

Here's some additional information that will guide you in the purchase of professional liability insurance.

- The insurance application is a legal document. If you provide any false information, it may void the policy.
- If you're involved in nursing administration, education, research, or advanced or nontraditional nursing practice, be especially careful in selecting a policy because routine policies may not cover these activities.
- After selecting a policy that ensures adequate coverage, stay with the same policy and insurer, if possible, to avoid potential lapses in coverage that could occur when changing insurers.
- No insurance policy will cover you for acts outside of your scope of practice or licensure. Nor will insurance cover you for intentional torts if intent to do harm is proved.
- Be prepared to uphold all obligations specified in the policy; failure to do so may void the policy and cause personal liability for damages. Remember that an act of willful wrongdoing on your part renders the policy null and void and may lead to a breach of contract lawsuit.
- Check out the insurance company by calling your state division of insurance to inquire about the company's financial condition.

The claims-made policy protects you only against claims made against you during the policy period. A claims-made policy is less expensive than an occurrence policy because the insurance company is at risk only for the duration of the policy. However, you can purchase an extended-reporting endorsement, or tail coverage, which in effect turns your claims-made policy into an occurrence policy.

Excess judgment

You're personally responsible for any *excess judgment* — a judgment exceeding the policy limits. Depending on the laws in your state, almost everything you own, except for a limited portion of your equity in your home and the clothes on your back, can be taken to satisfy the uninsured portion of a judgment.

SUBROGATION

Subrogation is defined as the act of substituting another (that is, a second creditor) with regard to a legal right or claim. Employers (or other defendants such as physicians), who have been found liable for damages can subsequently sue another involved in the incident to recoup their losses.

In a Pennsylvania case, *Mutual Insurance v. American Casualty Company of Reading* (1997), a patient underwent angioplasty and had a complication, which was treated. During a nurse-to-nurse report, the complication wasn't mentioned. The patient coded and died in less than 12 hours. The family sued the hospital and the physician, but the nurses weren't named. After the hospital was found liable,

the hospital's insurer filed suit against the nurses involved, saying the patient would have been more closely monitored if staff had known it hadn't been a routine angioplasty. The court ruled the suit was permissible.

INSURANCE COSTS

Fortunately, premiums for insurance coverage of $1 million aren't much greater than they are for smaller limits. Because a substantial part of the premium pays for the insurance company's assumption of risk, higher limits don't increase the premium disproportionately.

Insurance companies offer a variety of liability insurance policies at a variety of rates. If possible, choose an agent who is experienced in professional liability coverage. Organizations, such as the American Nurses Association and your state nurses' association, offer group plans at attractive premiums. You need to review the extent of coverage with your agent to make sure it's adequate for your needs.

INSURER'S ROLE IN A LAWSUIT

Professional liability insurance can supply you with more than just financial protection. The insurance company may also provide a defense counsel to represent you for the entire course of litigation, if this is included in your insurance contract. Some companies may even offer nurse-attorneys for defense counsel. Insurance companies aren't in business to lose money; they'll retain highly experienced attorneys with considerable experience in defending malpractice lawsuits.

When preparing your defense, attorneys will investigate the subject of the lawsuit, obtain **expert witnesses**, handle motions throughout the case, and prepare medical models, transparencies, photographs, and other court exhibits, if necessary. The costs incurred in preparing a defense can be covered by your insurance.

Out-of-court settlements

During litigation, and indeed even before a lawsuit is actually filed in court, your insurance company will first try for a dismissal. If that attempt is unsuccessful, the company may then seek an out-of-court **settlement** from the patient's attorneys. Although this saves time and money, it may not be in your best professional interests. In the United States, if you believe your professional reputation is at stake, you may be able to refuse to agree to an out-of-court settlement. If your policy contains a threshold limit, your insurer can't settle a case out of court for an amount greater than the threshold limit without your permission. Without a threshold limit, your insurer has total control over out-of-court settlements.

If the lawsuit against you goes to court and the insurance company is defending you, the insurer has the right to control how the defense is conducted. The insurer's attorney makes all the decisions regarding the case's legal tactics and strategy. You, however, have a right to be kept advised of every step of the case. Most insurers will keep you informed. After all, the insurer knows that a successful defense depends in part on the defendant's cooperation. Also, you can sue the insurance agency if it fails to provide a competent defense.

If you lose a malpractice lawsuit, the insurance company will cover you for jury-awarded general and special damages. In the United States, juries award **general damages** to compensate for:
● pain and suffering
● worsening change in lifestyle.
Juries award **special damages** to relieve:
● present and future medical expenses
● past and future loss of earnings
● decreased earning capacity.

Punitive damages

The court may award **punitive damages** to punish actions that involve malice or reckless disregard for another. Historically, insurance companies haven't had to pay punitive damages. But recently, courts have been forcing insurers to pay punitive damages if the policy states that the company will pay "all sums which the insured shall become legally obligated to pay as damages." The courts have also directed insurers to expressly exclude punitive damages from coverage when writing the policy, if that's the insurer's intent.

Multiple insurers

You may have more than one insurance policy covering a patient's claim against you. For example, you might have malpractice coverage through the facility where you work and through membership in a professional organization, in addition to your own insurance policy. All three insurance companies might well become involved in settling a lawsuit. Determining who pays is complex. However, you must be sure to promptly notify every insurance company you have a policy with that you're the target of a malpractice lawsuit. That will prevent any of the companies from using the *policy defense* of lack of notice or late notice. Such policy defenses frequently enable the insurance company to successfully avoid responsibility for providing coverage.

Indemnification suits

If several insurance companies are representing different parties in a malpractice lawsuit, they'll typically file counteractions against the other parties, seeking compensation, or *indemnification*, for all or part of any damages the jury awards.

Many states now permit damages to be apportioned among multiple defendants, with the extent of liability dependent on the jury's determination of each defendant's relative contribution to the harm done. This is called *comparative negligence*. For example, suppose you were the nurse responsible for the instrument count during surgery in a foreign-object case, and the court found you to be 75% responsible. Your insurance company would pay 75% of the total award. The other insurance companies would be held liable for the remaining 25%, in proportion to the percentage of harm attributed to each remaining defendant.

A plaintiff's acts or omissions (for example, failure to follow a physician's order) may also be considered by a jury in determining where liability lies. Any judgment would be reduced by the plaintiff's own negligence. If one of the codefendants — the surgeon, for example — decided that he had been judged negligent only because of your negligence, he could instruct his insurance attorneys to file a new, separate lawsuit in his name against you.

Indemnification suits are becoming increasingly common. Your own facility, a fellow nurse, or a laboratory technician — as long as each has individual professional liability insurance — can file an indemnification suit against you. This possibility strengthens the argument for having your own professional liability insurance.

CONTROLLING LIABILITY COSTS

Many states are taking steps to decrease malpractice litigation. In addition to establishing special statutes of limitations, some states have imposed a maximum limit on how much a jury can award in general damages. That restriction, however, has been challenged on the grounds that it's unconstitutional.

Medical associations and insurance companies are also trying to limit malpractice awards in other ways: by forcing malpractice claims into *arbitration*, thus removing them from the province of *lay juries*, and by requiring that claims be screened by a medical malpractice screening panel. A few states such as Ohio provide for submission to nonbinding arbitration panels if all parties agree. State laws may also provide for binding arbitration if specified by a written contract between a patient and the physician or facility.

If a malpractice screening panel decides the plaintiff's claim isn't valid, the plaintiff can't file suit unless he posts a bond to cover his court costs in advance. More than half the states have set up screening panels, although the panels have been criticized by consumer groups and plaintiffs' attorneys and challenged in court as unconstitutional. The Alaska courts have upheld the constitutionality of screening panels; an example is *Keyes v. Humana Hospital Alaska, Inc.* (1988).

YOUR EMPLOYER'S INSURANCE

Virtually all health care facilities carry insurance to protect against their liability for an employee's mistakes. Without professional liability insurance, the facility would have to pay damages awarded in a lawsuit out of its own funds, which could lead to bankruptcy.

You should make a point of finding out the degree of professional and financial protection you're entitled to under your employer's liability insurance. This information will help you to more accurately assess your own professional liability insurance needs.

Consider obtaining, if your employer will allow, a copy of the facility's insurance policy and letting your professional liability insurance agent review it. Your agent, usually without a fee, should be willing to determine the extent, limits, and exclusions of your employer's insurance coverage.

Coverage limits

Each health care facility's professional liability insurance policy has a maximum dollar coverage limit. Your employer can purchase coverage that exceeds the basic limit; many facilities do so for extra protection.

Deductible limit

Most facilities also have a deductible provision that makes them responsible for damages under a certain figure. The higher the deductible limit, the lower the premium charged by the insurer. You should pay careful attention to the deductible limit because your employer may be able to settle a claim against you, for which they may be held financially responsible, under that figure without consulting you or the insurer. Because you won't have a chance to defend yourself and because many people interpret a settlement as an admission of guilt, such an action could tarnish your professional reputation. A tarnished reputation, in turn, could jeopardize your ability to obtain your own professional liability insurance or a new job. Therefore, in the event of a lawsuit, you should maintain close contact with your employer's legal staff and insist on being informed about each step in the case.

Threshold limit

Most health care facilities demand control over when an insurer can settle a case. To gain this control, the employer normally sets a threshold limit, usually $3,000. The insurer can settle a case below the threshold without the employer's permission. To settle a case above the threshold, however, the insurer must get the employer's permission, but not the employee's permission. The employer wants the threshold to protect its reputation for safety and quality care, the same reason you have for not wanting your insurance provider to settle a lawsuit against you without informing you. If an insurer were allowed to settle cases behind an employer's back, the employer could become more prone to malpractice lawsuits as its reputation deteriorated. The insurer's ability to settle claims concerning your conduct without consulting you, however, can tarnish your reputation.

Provisions for your defense

If you're sued and your employer's insurance covers you, the insurer may have a duty to provide a complete defense, including assigning an attorney to handle the entire case. The insurer will pay the attorneys' fees as well as any investigation costs and expert witnesses' fees.

Keep in mind that you're a player in the lawsuit, but the defense counsel is for the health care facility first and the nurse incidentally. A nurse sued for malpractice needs her own attorney, whose primary concern is her defense. This attorney may work closely with the facility's counsel, but his loyalty is to the nurse. He'll provide you with an opportunity to confer with him and give your side of the story.

If your employer grants written consent to settle the case, the insurer may do so, or it may decide to try the case in court if its legal advisors overrule the employer. If the plaintiff wins the lawsuit, the insurer is obliged to pay damages awarded to the patient up to the insurance policy's coverage limit.

Stipulations for denying coverage

Insurance companies that provide professional liability coverage for hospitals and other health care facilities reduce the risk they assume under respondeat superior in several ways. One way is by stipulating a precise coverage period, typically 1 year. Another way is by defining the type of coverage they'll provide, whether, for example, it's an occurrence or claims-made policy.

A third way is by putting exclusions into malpractice policies. These exclusions vary considerably from policy to policy, but all list specific acts, situations, or personnel that the insurance doesn't cover. In addition to exclusions, insurers may deny coverage to you or your employer due to other circumstances, such as:

● The insurance policy lapses because your employer failed to pay the premiums.

● Your employer refuses to cooperate with the insurance company, for whatever reason.

● The insurer discovers that your employer made misstatements on the insurance application.

In some malpractice situations, an insurer could agree to provide you with a defense but refuse to pay damages awarded to a patient. The insurer agrees to defend you in this situation because he doesn't want to be accused of **breach of contract**. But he must notify you of his intention not to pay damages in a **reservation-of-rights letter**. This letter informs you and your employer that the insurer believes the case falls outside what is covered by the insurance policy. When your employer and the insurer disagree about whether insurance coverage exists, the dispute may have to be resolved through separate legal action. Similarly, you have the right to bring such action against your employer's insurance company if it refuses to cover you.

Special considerations

Keep in mind a few more concerns when reviewing your employer's policy. First, is the policy purchased for you as an employee benefit? If so, the insurer protects *you* and not the facility.

Second, the policy may only provide coverage for **incidents** that occur while you're on the job. You may be held liable for nursing actions off the job, unless your actions are covered under a **Good Samaritan act**, a state law that protects health care professionals who act in an emergency.

Third, many employers provide only a claims-made policy. If a suit is filed against you after you've stopped working for that employer, for an incident that took place while you were still an employee, you probably won't be covered by your former employer's insurance plan.

Fourth, if you're an independent contractor, such as a private-duty nurse, you usually aren't considered by the court to be under the health care facility's direct supervision and control. Consequently, the facility won't be considered responsible for your actions, and its insurance probably won't cover you. However, if the policy is yours with

the facility paying the premiums as an employee benefit, you're still covered.

Finally, in most cases, your employer wouldn't be liable for your intentional acts of harm, such as striking a patient. In such cases, you would be responsible for any criminal or **civil penalties** levied against you. Again, if the policy is yours and not the facility's, whether the liability is imputed to the employer is irrelevant. However, intentional acts of harm usually aren't covered by any professional liability policy.

S*elected references*

Carelock, J., and Innerarity, S. "Critical Incidents: Effective Communication and Documentation," *Critical Care Nursing Quarterly* 23(4):59-66, February 2001.

Clayton, M. "Consent in Children: Legal and Ethical Issues," *Journal of Child Health Care* 4(2):78-81, Summer 2000.

Collins, S.E. "Litigation Risks for Infusion Specialists. Understanding the Issues," *Journal of Infusion Nursing* 24(6):375-80, November-December 2001.

Collins, S.E. "Nursing Malpractice Insurance: Individual Insurance Policy Purchase," *Florida Nurse* 50(1):14-15, March 2002.

Exstrom, S.M. "The State Board of Nursing and Its Role in Continued Competency," *Journal of Continuing Education in Nursing* 32(3):118-25, May-June 2001.

Fanaeian, N., and Merwin, E. "Malpractice: Provider Risk or Consumer Protection?" *American Journal of Medical Quality* 16(2):43-57, March-April 2001.

Fiesta, J. "Nursing Malpractice: Cause for Consideration," *Nursing Management* 30(2):12-13, February 1999.

Gibson, T. "Nurses and Medication Error: A Discursive Reading of the Literature," *Nursing Inquiry* 8(2):108-17, April 2001.

Goudreau, K., and Chasens, E.R. "Negligence in Nursing Education," *Nurse Educator* 27(1):42-46, January-February 2002.

Helm, A., and Kihm, N.C. "Is Professional Liability Insurance for You? Before You Say No, Weigh These Considerations," *Nursing2001* 31(1):48-49, January 2001.

LaDuke, S. "What Should You Expect from Your Attorney?" *Nursing Management* 31(1):10, January 2000.

Lagana, K. "The 'Right' to a Caring Relationship: The Law and Ethic of Care," *Journal of Perinatal and Neonatal Nursing* 14(2):12-24, September 2000.

Sheehy, S.B. "Understanding the Legal Process: Your Best Defense," *Journal of Emergency Nursing* 25(6):492-95, December 1999.

Wassel, M.L., et al. "What are the Legal or Malpractice Issues Faced by Case Managers?" *AAOHN Journal* 49(8): 374-77, August 2001.

Chapter Two

MEDICATION ERRORS

UNFORTUNATELY, lawsuits involving nurses' drug errors are common. The court determines liability based on the standards of care required of nurses when administering drugs. In many instances, if the nurse had known more about the proper dose, administration route, or procedure connected with giving the drug, she might have avoided the mistake that resulted in the lawsuit.

Case studies

The following court cases illustrate how errors in medication administration can result in nurses going to court.

CASE 1

In *Voorhees v. the University of Pennsylvania* (1997), a judgment was rendered against the hospital for the widow of a former patient. The action was brought under the *wrongful death statute*, alleging that the hospital, through its nursing and medical staff, was negli-

gent. The patient developed pain after work-related injuries and was diagnosed with bilateral avascular necrosis of the femoral heads. The patient, who was admitted to the hospital, agreed to participate in a *randomized-controlled study* of prophylactic anticoagulation therapy to reduce the incidence of clot formation or pulmonary emboli while undergoing hip replacement surgery.

On the day of the left hip surgery, heparin was ordered; however, the patient didn't receive the medication due to a nursing error. The patient was removed from the study because of the missed medication dose and, although it was ordered, he didn't receive any prophylactic anticoagulation therapy until 36 hours after the surgery, when he was started on aspirin twice per day.

The right hip surgery was performed 7 days after the left hip surgery, and the only anticoagulation therapy given to the patient was aspirin. The next day, a venogram of the left leg revealed clots in several deep veins below the knee and a thrombus in multiple muscular branches. In spite of the venogram findings, heparin wasn't ordered for the clots present, and vascular studies of the right leg weren't ordered.

On the day of discharge, a nurse noted right ankle swelling; however, she failed to measure the patient's calves or notify the attending physician. The patient was discharged without additional studies or anticoagulation therapy to address the formed blood clots. The patient died at home several days later from bilateral pulmonary emboli and it was undisputed that a right lower leg clot was the cause of the embolism.

A physician **expert witness** for the estate of the patient testified that the nurses were negligent for:

• failing to administer the ordered medication that was intended to prevent clot formation on the day of surgery.

• failing to give any form of anticoagulant prophylaxis, whether it was heparin or a substitute, after the surgery for a period of 36 hours.

• failing to administer the ordered anticoagulant medication to patients under this protocol two times in the past. The incident with this patient was the third time a medication error had occurred. Therefore, the hospital should have known about the potential for this type of occurrence and provided some type of backup plan in the form of policies and procedures to address it. The hospital was legally "on notice."

• failing to notify the physician of the patient's clinical sign of ankle swelling.

CASE 2

In the case of *Wright v. Abbott Laboratories* (1999), a newborn went limp after birth and required resuscitation. The newborn was transferred to the neonatal special care unit for blood pressuring monitoring, temperature regulation, and I.V. fluids. The newborn's blood pressure was checked every 15 minutes and glucose monitoring was performed every hour. A resident was called about the newborn's low blood pressure and the resident ordered "I.V. piggyback normal saline, 20 cc over 30 minutes." Nurse Karen Diltz overheard Nurse Donna Benjamin repeating the order and asked if she could help. Nurse Diltz didn't read the physician's order (that was recorded by a third nurse, Nurse Rhonda Martin) and relied on what she heard Nurse Benjamin repeating.

Nurse Diltz removed a vial from the medication cart. The medication cart contained labeled vials of 0.9% sodium chloride and 14.6% sodium chloride. Nurse Diltz drew 25 cc of 14.6% sodium chloride from the vial and then gave the syringe to Nurse Benjamin, who injected the medication into a porthole in the newborn's I.V. tubing. Less than 1 hour later, the resident ordered another 20 cc of normal saline. Again Nurse Diltz used a vial of 14.6% sodium chloride from the medicine cart and drew up 25 cc with a syringe. Nurse Diltz again gave the syringe to Nurse Benjamin, who injected the medication into the I.V. tubing again. The newborn sustained severe permanent physical injuries as the result of the concentrated saline injections. Further complicating matters for

Nurse Diltz was the fact that Nurse Benjamin wasn't authorized to administer I.V. medications.

The hospital entered into a structured settlement with the family of the newborn after a medical malpractice action was filed. The family also sued the drug manufacturer, arguing that the manufacturer failed to warn the hospital that the concentrated saline could be mistaken for diluted saline, that the product warning was inadequate, and that the mistaken injection of concentrated saline was a foreseeable misuse. The drug manufacturer argued that it provided adequate warning to the hospital and that the manufacturer had a right to assume that hospital employees would follow warnings on the product, and that the absence of warnings didn't cause the injuries to the newborn. The court found for the drug manufacturer.

Legal issues

The National Coordinating Council for Medication Error Reporting and Prevention defines a medication error as any preventable event that may cause or lead to inappropriate use or patient harm while the medication is in the control of the health care professional, patient, or consumer. These preventable events may be related to professional practice, health care products, procedures, or systems (such as prescribing, order communication, compounding, dispensing, distribution, administration, education, monitoring, use, and product labeling, packaging, and nomenclature).

Appropriate medication administration requires consideration of the five "rights" of medication administration:

- right patient
- right medication
- right dosage
- right route
- right time.

Civil liability can result to the nurse and her employer from the failure to implement the five rights of medication administration, as illustrated by the case scenarios above. (See *Medication errors and nursing liability*.) The case studies deal with civil lawsuits instituted by a patient or a patient's family against a hospital for nursing *negligence* in the administration of medication.

CASE 1

In case 1 (*Voorhees v. the University of Pennsylvania* [1997]), the patient's family's attorney presented two theories of hospital liability for the actions of the nurses: ***respondeat superior*** and ***corporate liability***. The first doctrine, *respondeat superior,* holds that when an employee is found negligent, the employer must accept responsibility if the employee was acting within the scope of his employment. (See "Respondeat superior" in chapter 1, page 6.) The second doctrine, corporate liability, holds the hospital **liable** for its own wrongful conduct — for any breach of its duties as mandated by **statutory law**, **common law**, and applicable rules. Corporate liability creates a ***nondelegable duty*** (that is, the duty can't be delegated or assigned to another party) that the hospital owes directly to the patient to ensure the patient's well-being and safety while hospitalized. Corporate liability requires the patient to prove that the hospital knew or should have known about the breach of duty that was harming its patients.

The four general areas of hospital duties owed to a patient include:

● A duty to use reasonable care in the maintenance of safe and adequate facilities and equipment.

● A duty to select and retain competent physicians.

● A duty to oversee all persons who practice medicine within its purview as to patient care.

● A duty to formulate, adopt, and enforce adequate rules and policies to ensure quality care for patients.

In this case, *respondeat superior* liability of the hospital was attributed to the nurses' failure to administer the ordered prophylactic anticoagulant therapy, failure of the nurses to give an anticoagulant medication on the day of surgery and not until 36 hours after surgery, and failure of the nurses and physicians to manage the patient's ankle swelling. Corporate liability of the hospital was based on the failure of the nursing staff to administer the ordered medication in the protocol twice before this incident; therefore, the hospital was negligent for failing to take steps to avoid a recurrence of this medication error.

Let's explore the errors specific to the nurses involved in this case.

Failure to administer an ordered medication

The nurse failed to give the dose of heparin ordered for the patient on

RELATED CASES

Medication errors and nursing liability

When reviewing cases involving medication errors, one point becomes clear: The courts won't tolerate carelessness that harms the patient.

In a 1990 case, *Demers v. United States,* the patient was admitted to the hospital for pacemaker implantation. Following the procedure, he was erroneously administered diltiazem (Cardiazem), a drug intended for another patient. This error resulted in the patient's death; the suit was brought by the patient's wife.

Administering the right dose is also imperative. In an Ohio case, *Gallimore v. Children's Memorial Hospital* (1993), a nurse inadvertently gave a child 200 mg of gentamicin rather than the ordered 30 mg dose when she failed to securely clamp the I.V. tubing. The child suffered hearing loss as a result of the overdose and the nurse was found negligent.

Similarly, in *Dessauer v. Memorial General Hospital* (New Mexico 1981), an emergency department physician ordered 50 mg of lidocaine for a patient. However, the nurse, who normally worked in the hospital's obstetrics ward, gave the patient 800 mg. The patient died, the family sued, and the hospital was found liable.

Questioning a drug order

If you question a drug order, follow your hospital's policies. Usually, they'll tell you to try each of the following actions until you receive a satisfactory answer:

- Look up the answer in a reliable drug reference.
- Ask your charge nurse.
- Ask the hospital pharmacist.
- Ask your nursing supervisor or the prescribing physician.
- Ask the chief nursing administrator (if she hasn't already become involved).
- Ask the prescribing physician's supervisor (service chief).
- Get in touch with the hospital administration and explain your problem.
- Document all of these actions.

the day of the first hip surgery. A nurse is obligated to administer a prescribed medication unless she has reason to believe that the medication is contraindicated for the patient. In that event, the nurse should call the physician to clarify the prescribed medication order. (See *Questioning a drug order.*) If a nurse must refuse to give a medication because of a contraindication, she should discuss her concerns with the physician and her nursing supervisor. (See *Refusing to administer a drug.*)

A medication can be given within the time parameters noted by facility policy — some medications can be given 1 hour before or after the time written on the medication administration record and still be considered a timely administration of the medication. However, in this case, the nurse failed to give the drug at all.

Failure of the nurses and physicians to give prophylactic anticoagulation

The patient didn't receive anticoagulant medication until 36 hours after the first surgery. After a review of the medication administration record, the nurses caring for this patient postoperatively should have assessed that the patient wasn't receiving any type of anticoagulation therapy and should have notified the physician to investigate further.

Failure of the nursing staff to administer a medication on three separate occasions

Most hospitals have quality assurance committees or teams, consisting of nursing, pharmacy, medicine, legal, and risk management representatives, to identify, analyze, and formulate strategies to combat these types of repetitive incidents. Based on this hospital's failure to identify and appropriately correct these recurrent errors, the jury held the hospital corporately liable for the actions of the nursing staff.

Failure of the nursing staff to manage the clinical sign of ankle swelling

The discharge nurse noted swelling in the patient's right ankle, which is suggestive of a blood clot. Remember that a clot originating in the right lower leg caused the em-

Refusing to administer a drug

All nurses have the legal right not to administer drugs they think will harm patients. You may choose to exercise this right in a variety of situations:

- when you think the dosage prescribed is too high
- when you think the drug is contraindicated because of possible dangerous interactions with other drugs, or with such substances as alcohol
- because you think the patient's physical condition contraindicates using the drug.

In limited circumstances you may also legally refuse to administer a drug on grounds of conscience. Some states and Canadian jurisdictions have enacted *right-of-*

conscience laws. These laws excuse medical personnel from the requirement to participate in any abortion or sterilization procedure. Under such laws you may, for example, refuse to give any drug you believe is intended to induce abortion.

When you refuse to carry out a drug order, be sure to do the following:

- Notify your immediate supervisor so she can make alternative arrangements (assigning a new nurse, clarifying the order).
- Notify the prescribing physician if your supervisor hasn't done so already.
- Document that the drug wasn't given and explain why.

---

bolism. However, this nurse didn't notify a physician of the swelling, nor did she perform further assessment of the patient's legs, such as measuring the diameter of both calves, both of which constitute a failure to act in accordance with minimum acceptable levels of patient care.

LESSONS IN PRACTICE For safe practice, carefully review the medication administration record and the physician's orders at the start of every shift to determine if a medication is ordered, scheduled, or discontinued, or if the route, dosage, or time has been changed. When obtaining shift report from the nurse before you, ask whether there have been any

changes in the medications ordered. The patient's participation in research studies should also be communicated in the shift report. (See *Your role in drug experimentation,* page 40.) Remember to notify the physician of unusual or abnormal findings, especially if the patient is about to be discharged.

CASE 2

In case 2 (*Wright v. Abbott Laboratories* [1999]), the nurse administered concentrated sodium chloride I.V. to a newborn when normal saline solution was ordered. Nurse Diltz, who drew up the incorrect medication in the syringe, acknowledged in her testimony:

Your role in drug experimentation

At times you may participate in administering experimental drugs to patients or administering established drugs in new ways or at experimental dosage levels. Your legal duties don't change, but if you have any questions, you'll get your answers from the experimental *protocol* instead of the usual sources (such as books and package inserts). An institutional review board probably reviewed and accepted the protocol before it was instituted. This is another resource for the nurse, especially if ethical concerns regarding the treatment develop. It's important that you make sure no drug is given to a patient who hasn't consented to participate. Consent should be in writing for all experimental protocols.

● The hospital's policies and procedures held the nurse legally accountable to know, for each medication administered, the drug's action, adverse reactions, and implications for nursing care.
● The hospital's policies and procedures required the nurse to check the name of the patient, the patient's identification bracelet, and the drug, dosage, route, and time on the patient's record and medication label three times prior to administration.
● She had been taught, in nursing school and by the hospital, to check and double-check the five rights of drug administration: right patient, right drug, right route, right dose, and right time.
● The hospital's policies and procedures required her to read a medication order prior to administration of that medication.
● The newborn wasn't hyponatremic and there were no indications to administer concentrated sodium chloride.

● She knew that the normal saline solution and concentrated sodium chloride were stocked in the same medication cart but in different drawers; and she knew the difference between normal saline solution and concentrated sodium chloride, and the indications for each.
● She had administered concentrated sodium chloride more than 10 times but fewer than 100 times prior to the incident in question.
● She knew a medication error involving concentrated sodium chloride could result in serious injuries.
● She knew the order was for a volume expander and that concentrated sodium chloride wasn't a volume expander.
● She knew that a normal saline vial held only 10 cc, yet she drew up 25 cc of concentrated sodium chloride twice from a vial.
● She failed to follow nursing policies, failed to read the concentration on the vial, and handed the syringe to a nurse who wasn't authorized to administer the solution.

Nurse Diltz testified that she relied on what she overhead and that she didn't record or read the verbal order taken by Nurse Benjamin, the nurse who actually administered the concentrated sodium chloride. She also testified that it was her normal practice to read a drug label 3 times before administering that drug; however, she didn't read the label of the vial to determine the concentration of the sodium chloride in this case.

FAILURE TO OBSERVE DRUG SAFETY BASICS

Not only was Nurse Diltz questioned about the events that lead to the lawsuit, but her knowledge of her hospital's policies and procedures and her education in drug administration were also explored. In this case, Nurse Diltz failed to observe a number of basic drug safety principles, any of which may have prevented her from drawing up the incorrect medication and giving it to another nurse to administer.

The first mistake Nurse Diltz made was failing to review the verbal order taken and written by another person. Reviewing the written order may have helped Nurse Diltz identify her error as she checked the order against the medication she was preparing for administration.

Her second mistake was her failure to read the label of the concentrated sodium chloride. Neglecting to read the label breached the policies and procedures of the hospital, the standard of clinical practice taught in nursing school, and the

legal standard of care owed to the patient.

Her third mistake was handing the syringe to Nurse Benjamin for administration. Even though a medication may be needed emergently, nurses are still required to provide safe nursing care and to act in accordance with facility practices and general nursing parameters. Nurse Diltz should have taken the time to label the syringe with its contents, which would have given her another opportunity to realize she was drawing up the wrong medication.

Nurse Diltz' fourth mistake was giving the syringe to a nurse who wasn't authorized to administer I.V. medications. (Nurse Benjamin was also negligent for accepting an unlabeled syringe and administering its contents without question.)

If you're unsure of the **licensure** and **scope of practice** of another nurse, you should speak with the nurse and with your nursing supervisor. Your goal is to avoid asking other nurses to perform tasks that they may not legally be entitled to perform. Because of the their actions, Nurse Diltz and Nurse Benjamin could have also faced license sanctioning by their state board of nursing. Each of the mistakes detailed above is a breach in **standard** nursing practice.

●◗▶ **LESSONS IN PRACTICE** As a nurse, you can learn a great deal from Nurse Diltz' mistakes. First, a verbal order should always be written by the nurse taking the order and repeated back to the person giving the order to avoid misinterpretations. (See *Documenting verbal drug orders,* page 42.) The order should be re-

Documenting verbal drug orders

When a physician writes a drug order for the patient and signs it — or when another health care professional writes an order and the physician countersigns it — the courts usually won't question the legality of the order. However, if a physician gives you a verbal drug order — either in person or by telephone — protect yourself legally, as follows:

- Write down the order exactly as he gives it, the date, and the time.
- Repeat the order back to him so that you're sure you heard the physician correctly.

Documentation guidelines

After you have given the drug to the patient, make sure you document all the necessary information:

- Record in ink the type of drug, the dosage, the time you administered it, and any other information your facility's policy requires.
- Sign or initial your notes.
- Make sure the physician cosigns the drug order as soon as possible.

If your facility keeps drug orders in a special file, make sure you transfer the physician's drug order, which you wrote on the patient's chart, to that file.

If a physician orally gives a drug order during an emergency, your first duty is to carry it out at once. When the emergency is over, document what you did.

The danger of poor documentation

Here's what can happen if you don't document drug orders:

- You could face disciplinary measures for failing to document.
- You could damage your defense or your facility's in a malpractice suit.
- Other nurses, not knowing what drugs have been given, may administer other drugs that could result in harmful interactions.
- If controlled substances are given, suspicions could be raised that you're diverting drugs for your own use.

viewed and the medication administration record checked (if necessary) prior to giving the medication. Also, don't forget to check (and double-check) the five rights of medication administration. If she had followed these steps, Nurse Diltz might not have been sued.

University of Texas Medical Branch v. Danesi (1999) demonstrates that medication errors may lead to lawsuits resulting not only from physical problems, but emotional problems as well. In this case, the patient sued the hospital for negligence after he was given the wrong medication by the nursing staff. He was informed about the medication error by a physician. The patient alleged that the nursing staff's negligence in administering the wrong medication caused him to suffer from anxiety, shortness of breath, and emotional distress. The jury found for the patient, awarding him with mental anguish *damages*, a finding that the hospital *appealed*. However, the patient again presented direct evidence of the nature, duration, and severity of his mental anguish with his testimony, which included:

• the medication error frightened him and caused him stress and anxiety because he thought he was going to die

• the medication error still causes a disruption in his life as he fears taking the wrong medication; as a result, he has his wife carefully monitor his medication.

His wife also testified about the stress associated with the incident, and a nurse expert testified that patients who know they have received the wrong medication suffer from anxiety. The jury upheld its original verdict.

Avoiding litigation

Nurses who are involved in medication errors may be counseled, disciplined, even discharged, depending on the nature and severity of the incident and the employer's policies and procedures.

LOSS OF BENEFITS

Depending on the law in her state, the nurse may be denied unemployment compensation benefits if she's discharged for a medication error, especially if that error was committed by an act of *willful conduct*. Willful conduct refers to an intentional act, as opposed to negligence — committing an inadvertent

mistake. A nurse still may be denied unemployment benefits, even when her conduct wasn't willful, depending on the wording and the case law associated with her state's unemployment statute.

Take the case of *Anderson v. Commission of Labor* (1998), in which a licensed practical nurse was discharged from her employment for failing to administer a scheduled medication to a diabetic patient. This was her second offense in the facility; she had previously been suspended for a medication error involving insulin. The nurse applied for unemployment compensation benefits, but her claim was denied by the Unemployment Insurance Appeal Board because she had lost her employment under disqualifying circumstances. The court found that the nurse's negligence had persisted after her first error, despite prior warning and remedial action by the facility, and that this constituted disqualifying conduct. The order of the Unemployment Insurance Appeal Board that denied benefits to the nurse was upheld on appeal.

LOSS OF LICENSE

A nurse involved in medication errors may also be the subject of investigation by the board of nursing in the state in which she's licensed, which may result in *licensure sanctions*. The role of the state board of nursing is to protect the public from unsafe nursing care. The improper administration of, or failure to administer, a medication may be considered unsafe nursing care, depending on the state's nurse practice act.

An example of this is *Hicks v. the State of Delaware* (1994), wherein the state filed a ***complaint*** with the Delaware Board of Nursing alleging that a licensed practical nurse (LPN) was guilty of unprofessional conduct, rendering her unfit to practice nursing. The complaint alleged that the LPN:

● committed several errors while dispensing medication

● charted medications as given, when, in fact, the medications hadn't been given (this conduct is criminal as well as unprofessional)

● gave medications without documentation of such

● failed to document and transcribe information into the patient's record.

The Delaware Board of Nursing suspended the nurse's license for 3 years because she committed medication and documentation errors on multiple occasions, against sound nursing practice and against the established policies and procedures of the facility in which she worked. The nurse appealed; however, the Board's decision was upheld because the suspension was supported by testimony and because the sanction imposed by the Board was within the parameters of the Delaware Nurse Practice Act.

Administering drugs to patients continues to be one of the most important — and, legally, one of the most risky — tasks nurses perform. Since the release of the Institute of Medicine's report, *To Err Is Human: Building a Safer Health System* (2000), which noted adverse medical errors are responsible for at least 44,000 and as many as 98,000 deaths in the United States, medication errors are receiving a great deal of attention.

Over time, nurses' responsibilities with regard to drug administration have increased. For many years, U.S. and Canadian nurses were only permitted to give drugs orally or rectally. Today nurses give subcutaneous and intramuscular injections, induce anesthesia, and administer I.V. therapy. In some states, nurses may even prescribe drugs, within certain limitations. Both U.S. and Canadian laws, however, continue to strictly guard the nurse's role in drug administration. Within this limited scope, the law imposes exceptionally high standards.

To guard yourself against litigation involving the medications you administer, become familiar with the rules and laws governing drugs and medication administration.

FIVE RIGHTS FORMULA

In the case studies presented above, the nurses could have avoided the medication errors they made by following the five rights of medication administration. Following these simple steps — checking that you have the right drug, given to the right patient, at the right time, in the right dosage, by the right route — is an easy way to guard against malpractice liability. You would be wise to add a sixth right to this checklist: *by the right technique.*

DRUG CONTROL LAWS

Legally, a drug is any substance listed in an official state, jurisdictional, or national ***formulary***. A drug may also be defined as any substance (other than food) "intended to affect the structure or any function of the body... (or) for use in the diagnosis, cure, mitigation, treatment, or prevention of disease."

A *prescription drug* is any drug restricted from regular commercial purchase and sale. A state, jurisdictional, or national government has determined that this drug is, or might be, unsafe unless used under a qualified medical practitioner's supervision.

FEDERAL LAWS

The Comprehensive Drug Abuse Prevention and Control Act and the Food, Drug, and Cosmetic Act are two important federal laws governing the use of drugs in the United States. The Comprehensive Drug Abuse Prevention and Control Act (incorporating the Controlled Substances Act) seeks to categorize drugs by how dangerous they are and regulates drugs thought to be most subject to abuse. The Food, Drug, and Cosmetic Act restricts interstate shipment of drugs not approved for human use and outlines the process for testing and approving new drugs.

STATE LAWS

At the state and jurisdictional level, pharmacy practice acts — state and jurisdictional laws that mirror federal laws — are the main laws affecting the distribution of drugs. Through these acts, criminal penalties attach under state or jurisdictional law for similar violations. These laws give pharmacists (in Canada, sometimes physicians as well) the sole legal authority to prepare, compound, preserve, and *dispense* drugs. Dispense refers to taking a drug from the pharmacy supply and giving or selling it to another person. This contrasts with administering drugs — actually getting the drug into the patient. Your nurse practice act is the law that most directly affects how you administer drugs.

Most nursing, medical, and pharmacy practice acts include:
• a definition of the tasks that belong uniquely to the profession
• a statement saying that anyone who performs such tasks without being a licensed or registered member of the defined profession is breaking the law.

In some states and jurisdictions, certain tasks overlap. For example, both nurses and physicians can provide bedside care for the sick and patient teaching.

In many states, if a nurse prescribes a drug, she's *practicing medicine without a license*; if she goes into the pharmacy or drug supply cabinet, measures out doses of a drug, and puts the powder into capsules, she's practicing pharmacy without a license. For either action, she can be prosecuted or lose her license, even if no harm results. In most states and Canadian jurisdictions, to practice a licensed profession without a license is, at the very least, a *misdemeanor*.

YOUR RESPONSIBILITY FOR KNOWING ABOUT DRUGS

When you have your nursing license, the law expects you to know about any drug you administer. If you're an LPN you assume the same legal responsibility as a registered nurse once you've taken a pharmaceutical course or obtained authorization to administer drugs. More specifically, the law expects you to:

● know a drug's safe dosage limits, toxicity, potential ***adverse reactions***, and indications and contraindications for use

● refuse to accept an illegible, confusing, or otherwise unclear drug order

● seek clarification of a confusing order from the physician and not to try to interpret it yourself.

Increasingly, judges and juries expect nurses to know what the appropriate observation intervals are for a patient receiving any type of medication. They expect you to know this even if the physician doesn't know or if he doesn't write an order stating how often to check on the newly medicated patient.

LPN'S ROLE IN ADMINISTERING DRUGS

Most nurse practice acts now permit LPNs with the appropriate educational background or on-the-job training to give drugs under the supervision of a registered nurse, physician, or dentist. What constitutes appropriate training or educational background? No clear-cut definitions exist, but most courts probably would be satisfied if an LPN could prove that her supervising registered nurse or physician had watched her administer drugs and had judged her competent. For tasks that require instruction and experience beyond the nurse's academic training, health care facilities usually develop didactic training with goals and proficiency tests. Additionally, skills testing should be documented through proficiency checklists. This provides objective documentation in case of a lawsuit. (Note, however, that some states prohibit LPNs from inserting I.V. lines.)

PROTECTING YOURSELF FROM LIABILITY

If you make an error in giving a drug, or if your patient reacts negatively to a properly administered drug, inform the patient's physician immediately and protect yourself by documenting the incident thoroughly. Besides normal drug-charting information, include information on the patient's reaction and any medical or nursing ***interventions*** taken.

In the event of an error, you should also file an incident report. Identify what happened, the names and functions of all persons involved, and what actions were taken to protect the patient after the error was discovered.

SOUND ADVICE

Follow these general tips to help you avoid medication errors.

● Check the five "rights" of medication administration each and every time you administer a drug.

● Double-check all medication calculations and fluid rates. When in doubt, have another nurse check your calculations before you administer the drug.

● If you aren't familiar with the medication, look it up in a current drug reference book. Be sure you know why you're giving the drug, and check that the dose is appropriate.

• Educate the patient on the medication use process. Inform and provide the patient with literature on the side effects and complications of a particular medication. Involve the family, if applicable.

• If applicable, allow the patient to view the medication prior to administration so that he can start to identify the medication as the "small red pill" or the "horse pill." The patient will then be in a better position to know if he's being administered the wrong medication.

• Ask patients who are routinely admitted to a unit to bring with them their medication prescription bottles from home so that hospital staff can determine what medications the patient has been prescribed.

• Ask for clarification if a physician writes "resume home medications" on the discharge summary. It's well worth the extra time spent reviewing the medical record and discussing the medications with the physicians involved in the patient's care to determine what medications were taken preadmission and if those medications were discontinued or are contraindicated based on the current treatment plan, to determine what new medications were ordered for the patient as a result of the admission, and to clarify which medications the patient will take at home upon discharge. The discharging physician and nurse both have duties here. You don't want a patient going home to take the wrong medications.

• Don't administer a medication for a colleague without checking the medication administration record or physician's order first. Follow the five rights of medication administration here as well.

• Don't allow the patient to take medications from home unless you have a physician's order, the pharmacy is notified, and facility policy and procedure allow the patient to take medications from home. The medication should be kept with the rest of the patient's scheduled medication.

• On admission, ask patients specifically about prescription medication, over-the-counter (OTC) medication, and herbal remedies being taken. A patient may not consider an herbal remedy or an OTC preparation to be a medication, and he may forget to tell you unless specifically asked about each.

• When administering blood products and other high-risk products and solutions, follow facility policies and procedures for administrating, charting, and monitoring.

• Develop a proactive nursing practice by staying informed on the latest and current developments in your field and reading up on the medications most commonly given in your practice setting.

• If you're a home health care nurse, assess the patient's compliance with medication administration, knowledge about the medication and side effects, and the caregiver's knowledge about the patient's medication regimen.

• If you're a long-term care nurse, assess and report the effectiveness of medication being administered to residents (as should be done in any setting). Medication administration is an important and vital component of the services being provided to the residents.

The practice of nursing can be very rewarding, yet it's also fraught with potential liability for the nurse. Taking a proactive approach to medication safety will reduce the risk of civil, criminal, and administrative liability for a nurse and the risk of civil liability for the employer.

Selected references

Anderson, D.J., and Webster, C.S. "A Systems Approach to the Reduction of Medication Error on the Hospital Ward," *Journal of Advanced Nursing* 35(1):34-41, July 2001.

Antonow, J.A., et al. "Medication Error Reporting: A Survey of Nursing Staff," *Journal of Nursing Care Quality* 15(1):42-48, October 2000.

Aufseeser-Weiss, M.R., and Ondeck, D.A. "Medication Use Risk Management: Hospital Meets Home Care," *Journal of Nursing Care Quality* 15(2):50-57, January 2001.

Benner, P. "Creating a Culture of Safety and Improvement: A Key to Reducing Medical Error," *American Journal of Critical Care* 10(4):281-84, July 2001.

Bond, C.A., et al. "Medication Errors in United States Hospitals," *Pharmacotherapy* 21(9): 1023-1036, September 2001.

Cavell, G.F. "Drugs: The Nurse's Responsibility," *Professional Nurse* 15(5):296, February 2000.

Cox, J. "Quality Medication Administration," *Contemporary Nurse* 9(3-4):308-13, September-December 2000.

Gibson, T. "Nurses and Medication Error: A Discursive Reading of the Literature," *Nursing Inquiry* 8(2):108-17.

"Infusion Pumps: Preventing Future Adverse Events," *Sentinel Event Alert* (15):1-3, November 2000.

McCarthy, A.M., et al. "Medication Administration Practices of School Nurses," *Journal of School Health* 70(9):371-76, November 2000.

"Medication Errors Related to Potentially Dangerous Abbreviations," *Sentinel Event Alert* (23):1-4, September 2001.

Morris, M.R. "Preventing Med Errors," *RN* 62(9):69-73, September 1999.

O'Shea, E. "Factors Contributing to Medication Errors: A Literature Review," *Journal of Clinical Nursing* 8(5):496-504, September 1999.

Pape, T.M. "Searching for the Final Answer: Factors Contributing to Medication Administration Errors," *Journal of Continuing Education in Nursing* 32(4):152-60, July-August 2001.

"Reports Spotlight Medication Errors: Make Changes Before Tragedy Strikes," *ED Management* 12(6):61-66, suppl 1-2, June 2000.

Wolf, Z.R., et al. "Responses and Concerns of Healthcare Providers to Medication Errors," *Clinical Nurse Specialist* 14(6):278-87, November 2000.

Zuzelo, P.R., et al. "Content Validation of the Medication Error Worksheet," *Clinical Nurse Specialist* 15(6):253-59, November 2001.

FAILURE TO COMMUNICATE INFORMATION

CLINICAL NURSING PRACTICE involves different types of communication with a variety of health care professionals. Communication may be verbal, nonverbal, or written between nurses and nurses, nurses and other members of the interdisciplinary health care team, and nurses and patients and their family members. In each type of communication and with each individual involved in the communication process, there's the possibility that information will be miscommunicated, misunderstood, or not communicated. This chapter examines some of the more common areas of failure to communicate information in health care settings and presents tips for preventing potential *liability*.

Case studies

The following court cases illustrate the importance of nurses communicating clearly and fully with staff, patients, and families.

CASE 1

Nurses have a responsibility to communicate with each other as well as other members of the health care team, especially if there's a change in a patient's status. *Holton v. Memorial Hospital* (1997) aptly illustrates the tragic outcomes that are possible when there's a failure to communicate changes in a patient's status.

In late November or early December 1991, Patricia Holton began to suffer severe back pain. Her physician ordered X-rays and a bone scan of her spine. These tests revealed that Mrs. Holton suffered from either a degenerative process or a compression fracture of the vertebrae in her thoracic spine. She was scheduled for magnetic resonance imaging (MRI) to be performed on January 4, the earliest available date for a nonemergency MRI. Her physician instructed her to go to the emergency department (ED) if her pain worsened.

On the evening of December 26, Mrs. Holton went to the ED of Memorial Hospital, complaining of numbness below the waist and a tingling sensation in her left leg. The ED physician, Dr. Jergens, examined the patient and found that she had a low-grade fever and an elevated white blood cell count, indicating the presence of an infection. There was no evidence of any loss of motor skills on examination. A blood culture and computed tomography (CT) scan were ordered. Dr. Jergens wrote in his admitting note that a spinal epidural abscess was a possible explanation for the patient's signs and symptoms.

Mrs. Holton was admitted to the hospital under the care of Dr. Doubek, her primary care physician. He examined her early on the morning of December 27 and noted she had numbness, tingling, and weakness in her lower extremities. He then ordered a neurologic consultation.

Dr. Murphy, a neurosurgeon, examined Mrs. Holton late in the afternoon of December 27. She complained of numbness in her abdomen and legs, but could still move her lower extremities. The CT scan confirmed the existence of a compression fracture and the radiologist who interpreted the CT scan noted that her pain was most likely due to a cancerous tumor.

During the day of December 27, Mrs. Holton noted increasing difficulty moving her left leg. She brought this to the attention of the nurse caring for her. There was no indication in the **nurses' notes** of this new symptom; the only documentation was that the patient didn't experience any significant change in her condition during the day. Between 6 p.m. and 7 p.m. on that same day, Mrs. Holton walked to the bathroom unassisted. When she attempted to return to her bed, she noted that the numbness in her left leg had greatly increased and she couldn't move her legs or stand up. She rang for assistance and two nurses' aides helped her into a wheelchair and then back to bed. The nurses' aides failed to report this incident to the nurse or to the physician.

The night shift nurse who cared for Mrs. Holton noted that she was having difficulty moving her leg, but she didn't believe this to be a significant change in the patient's status. The next morning, December 28, Mrs. Holton complained of numbness from the waist down and was only able to move her right leg slightly. She also had lost bowel and bladder control. The nurse caring for Mrs. Holton reported these symptoms immediately to Dr. Doubek and the neurosurgeon on call. Tests were ordered to determine where the pressure on the spinal cord was located.

Dr. Doubek testified at trial that at the time of his diagnosis he was operating under the assumption that Mrs. Holton had suffered a sudden onset of paralysis because he hadn't been informed that her sensory deficits had been progressing over several hours. Accordingly, he thought her condition was caused by a tumor-induced infarct of the blood supply to the spinal cord, which would be consistent with sudden and complete loss of motor function. In fact, the escalation from numbness and tingling to paresis indicates spinal cord compression caused by osteomyelitis. Osteomyelitis can cause inflammation or an abscess, both of which can place pressure on the spine. Because Dr. Doubek determined that a tumor was the more likely cause of the patient's condition, he felt that radiation was the best course of treatment.

Similarly, the neurosurgeon on call testified that he would have examined Mrs. Holton immediately if he had been informed that she was beginning to have difficulty ambulating and moving her legs. According to the neurosurgeon, by the time Mrs. Holton lost bowel and bladder control her condition was irreversible. Had the condition been correctly diagnosed and treated when her signs and symptoms first appeared, she could have had an

excellent neurologic recovery.

On January 21, 1991, Mrs. Holton was transferred to a second facility because her condition wasn't improving. At that hospital, she was diagnosed and treated for osteomyelitis. She's currently a paraplegic with bowel and bladder involvement. At trial, the jury returned a verdict against the hospital in favor of Mrs. Holton, primarily due to the nurses' lack of communication with the physicians.

CASE 2

Nurses also have a *duty* to communicate with the patient and his family members. Not listening to what the patient is trying to communicate can have disastrous consequences. In *McCrystal v. Trumbull Memorial Hospital* (1996), Mrs. McCrystal was pregnant with her fourth child. Her other three children were all delivered at term by cesarean delivery.

Mrs. McCrystal learned that she was pregnant in December 1989. During this pregnancy, Mrs. McCrystal was cared for by Dr. Lee. Early in the pregnancy, Mrs. McCrystal informed Dr. Lee that she wished to have a tubal ligation following the birth of the child. This necessitated the delivery of the child at Trumbull Memorial Hospital rather than the facility where Dr. Lee usually admitted patients, St. Joseph's Hospital. Mrs. McCrystal was told that this baby, like her other children, would be delivered by cesarean delivery.

During most of her pregnancy, Mrs. McCrystal had no problems. On May 10, 1990, however, she went to the ED at Trumbull Memorial Hospital complaining of cramping. After being examined, she was told she had a bladder infection, medication was given for the infection, and she was released. Four days later, at a scheduled checkup with Dr. Lee, Mrs. McCrystal was told that she and the baby were fine and that she wouldn't need to return until her next scheduled appointment.

On the morning of May 16, she again began experiencing cramping and returned to the ED of Trumbull Memorial Hospital. She was examined, assured that she wasn't going into labor, and sent home. Later that same day, she returned to Trumbull Memorial Hospital. This time the staff performed tests to see if her contractions were beginning. The test results were negative, and she was again released to go home.

Immediately after returning home, she noted the appearance of vaginal bleeding. Instead of returning to Trumbull Memorial Hospital, she called the Women's Care Center at St. Joseph's Hospital and spoke with a nurse. Based on advice from this nurse, Mrs. McCrystal stayed at home and waited to see if the bleeding would stop.

When the bleeding persisted, she called Dr. Lee's answering service. He returned her call and, following his advice, she stayed at home and tried to relax. Although she tried to rest, Mrs. McCrystal had to get up and go to the bathroom because of vomiting. She also began to experience more intense vaginal bleeding. At approximately 11 p.m., she experienced what she termed "a lot of fluttering in her stomach" and her husband drove her to Trumbull Memorial Hospital.

An emergency cesarean delivery was performed on Mrs. McCrystal after Dr. Lee arrived at the hospital. The surgery revealed that her uterus had ruptured along the scar line from a previous cesarean delivery. The baby had suffered prolonged hypoxemia and, as a result, lived only about 3 months. Mrs. McCrystal recovered fully and filed suit for the injuries she had received under the ***wrongful death statute*** for the death of her daughter. One of her major ***complaints*** in this lawsuit was against the nurse at the Women's Center for ***negligence*** in not properly handling her phone call.

In her testimony at trial, Mrs. McCrystal stated that when she spoke to the nurse at the Women's Care Center, she specifically told the nurse that she was bleeding to such an extent that the blood was clotting. Mrs. McCrystal further testified that the nurse asked no further questions and that the only ad-

vice the nurse gave to her was to call back if the bleeding increased.

The nurse testified that she interpreted Mrs. McCrystal's statement as meaning she was "spotting" and thus there was no need to question her further about the bleeding. The nurse also testified that one of the tests that Mrs. McCrystal had done earlier that day at Trumbull Memorial Hospital commonly causes some minor spotting. Thus, she advised the patient to return to the hospital only if the bleeding persisted.

The court held that the nurse at the Women's Care Center was negligent for not listening fully to the patient's description of her bleeding and for not asking additional questions. There was also liability on the part of the physician, who advised her to wait and see if the bleeding ceased before coming to the hospital. Interestingly, the case was sent back to the trial level on the issue of ***comparative negligence***, as the patient and her husband should have returned to Trumbull Memorial Hospital sooner, instead of waiting until her symptoms became life-threatening to her baby.

Legal issues

The following court cases illustrate important communication lessons for nurses.

CASE 1

Case 1 (*Holton v. Memorial Hospital* [1997]) illustrates several instances of lack of communication. The most obvious instance is between

The dangers of ambiguous communication

Wingo v. Rockford Memorial Hospital (1997) illustrates the importance of a nurse not only communicating a change in condition, but also communicating clearly using unambiguous wording. In this case, the patient was sent home on the physician's belief that a rupture of membranes in a term pregnancy had sealed over and that labor contractions had ceased. Mrs. Wingo was first admitted to the hospital with an initial rupture of her membranes and irregular contractions. The physician examined the patient early in the day and, noting no leakage of fluid, assumed that either her membranes had not ruptured or that the leak had sealed itself. However, the nurse caring for the patient had assessed amniotic fluid continuing to leak from the patient all day. When the physician called the nurse caring for Mrs. Wingo to inquire about her condition, the nurse reported that there was "no change" in her condition. Thus, he believed that the patient had stabilized and that it was safe to discharge her, when in fact she continued to leak amniotic fluid and have more regular contractions, signaling the onset of labor. Mrs. Wingo's daughter was born later that night after showing signs of fetal distress, and she now has severe brain damage. The court concluded that the nurse must take responsibility for reporting a patient's condition in a manner that will be understood by the physician. "No change in condition" could have different meanings, depending on the perspective of the person observing the patient. It's up to the nurse to be as clear as possible in her description when communicating her findings.

the physician and the nurse. Changes occurring in the patient's condition weren't reported by the nurses to the physician, nor were any changes noted in the patient's medical record. Equally important, however, was the failure of the nurses to report changes in the patient's condition to each other at change of shift, which would have allowed them to accurately follow her developing symptoms. Note that the nurses failed to communicate both orally and in writing. No mention was made in the medical record of such significant events as Mrs. Holton needing complete assistance from the bathroom back to bed.

The night shift nurse also failed to communicate with the patient. This nurse was aware that Mrs. Holton was experiencing increasing numbness and difficulty moving her leg, yet she documented that there was no significant change in her condition. (See *The dangers of ambiguous communication.*) Had she communicated more with the patient, she would have known that

Protecting the patient

Your first duty is to protect your patient, not his physician. If your judgment says your patient's condition warrants a call to his physician, don't hesitate — in the middle of the day or in the middle of the night.

If your hospital doesn't already have a policy covering nurse-physician communications, ask for one and keep asking until you get one. Meanwhile, for your own protection, carefully record all contact with physicians, including the date, time, and substance of the communication.

Mrs. Holton was experiencing significant changes.

◐◖▶ LESSONS IN PRACTICE Lines of communication among members of the health care team must remain open to ensure the safest care for the patient. As a nurse, you must communicate changes in a patient's condition to the physician, even if you aren't sure how important those changes may be. Remember, it isn't the physician's responsibility to call you to check about changes in a patient's condition. It's the nurse's duty and responsibility to keep the physician informed so that care may be directed appropriately. (See *Protecting the patient.*)

Not only must the nurse inform the physician of changes in a patient's condition, she's also responsible for informing him when a patient's condition doesn't respond to ordered treatments. Such was the case in *Glassman v. St. Joseph Hospital* (1994). In this case, Mr. Glassman was admitted to the intensive care unit after an uneventful coronary artery bypass surgery. He developed a fever, which, despite medication and other interven-

tions, rose to 106° F (41.1° C). Soon after, the patient developed seizures, for which he also received medication. During that evening, the physician dictated the following order: "If patient has another seizure in the next one-half hour, give 200 mg phenobarbital I.M.; then if he seizes in the next 4 hours, please repeat with 200 mg phenobarbital I.M." (*Glassman v. St. Joseph's Hospital* [1994]). The nurse gave the patient the proper dose of phenobarbital when he had another seizure at 10 p.m. However, he had two more seizures in the next hour, and the nurse didn't notify the physician. She observed further seizures throughout the night, for which she only notified the physician twice, and the patient eventually lost consciousness.

Subsequently, Mr. Glassman didn't receive additional medications that may have controlled his seizures. When Mr. Glassman regained consciousness 2 days later, he had no idea who or where he was, and he was diagnosed with severe, permanent, diffuse brain damage. His wife sued on his behalf, and following a lengthy trial, the court concluded that there was negligence on the part of the hospital and its employees.

This case illustrates the essential need to communicate the patient's lack of response to administered medications. Since the patient obviously wasn't responding to the phenobarbital, as evidenced by his continued seizures, the nurse was obligated to notify the physician.

● ▶ **LESSONS IN PRACTICE** Know the purpose of the medications you administer and how to evaluate their effectiveness. If you're unsure about the desired effect of medications or treatments, ask the physician what his expectations are — then you'll know when to notify him. In this case, the physician expected the patient to stop having seizures after being given the medication; the patient's nurse should have informed him when this didn't occur.

FOLLOW THE CHAIN OF COMMAND

Keep in mind that you may not always get an appropriate response to your communication. When you aren't satisfied with the response, follow your chain of command. A landmark case illustrating the importance of following the chain of command is *Darling v. Charleston Community Memorial Hospital* (1965). On November 5, 1960, 18-year-old Dorrence Darling broke his leg while playing in a college football game. He was taken to Charleston Community Memorial Hospital where his leg was casted in the ED by Dr. Alexander, and the patient was admitted to the hospital for observation. Shortly after the cast was applied, the patient complained of increasing leg pain. The toes below

the cast became swollen and dark in color and, shortly thereafter, cold and insensitive to touch.

On November 6, Dr. Alexander "notched" the cast around the toes and, the next day, he removed the lower 3″ (7.6 cm) of the cast. On November 8, he split the sides of the cast with a Stryker saw; in the course of splitting the cast, the patient's leg was cut on both sides. The nursing staff noted blood and serous drainage and an unpleasant odor.

During Mr. Darling's hospitalization, the nursing staff carefully charted the extent of his pain, the low-grade to severe fever he continued to have, and the fact that Dr. Alexander was continually notified of the course of the patient's recovery. Dr. Alexander continued to order antipyretics for the fever and increasingly greater amounts of pain medication, neither were effective in temperature or pain control. The nurses also notified the nursing supervisors of the patient's deteriorating condition and the increasingly foul odor coming from the casted leg.

Mr. Darling remained in Charleston Community Memorial Hospital until November 19, 1960, when he was transferred to Barnes Hospital in St. Louis. Dr. Fred Reynolds, head of orthopedic surgery at Washington University School of Medicine, assumed Mr. Darling's care. He found that the fractured leg contained a considerable amount of dead tissue which, in his opinion, resulted from the interference with the circulation in the leg caused by swelling or hemorrhaging of the leg against the side of the cast. He performed several operations in an attempt to save the leg, but it was ul-

---

Dealing with inadequate care

If you judge the care of the patient to be inadequate, discuss your concerns with the involved health care team member and notify your unit manager or nursing supervisor of your concerns, citing specifically when the incompetent care occurred, what it consisted of, and the outcome to the patient or patients. Document that you have discussed the patient's condition with the physician and the nursing supervisor or unit manager. If you don't obtain a satisfactory response, continue to express your concerns, following the chain of command in your facility, so that appropriate action can be initiated. The more likely serious consequences for the patient will ensue, the greater your need to communicate your findings.

---

timately amputated about 8″ (20 cm) below the knee.

WHO'S AT FAULT?

After the loss of the leg, the patient's father brought a ***claim*** against Dr. Reynolds and Charleston Community Memorial Hospital, its board of directors, and the nurses caring for the patient.

Although Dr. Alexander settled out of court, the hospital and nurses pursued this case for two reasons. The nursing care had been competent, with the physician having been informed of all changes in the patient's condition. The nurses had also adequately documented the nursing care of the patient, including the number of times that Dr. Alexander had been called about Mr. Darling's condition. The court noted that skilled nurses would have promptly recognized the conditions that signaled a dangerous impairment of circulation in the patient's leg and would have known that the condition would be

irreversible within a number of hours. At that point, "it became the nurses' duty to inform the attending physician, and if he failed to act, to advise the hospital authorities so that appropriate action might be taken" (*Darling v. Charleston Community Memorial Hospital* [1965]). The court recognized that the staff directly caring for Mr. Darling could only notify their supervisors. The supervisors, however, have the authority to notify the administrator. (See *Dealing with inadequate care.*)

Nurses have a greater responsibility than merely notifying physicians regarding a patient's care. They're accountable to ensure that nursing supervisors are also fully aware of the care being given to the patient, and to see that someone with authority, such as the medical chief of staff, is also aware of the patient's condition to allow for the initiation of timely and competent care.

CASE 2

As case 2 (*McCrystal v. Trumbull Memorial Hospital* [1996]) illustrates, nurses also have a duty to communicate with patients and their family members. This case vividly highlights the need for nurses to carefully listen to the patient and to question the severity of his symptoms. Perhaps, if the nurse had known of the patient's history of cesarean deliveries, she would have asked her more probing questions regarding her signs and symptoms. (See *Nurse-patient communications,* page 58.)

Defamation and privileged communications

Defamation encompasses the torts of **libel** and **slander**. Defamation is wrongful injury to another's reputation through either oral or written words. Claims of defamation may be brought by patients against health care providers or by health care providers against other health care providers. Nurses are frequently cautioned about statements they make in documentation such as charting that the patient is "crazy."

A successful claim of defamation must meet five conditions:
• language that would adversely affect one's reputation
• defamation about or concerning a living person
• publication to a third party or to several persons but not necessarily to the world at large
• damage to the person's reputation as seen by adverse, derogatory, or unpleasant opinions against the person defamed

• fault on the part of the defendant in writing or telling another the defamatory language.

LANDMARK CASE

Although lawsuits charging negligence are more common, there have been cases of defamation involving nurses. The landmark case in this area of the law is *Schessler v. Keck et al.* (1954).

Miss Schessler, a single woman, worked as a cook and caterer in Beverly Hills and Bel Air, California, from 1946 to 1948. She had served in the armed services during World War II. Sometime during 1943 or 1944, it was discovered that she had a biological false positive reaction to blood tests for syphilis. A memorandum was issued by the Chief, Division of Serology, Army Medical Center in Washington, D.C. to this effect. In 1946, Miss Schessler, in an attempt to eliminate this false positive type of response, sought treatment at the Mayo Clinic in Rochester, Minnesota. She underwent examinations that resulted in the same type of diagnosis that she had received in the military; she had a non-syphilitic reaction to syphilis blood tests. These results were sent to her primary physician, Dr. Clyde Wood, in California.

In September 1946, Miss Schessler consulted Dr. Wood and presented him the memorandum given her by the army. She also began treatment to eliminate the false positive readings and was seen by Dr. Wood's office for this treatment between the years 1946 and 1950. Dr. Wood's office nurse, Jean Keck, had access to the patient's files and test results. The plaintiff discussed

RELATED CASES

Nurse-patient communications

Two related cases concerning the importance of nurse-patient communications are *Lopez v. Southwest Community Health Service* (1992) and *Parker v. Bullock County Hospital Authority* (1990). In each case, there was a lack of documented communication between the nurse and the patient that lead to a tragic outcome.

In the *Lopez* case, Mrs. Lopez, who was 28 weeks' pregnant at the time, contacted her physician's office because she was having pain. Mrs. Lopez was instructed to go to the hospital, and the office nurse called the hospital to inform them that the patient was to be admitted and that she was in active labor.

Two nurses saw Mrs. Lopez when she arrived at Southwest Community Health Service. The first nurse did not examine the patient, and the second nurse, after examining Mrs. Lopez, determined that Mrs. Lopez was 10 cm dilated and that the membranes were "bulging." When the physician was notified of these results, he ruptured the membranes and delivered the baby, who is now a quadriplegic, deaf, blind, and brain damaged.

Neither of the nurses questioned the patient or her support person about their understanding of why Mrs. Lopez was sent to the hospital.

When they arrived at the hospital, no history was taken and no one seemed to have spoken to the patient or her support person. If one of the nurses had asked, both the patient and her support person would have explained that they were concerned about the pains, but didn't believe Mrs. Lopez to be in active labor because the pains were irregular. Arguably, the physician wouldn't have delivered the child had he not listened to the nurses. This child's injury and the lawsuit may well have been prevented if the nurses in the hospital had listened to the patient, rather than relying solely on the description of the patient's symptoms provided by the office nurse.

In the *Parker* case, the patient fell while taking a shower in the hospital. The patient, who was recovering from surgery, informed the nurse who helped her to the shower that she was feeling light-headed and dizzy. The nurse, seemingly ignoring the patient's statement, left the patient unassisted in the shower. Liability could have been avoided if the nurse had assessed the patient after she reported feeling light-headed and dizzy. The nurse could have postponed the shower until the patient was more steady on her feet, or an alternate means of bathing the patient could have been used.

her "non-syphilis" blood tests with the office nurse during 1946 to 1948. Miss Schessler specifically told this nurse that she didn't have syphilis, but was in treatment solely for the purpose of eliminating the false positive result she was getting to syphilis tests.

In August 1948, Jean Florian was dating William Keck, whom she would later marry. He had a comfortable home in Bel Air, California, where he employed a variety of domestic servants. One of the times that Miss Florian was present in William Keck's home, they had a lengthy discussion about Miss Schessler, her treatment for syphilis, and the fact that she shouldn't be employed as a cook. This conversation was overheard by the domestic staff in the home and they repeated the conversation to friends. As a result of these latter conversations, Miss Schessler was no longer able to find work as a cook and caterer. Miss Schessler then brought action for defamation.

Still applicable today

Today, it isn't hard to imagine similar cases involving harm to a person's reputation from hall, elevator, or cafeteria conversations about a patient who is human immunodeficiency virus (HIV) positive or who has acquired immunodeficiency syndrome. Indeed, even mentioning that a patient was tested for HIV may be seen as harmful to his reputation.

PRIVACY TIPS

Think of the number of times that nurses and other health care providers discuss confidential patient information without ensuring that no one will overhear the conversation. It doesn't have to be another patient or visitor who overhears confidential information; it could be the housekeeper or the pharmacist. For defamation to occur, it must be published — that is,

revealed — to a third party who has no right to the information, and it must lessen the person's reputation, his esteem in the community, or his good name.

●▶▶ **LESSONS IN PRACTICE** All members of the health care team are cautioned to avoid discussing patient information in any place that isn't confidential. If a patient conference is important, use the conference room rather than the nurse's station for such discussions. When you're giving a shift report to the oncoming nurse, keep in mind the type of information you're passing on and the ability of others to hear what you're saying. Also remember these key points:

● Respect the patient's right to the confidentiality of information about his character and refrain from discussing such information in areas where the conversation could be overheard.

● Don't repeat information that could be considered defamatory and isn't relevant to a patient's care, even if there's no one to overhear the conversation.

● Ensure that potential defamatory comments aren't placed in the patient's record; document as though the patient or a family member would be reading the chart.

NURSES BRINGING SUIT

A precedent-setting case illustrating that defamatory cases may also be initiated by the nurse is *Farrell v. Kramer* (1963). Ms. Farrell was a registered nurse who had been the head nurse in the recovery room of a large metropolitan hospital before moving to Maine. Her competence as a nurse wasn't disputed at trial.

In 1953, she joined the staff of the Cary Memorial Hospital, and in 1956 she became the night supervisor. The defendant, Dr. Kramer, was a competent and experienced physician and surgeon.

In April of 1959, Dr. Kramer performed a surgical operation on a patient at the hospital. Ms. Farrell became critical of the postoperative care of the patient and made a series of complaints to the chief of nurses, the hospital administrator, the patient's attending physician, the chairman of the hospital board, and the town manager, who was also a member of the hospital board of directors. In effect, these multiple complaints charged the physician with patient neglect. The making of these complaints began a personal feud between Ms. Farrell and Dr. Kramer. In July 1959 she was dismissed from her employment at the hospital.

Although no reason was given for her *termination*, the hospital officials were convinced that she had discussed the hospital and the treatment of specific patients in such places and in such a manner as to constitute unprofessional conduct on her part. Ms. Farrell unsuccessfully lodged a request for a hearing with the hospital Board of Directors. In September 1959 she appealed to the town council for a review of her discharge, but the town council disclaimed any authority to act in conjunction with the hospital. In the same month, Ms. Farrell wrote to the Maine Medical Association, charging Dr. Kramer with neglect of his professional duty and having used his influence to contribute to her discharge. In response to these latter charges, a hearing was held by the Grievance Committee of the Aroostook County Medical Association; the charges against the physician were dismissed.

Defamed by a colleague

In August 1960, Ms. Farrell was rehired by the hospital on the stated condition that she not discuss hospital business outside of the hospital. On August 20, Dr. Kramer discovered that she had been reinstated at the hospital. He immediately called the hospital administrator and made derogatory comments about Ms. Farrell and the following statement, "She is unfit for the care of patients and I can prove that." These comments are the basis of this cause of action (*Farrell v. Kramer* [1963]). The conversation was reported by the hospital administrator at the next meeting of the hospital directors, and Ms. Farrell continued to be employed by the hospital. In the spring of 1961, Ms. Farrell read the minutes of the hospital board meeting and initiated the action for defamation. The court upheld a verdict for the nurse against the physician, finding that his remarks were defamatory and that malice was implied.

This case illustrates that defamation can involve health care providers as well as patients. It also illustrates that nurses have the same rights as others, especially to their good name and esteem within the community. The damage award in this case would be considered small today, as Ms. Farrell was awarded $5,000, but the principle is significant.

REPORTING ABUSE

Qualified privilege is a defense against defamation. Privilege is a disclosure that might ordinarily be defamation under different circumstances, but such disclosure is allowable to protect or further public or private interests recognized by law. Examples of *privileged communication* include reporting persons with certain diagnoses, such as communicable diseases, gunshot wounds, and suspected abuse. A leading case in this area is *Kempster v. Child Protective Services of the Department of Social Services of the County of Suffolk* (1987).

On August 24, 1981, a 14-month-old child was brought to the John T. Mather Memorial Hospital by her parents because of swelling of her nose. The child's mother advised the nurse that the child had fallen after tripping over the leg of a kitchen chair 2 days previously. The hospital proceeded to take X-rays of the child's head, nasal area, and wrists. The X-rays revealed a partially healed wrist fracture of the child's right wrist, for which the mother had no explanation. A physical examination revealed abrasions on various parts of the child's body, which appeared to have been sustained on diverse occasions.

Based on these findings the nurse, having reasonable cause to suspect that the child might have been abused or maltreated, reported the incident to the Albany Registry of Child Protective Services. Upon discharge from the hospital, the child was temporarily placed in the custody of the Suffolk County Department of Social Services pursuant to an order of the Family Court.

Duty to report

The parents initiated the lawsuit in 1982, charging that the hospital and its staff had wrongfully and falsely accused the mother of abusing her child. The lawsuit further asserted that the parents were subjected to ridicule and humiliation and suffered mental and bodily distress because of the actions of the defendants. The court found for the defendants in all aspects of the lawsuit, stating that the hospital, through its employees, had reasonable cause to suspect possible *child abuse* and was therefore entitled to qualified immunity or privileged communication.

Nurses have a duty to disclose to the proper authorities information about suspected child abuse and *child neglect*. (See *Responding to suspected child abuse,* page 62.) In fact, nurses are more open to litigation if they fail to report the abuse; the appropriate state agency may file suit for nondisclosure of the abuse and any subsequent injury to the child.

Nurses are also protected when they report potential child abuse, even if a subsequent investigation shows the allegations to be false. In *Heinrich v. Conemaugh Valley Memorial Hospital* (1994), a Pennsylvania court granted *liability immunity* to the hospital and its staff members for filing a child abuse report that later proved groundless. The child protective law in that state mandates that suspected child abuse must be reported and that a parent or guardian seeking to prove injury due to a false report must also show bad faith on the part of those reporting the abuse.

●●◗ **LESSONS IN PRACTICE** Diseases and conditions that are mandated

Responding to suspected child abuse

You suspect your pediatric patient has been abused. What should you do next? Follow these guidelines:

- Tell the physician your reasons for suspecting child abuse and ask him to order a total-body X-ray. Also inform your supervisor of the situation.
- If you suspect the child has been forced to ingest drugs or alcohol, get an order for toxicology studies of the child's blood and urine.
- If the child is severely bruised, get an order for a blood coagulation profile.
- If X-rays or other studies suggest the child has been abused, talk with the physician about con-

fronting the parents. Ask how you might help him do this.

- If a parent admits to abusing the child and appears to want help, give the address and telephone number of a local group, such as a local chapter of Parents Anonymous, and encourage the parent to call.
- Whether the parent admits to abusing the child, report all suspected abuse to the state-designated agency empowered to investigate the situation. Keep in mind that in many states, failure to report suspected abuse is a crime.

by state or federal law as reportable must be reported to the correct agency. Suspected abuse of children, spouses, partners, and elders is a reportable condition. (See *Elder abuse.*) Failure to report such conditions or diseases leaves you more open to liability than if you had reported, even if a later investigation proves groundless.

Communication and cultural considerations

A new, slowly emerging area is the responsibility of nurses in communicating with culturally and ethnically diverse patients and health

care workers. A nurse today is likely to encounter patients and other members of the health care team who don't speak English as their primary language or don't share the nurse's cultural values. There's some limited case law to support not hiring personnel because of their inability to communicate effectively with patients and patients' families, an essential requirement of employment settings (*Fragante v. County of Honolulu, et al.* [1989]). In that case, Ms. Fragante was denied employment at a public hospital because of her inability to speak fluent English. The court upheld the hospital's position that the ability to communicate was an essential job function.

In *Dimaranan v. Pomona Medical Center, et al.* (1991), nurses weren't

Elder abuse

Elder abuse has reached alarming proportions, having increased 150% between 1986 and 1996. Estimates range from 700,000 to 2 million annual cases of mistreatment in the United States alone. A study by the Administration on Aging and the Administration for Children and Families estimates that more than 500,000 older persons in domestic settings were abused or neglected during 1996 and that for every reported incident, about five went unreported.

The greater an elderly person's disabilities, the more vulnerable he is to abuse or neglect by caregivers — usually his relatives. Family members provide about 80% of all care given to older people, and about 85% of all reported abuse involves a family member's behavior.

Defining abuse and neglect

Nearly every state has laws mandating that suspected elder abuse be reported to the authorities. However, not all states define elder abuse. Instead, they leave its diagnosis to health care professionals. One definition of abuse and neglect is as follows:

- Elder *abuse* is destructive behavior that's directed at an older adult, carried out in a context or relationship of trust, and occurring intensely or frequently enough to produce harmful physical, psychological, social, or financial suffering and a decreased quality of life.

- Elder *neglect* is harm caused by failure to provide prudently adequate and reasonable assistance to meet the elderly person's basic physical, psychological, social, and financial needs.

Detecting abuse

As a nurse — especially if you're in an outpatient or acute care setting — you have more contact with patients than most other members of the health care team. You may be the first to notice or suspect mistreatment of an elderly patient. In fact, in hospitals with special Elder Assessment Teams, most abuse referrals are generated by nurses — especially those in the emergency department. If you suspect elder abuse, report it according to hospital or agency policy.

Signs and symptoms

Detecting abuse in a frail, elderly person with multiple health problems can challenge your assessment skills. A situation or condition that suggests mistreatment may actually represent the progression of disease. For example, you may suspect that an elderly woman covered with bruises is battered when in fact she has a coagulation disorder caused by the medication she takes for heart disease.

The following signs and symptoms, although not definitive for abuse, call for further investigation and reporting:

(continued)

Elder abuse *(continued)*

- unexplained bruises, fractures, or burns
- poor hygiene or nutritional status
- pressure ulcers or other evidence of skin breakdown or infection
- dehydration
- fear of a family member or caregiver

- indications of overmedication or undermedication, such as grogginess or decreased level of consciousness
- unusual listlessness or withdrawal
- signs and symptoms of sexually transmitted disease.

allowed to converse in their native language, but were requested to use English for all communications. The hospital argued that allowing the nurses to converse in their native Philippino dialect created differential treatment for the nurses and adversely affected worker morale and supervision. The court noted that this language restriction did not infringe on the nurses' civil rights because it was motivated by the desire to eliminate dissension that could have compromised patient safety and quality health care delivery.

The Americans with Disabilities Act of 1990 requires that means of communication be made available to the disabled. This is seen in patient access to specially equipped telephones or interpreters for those with a hearing or speech impediment.

USING INTERPRETERS

Some state laws, as well as mandates of the Joint Commission for Accreditation of Healthcare Organizations and the American Hospital Association's Patient's Bill of Rights,

have provisions for ensuring that patients who don't speak English or who don't speak it well enough to express themselves or understand what is said to them, have access to interpreters.

Many facilities now provide interpreters for non-English speaking individuals, and nurses must make reasonable efforts to ensure that patients understand care issues and patient education instructions.

To prevent liability in this area of the law, the nurse should document who served as interpreter — whether it be a family member or an employee of the hospital — the instructions given, and how the nurse evaluated patient understanding. To ensure understanding, have the patient repeat information back to you, ask him questions (through the interpreter) to ascertain his understanding, and listen carefully to the questions that he asks. As more non-English speaking patients enter the health care system, there may be further litigation in this area.

Avoiding litigation

Nurses and other health care providers must communicate in a timely manner, reporting patients' signs and symptoms accurately and completely. It's equally important that changes in the patient's status are reported to the physician as well as when expected changes don't occur. Should the care of the patient be compromised by incompetent care, nurses must follow their facility's chain of command to ensure that the patient receives the safest care possible. Nurses should also communicate with patients to ensure that the patient's needs, and changes in condition, are addressed and documented. Emerging areas of essential communication include working with patients for whom English isn't the primary language and for those who have different cultural expectations.

The law doesn't allow the reputation of another person to be tarnished during communication, whether that person is a patient or another member of the health care team. There are, however, exceptions in which the reporting of information that could be considered defamatory is required by law, such as with suspected abuse of another or when the health of the public is endangered such as with communicable diseases.

Selected references

Carelock, J., and Innerarity, S. "Critical Incidents: Effective Communication and Documentation," *Critical Care Nursing Quarterly* 23(4):59-66, February 2001.

Duffy, M.M., and Alexander, A. "Overcoming Language Barriers for Non-English Speaking Patients," *ANNA Journal* 26(5):507-10, 528, October 1999.

Freed, P.E., and Drake, V.K. "Mandatory Reporting of Abuse: Practical, Moral, and Legal Issues for Psychiatric Home Healthcare Nurses," *Issues in Mental Health Nursing* 20(4): 423-36, July-August 1999.

Kleinpell, R.M., et al. "Translating Spanish: A Brief Guide for Intensive Care and Acute Care Nurses," *Critical Care Nurse* 20(2):100-104, April 2000.

Kruijver, I.P., et al. "Communication Skills of Nurses During Interactions with Simulated Cancer Patients," *Journal of Advanced Nursing* 34(6):772-79, June 2001.

LaDuke, S. "It Can Happen to You: The Firsthand Accounts of Six Nurses Accused of and Disciplined for Professional Misconduct," *Journal of Emergency Nursing* 27(4):369-76, August 2001.

Sheehan, J.P. "Caring for the Deaf. Do You Do Enough?" *RN* 63(3):69-72, March 2000.

Sundin, K., et al. "Communicating with People with Stroke and Aphasia: Understanding Through Sensation without Words," *Journal of Clinical Nursing* 9(4):481-88, July 2000.

Tammelleo, A.D. "Terminated Nurse Sues for Breach of Contract and Defamation. Case on Point: *McCullough v. Visiting Nurse Serv. of So. Maine* 691 A.2d 1201 — ME (1997)," *Regan Report on Nursing Law* 38(1):2, June 1997.

Chapter Four

FAILURE TO DOCUMENT INFORMATION

THE TREND toward increasing specialization means that patients are being assessed, cared for, and treated by more health care professionals than ever before. Complete, accurate, and timely documentation is crucial to the continuity of each patient's care. The medical record is also a legal and business record with many uses.

Nurses have been individually named in lawsuits for neglecting to document information as well as being involved in litigation through their employers that have been named in lawsuits. Not only does a failure to document information increase a nurse's risk of litigation, but so can the failure to adequately prepare documentation after an adverse event.

Case studies

The following court cases illustrate how critical it is for nurses to document every aspect of care.

CASE 1

The Federal court lawsuit of *Harriet G. Woodward v. Alan Myres, Karen Dean, RN, and Correctional Medical Services of Illinois* (2001) arose from the October 1998 death of Justin Farver, who committed suicide while awaiting trial in the Lake County (Illinois) Jail as a pretrial detainee. The administrator of Farver's estate sued Officer Alan Myres, Karen Dean, a registered nurse, and their employer, Correctional Medical Services of Illinois, a state entity paid to provide medical and psychological services at the jail.

Nurse Dean and Correctional Medical Services of Illinois (CMS) were sued on a claim that they deprived Farver of his right to due process guaranteed by the Fourteenth Amendment of the United States Constitution. The plaintiff also claimed that Nurse Dean, Officer Myres, and CMS violated Farver's Eighth Amendment right to protection against cruel and unusual punishment.

The court determined that Farver was a pretrial detainee who didn't require protection under the Eighth

What is a pretrial summary judgment?

A pretrial **summary judgment** granted to a defendant precludes the defendant from having to stand trial for the issue raised in the summary judgment motion. To grant a summary judgment, the court must look at all of the evidence in the light most favorable to the plaintiff. The request for a summary judgment is made by a defendant in a written motion filed with the court before trial. There is no verbal testimony by witnesses, but there is a review by the court of **witness** depositions as well as other documents submitted by both parties. A **deposition** is written documentation of a witness's testimony with **cross-examination** by the opposite party, made under oath in a pre-trial proceeding. If the court finds that the evidence leaves open genuine issues of material fact, the lawsuit goes to trial on that issue. During trial more evidence is introduced, and witnesses will testify in person and have their testimony cross-examined by opposing attorneys. If it's a trial by jury, and not by a judge only, the jury evaluates all of the testimony and evidence. Most trials for medical negligence or injury to a patient claimed to be a result of mismanaged medical care go to a jury, since it's typically a plaintiff's choice to have a jury instead of a judge.

Amendment because a detainee hasn't been found guilty of a crime and therefore may not be 'punished' by the state. However, as a pretrial detainee rather than a convicted inmate, the United States District Court determined Farver was protected from prison officials' deliberate indifference to his medical needs under the Due Process clause of the Fourteenth Amendment.

The defendants made a pretrial motion requesting the court to make a **summary judgment** in their favor on the Fourteenth Amendment violation claim against them because they believed the plaintiff's evidence raises no genuine issue of material fact for a judge or jury to decide. (See *What is a pretrial summary judgment?*) It was then up to the court to decide whether the lawsuit should go to trial.

In the fall of 1998, Farver was a 23-year-old male afflicted with cerebral palsy who had finished 1 year of college and was living with and helping his brother and sister-in-law raise their six children. In September 1998, a seven-count felony indictment was lodged against Farver, alleging he attempted to rape his 12-year-old niece at knifepoint, and he was arrested and taken to Lake County Jail. At the jail, Nurse Dean, who had been a registered nurse for about 2 years, evaluated Farver for a medical history, medical screening, and mental health screening. Nurse Dean had conducted 30 to 40 similar evaluations before evaluating Farver.

Assessment findings

During her evaluation of Farver, Nurse Dean learned that he had cerebral palsy, had attempted suicide in 1995 by jumping in front of a train, was later hospitalized for psychiatric problems, and had received outpatient mental health treatment at Dixon Correctional Center in May 1998. Nurse Dean also learned that Farver's worries extended beyond his legal issues (she stated that he said he was "always worried"), that one of his parents had attempted suicide, and that he had a history of violent behavior. Along with noting this information on the CMS Mental Health Screening Form, Nurse Dean circled "yes" to question number eight, which asked whether Farver "Expresses thoughts about killing self."

According to the form, since question eight was answered "yes," Nurse Dean was to "alert Shift Commander and refer [Farver] for Mental Health Evaluation." Nurse Dean didn't refer Farver to the shift commander, because, according to her deposition testimony, she checked "yes" in reference to Farver's past thoughts of suicide. Nurse Dean also said she didn't tell the shift commander about Farver's suicide risk because:

A: "I wasn't concerned. There was no trains. If that's his mode of killing himself, he wasn't going to find one in the jail. It seemed irrelevant at the time, okay?"

Q: "Why do you say that?"

A: "He wasn't suicidal when we spoke. He wasn't suicidal when I spoke to him. It was many, many,

many days later [that he committed suicide] and [after our meeting] he was...seen by other people, and evaluated, and he was going to medical [the medical unit in the jail], where he would have proper attention."

Failure to summarize

Nurse Dean failed to fill out the "Summary" and "Disposition" sections on the mental health intake screening form, indicating her overall findings regarding Farver's mental health and her recommendation for his future psychological treatment. Thus, Nurse Dean didn't refer Farver for mental health treatment of any kind.

The form's "Summary" portion allows the writer to select an option in rating the detainee:
● No mental health problems
● Mental health problems requiring routine follow-up
● Chronic mental health problem or mental illness; developmental disability; or other
● Acute mental health problem — psychosis; suicidal; or other
● Potential withdrawal from substance abuse.

Similarly, the "Disposition" section of the form gives the writer the following options:
● Approved for general population: No mental health referral
● Approved for general population: Routine mental health referral
● Special housing: Mental health referral ASAP
● Suicide precaution procedures: Mental health referral ASAP
● Psychiatric referral
● Medical monitoring for potential withdrawal.

Also, although the mental health screening form includes a "Reviewed by" signature line (for a supervisor's review), that line is left blank, indicating that Nurse Dean's supervisor didn't review Nurse Dean's screening.

Delayed reevaluation

Farver was housed in the medical unit, but wasn't put on suicide watch (which requires detainees to be individually checked every 15 minutes) and didn't receive further mental health examination until 7 days later when the jail's licensed clinical social worker (LCSW) evaluated him.

The LCSW completed a "Mental Health Intake Evaluation Form," writing most of the same information Nurse Dean noted on her form previously. The form notes Farver had a psychiatric history for about 10 years with the most recent inpatient care in 1995, following his attempted suicide by "playing on train tracks." The form also notes Farver wasn't on psychotropic medication and although the LCSW found Farver to be coherent, oriented, and rational, he felt "anxious, depressed, and not himself." In response to the question, "History of suicidal ideation or behavior?" a "yes" was circled and the following noted:

"Over 10 self-destructive episodes. Most recent 1995. Feels current suicidal proclivities as he knows what he did was wrong [and he is] not looking to spend rest of his life in prison. Over 10 psychiatric hospitalizations, the most recent [4/95], for suicide attempt. Single, no children. Employed in child care [and] has cerebral palsy. Felt anxious." Farver was then referred to the jail psychiatrist, and the

LCSW didn't request that Farver be placed on suicide watch.

Still no suicide watch

Eleven days later, Farver was seen and evaluated by the jail psychiatrist who noted that he was "requested to see [Farver because] of recent suicidal thinking in context of past attempts and multiple psychiatric hospitalizations." The psychiatrist also wrote that Farver "reports multiple psychiatric hospitalizations for suicide attempts including [an overdose] on pills, cutting wrists, running in front of a train," and that Farver "feels hopeless, helpless, worthless" and was suicidal. The psychiatrist diagnosed Farver as having a major depressive disorder and prescribed Farver an antidepressant and a tranquilizer, but didn't order that Farver be placed on suicide watch.

Meanwhile, after being admitted to the jail and up until his suicide, Farver made several attempts to reach his niece (his alleged victim). A fellow inmate made a statement that Farver spent the better part of the day before his suicide lying in bed, but came out to use the phone very abruptly twice that evening. He apparently phoned his brother, who refused to take the call or allow Farver to speak to his niece. Jail staff was notified of Farver's phone call and he was placed on "lockdown" (meaning that he wasn't allowed to leave his cell for any reason) as a result.

The next morning, the same inmate heard a deputy tell Farver that he was warned enough and that this time his lockdown period would be indefinite. That same inmate saw Farver "pacing and staring at the hooks" on the wall of his cell (presumably for hanging towels) between 11 a.m. and noon. Officer Myres entered the medical unit after noon that day on other business. According to Officer Myres, Farver was lying in his bed under his blanket, moving a little. About 9 minutes later, another inmate alerted Officer Myres that Farver had hanged himself. Although Myres and others attempted to revive Farver, he was pronounced dead on arrival at the local hospital.

Failure to document

Officer Myres testified Farver was "happy-go-lucky" and never appeared suicidal or behaved strangely. Farver's brother, who spoke by phone to Farver shortly after he was admitted to the jail also testified that his brother didn't seem depressed or suicidal when they spoke.

In its review of the pretrial evidence presented by both parties of the lawsuit, the Woodward court considered the pretrial record as a whole and drew all reasonable inferences in the light most favorable to the plaintiff, Farver's estate. (See *Court arguments.*) Using this standard, the court must find that Nurse Dean and the other defendants can prove that the plaintiff had no genuine issues of material fact in order to grant, as a matter of law, a summary judgment to the defendants.

The defendant's request for summary judgment was denied and Nurse Dean was to proceed to trial on the plaintiff's claim that her actions, as demonstrated by neglecting to document information in Farver's medical record, constituted a denial of Farver's rights under the Fourteenth Amendment to the United States Constitution.

CASE 2

In the Florida case of *Long Term Care, Inc. v. Winifred W. Martin* (2001), the Long Term Care Foundation appealed a judgment in favor of Mrs. Martin and her husband, James. The court, however, reversed the judgment, not on the issue of negligence, but on the issue of monetary damages due to the plaintiff.

Winifred Martin was hospitalized for surgery after fracturing her hip. While at the hospital she developed a sore on one of her toes. Her physician noticed the sore but did nothing to determine its etiology. She was discharged from the hospital and admitted to one of the defendant's inpatient rehabilitation centers on August 28, 1996.

Neither the hospital nor Martin's physician relayed information about the sore. However, a nurse at the center noticed the sore during the initial medical assessment. The nurse checked "yes" for "circulatory" on Martin's Medicare Screening and Charting Guide. Doing so required the nurses to monitor Martin's circulation daily by checking the color and warmth of her feet, and by taking the pedal pulses. During Martin's entire stay at the center, no nurse indicated on the chart that the pedal pulse had been checked.

Additional evaluation

From August 29, 1996, the day after admission, until September 1, 1996, the nursing notes indicate no complaints of pain by Mrs. Martin. On September 3, a nurse called Mar-

Court arguments

In the case of *Harriet G. Woodward v. Alan Myres, Karen Dean, RN, and Correctional Medical Services of Illinois* (2001), the defendants made several arguments urging the court to grant them summary judgment, which would prevent the case from going to trial.

The defendants' first argument was that the plaintiff's evidence didn't support the claim against Nurse Dean of denial of **due process rights** (rights that protect a pretrial detainee from deliberate indifference by prison officials to his medical needs). Nurse Dean and Correctional Medical Services claimed that the plaintiff only supported a medical malpractice action and that Farver wasn't denied his due process rights as guaranteed by the Fourteenth Amendment to the United States Constitution. The defendant's second argument stated that there was no evidence that Nurse Dean was actually aware of Farver's suicidal tendencies, which put him at risk for committing suicide, when she did her initial evaluation.

The plaintiff responded to the first argument that the question of whether Nurse Dean was deliberately indifferent was a question of fact for the court to decide. The plaintiff maintained that sufficient evidence had been produced for a reasonable jury to find deliberate indifference and, secondly, enough evidence had been presented to lead a jury to reasonably conclude that Nurse Dean knew of and deliberately disregarded Farver's need for mental health care.

The court reasoned that Nurse Dean's testimony in court wasn't a deposition, and she would have to appear before a jury to testify, and the jury may not believe her. The court further noted that the form posed a simple question in present tense and Nurse Dean made no effort on the form to modify the response she gave to that question to indicate that it referred to past events. Nurse Dean had, however, made modifications to her responses to other questions (such as for the question "Worried about major problems other than legal situation" she wrote that Farver is "always worried").

The court further concluded that regardless of what Nurse Dean would say on the witness stand, a jury could also reasonably find that based on what Nurse Dean learned during her evaluation of Farver, the risk of him committing suicide was obvious. She knew that he was "always worried," had a history of psychiatric treatment, had attempted suicide in the past, and that one of his parents had committed suicide.

The defendants further argued that Nurse Dean should be released from the denial of due process claim due to the following facts:

- Farver did not kill himself until 19 days after he met with Nurse Dean.
- Farver was housed in the medical unit where he would have constant monitoring.
- Farver would eventually receive a mental health evaluation.

(continued)

Court arguments *(continued)*

The court reasoned that Farver could have committed suicide within a few days of his meeting with Nurse Dean, but the fact remains that Nurse Dean failed to notify the shift commander of Farver's suicide risk (as directed by the form she filled out during her examination of Farver), she failed on that form to summarize or recommend a disposition as to the level and type of care Farver needed, and she failed to have that form reviewed and signed by her supervisor. Consequently, Farver wasn't placed on suicide watch, he wasn't given an immediate mental health screening, and he was not placed on an immediate treatment program. He was placed in the medical unit only by order of the court. The court concluded that the fact that Farver waited 19 days to commit suicide changed nothing about the facts Nurse Dean had at her disposal when she evaluated him.

The court examined the form Nurse Dean filled out in detail to determine whether her decisions were a substantial departure from accepted professional judgment, practice, or standards. The court noted the form had "Summary" and "Disposition" sections that were not completed. Furthermore, the place on

the form for Nurse Dean's supervisor's signature, which would have indicated that the form was reviewed, was blank. Therefore, the court found that the plaintiff presented enough evidence for a reasonable jury to conclude that Nurse Dean's decisions were a substantial departure from accepted professional judgment, practice, or standards.

The defendant's final argument was that Nurse Dean took reasonable steps to prevent Farver's death, supported by the facts that Farver was housed in the medical unit, was examined by the jail's licensed clinical social worker, and was examined by the jail psychiatrist. These facts were undisputed, but the court determined it was also undisputed that the steps taken didn't result from any action taken by Nurse Dean. The court concluded that Nurse Dean couldn't take credit for a decision and ensuing events that she didn't initiate.

Therefore, the court ruled that there was a genuine issue of material fact as to whether Nurse Dean acted with deliberate indifference to Farver's medical and mental health needs while he was an inmate at the Lake County Illinois Jail.

tin's physician to set up consultation with a podiatrist. The podiatrist saw Martin on September 7, and ordered X-rays and a culture with sensitivity. The podiatrist thought the bone could be infected,

and suggested to the physician that an antibiotic be prescribed. The podiatrist found pulses in both feet, but he also found distal cooling, which indicated insufficient blood flow. The podiatrist testified that he advised the physician to order a peripheral vascular study, a claim the physician denied. Ultimately, the tests ordered by the podiatrist proved negative for infection.

Delays for a worsening problem

The nursing notes show administration of antibiotics through September 14, at which point Martin complained of pain. Two days later, the toe began to turn green. On September 20, Martin complained of pain frequently. On September 22, the day after she revealed that her toe had been run over by a wheelchair, the toe was black. On September 25, she complained of increased pain, and a nurse called the physician for authorization to set up a consultation with a foot surgeon. On September 28 the physician went to the center to see Martin.

On October 1, the foot surgeon, who had been called on September 26, saw Martin, diagnosed gangrene, and concluded that the toe should be amputated. The foot surgeon referred Martin to a general surgeon, who saw Mrs. Martin on October 3 and ordered a vascular laboratory study. The study, performed on October 10, reported very bad circulation.

Failure to document

According to the center's defense expert, this information should have been discovered in August. In addition, according to the expert, the general surgeon should have ordered an arteriogram to determine the condition of the arteries. Instead, the general surgeon concluded (incorrectly, according to the expert) that Mrs. Martin had no pulse

in the leg, so the entire leg had to be amputated. Martin's experts testified that had the nurses monitored her pedal pulses, they would have noticed a lack of pulse, and surgical intervention would have saved the leg. Mrs. Martin's leg was amputated on October 18, 1996.

At trial, Mrs. Martin won her case against Long Term Care, Inc. on her claim of negligence by the nurses. Neglecting to document information about Mrs. Martin's circulation and pedal pulses, according to the expert witness, prevented the timeliness of an appropriate diagnostic work up and treatment that would have prevented the amputation of her leg.

Legal issues

As nursing documentation has become increasingly scientific and complex, its quality has taken on greater legal significance.

LEGAL SIGNIFICANCE OF THE MEDICAL RECORD

The medical record provides legal proof of the nature and quality of care the patient received. The weight it carries in legal proceedings can't be overemphasized. The record may become the focus of inquiry in personal injury, professional malpractice, or product liability claims as well as in workers' compensation, child custody, and employment disputes.

A factual, consistent, timely, and complete record defends you against allegations of negligence, improper treatment, and omissions in care. Health care professionals have a legal duty to maintain the medical record in sufficient detail, and inadequate documentation of care may result in liability or non-reimbursement by third-party payers.

In fact, documentation of care has become synonymous with care itself, and failure to document implies failure to provide care. Despite the introduction of charting by exception — a documentation system that implies all standards have been met with a normal or expected response unless otherwise documented — the prevailing rule is: "If it isn't documented, it hasn't been done."

CONTENTS OF THE MEDICAL RECORD

Federal regulations, such as those governing Medicare and Medicaid reimbursement, partially determine the form and content of the medical record. Although state laws vary in their stringency and specificity, all states require health care facilities to maintain the medical record in sufficient detail. (See *Legal risks of charting by exception.*)

The following documents are usually included in the medical record:

- patient admission and history
- physician's order form and progress notes
- nursing assessment and nursing diagnoses
- patient's medication record
- nurses' notes and progress notes
- diagnostic and laboratory test results
- X-ray and other radiologic reports
- operative and other treatment reports

- flow sheets, checklists, and graphic sheets
- discharge summary
- referral summaries
- consent forms, such as advance directives, living wills, do-not-resuscitate orders, and name of health care proxy or legal guardian
- home care instruction sheet.

(See *Using flow sheets,* page 76.)

Failure to properly maintain the medical record

As a general rule, the medical record is presumed to be accurate if there is no evidence of *fraud* or *tampering*. Evidence of tampering can cause the record to be ruled inadmissible as evidence in court. Medical records may be corrected if the portion in error remains legible; deleting or rendering the entry illegible can impose liability. Late entries are usually acceptable if they're clearly marked "late entry" when made. Loss of the medical record raises a *rebuttable presumption* of negligence (which may be overcome by contrary evidence).

ELEMENTS OF NEGLIGENCE

One of the major elements to be met to prove negligence in a medical malpractice case is whether the *standard of care* was met. Once it's established that a nurse has a professional duty to perform acceptable standards of care (demonstrated by a professional relationship such as a nurse-patient relationship), the next question is whether the standard of care was met. Not meeting the standard of care is considered a *breach of duty*. If it can be proven that the breach of duty to

Legal risks of charting by exception

Charting by exception (CBE) omits all charting related to routine nursing care. Instead, it relies on written standards of practice that identify the nurse's basic patient responsibilities.

Because this charting system requires the nurse to document only information that deviates from the expected, it can raise legal concerns. To ensure a legally sound patient record, well-defined guidelines and standards of care for its use must be understood by all nursing staff members and used consistently.

When CBE violates the law

Lama v. Boras (1994) illustrates what can go wrong when nurses don't follow accepted standards of care when using CBE. Roberto Romero Lama had surgery for a herniated disk. Two days later, a nurse wrote in his chart that the bandage covering the surgical wound was "very bloody." An entry the next day indicated he had pain at the incision site.

Several days later, a nurse documented the bandage as "soiled again." The next day, Mr. Romero began to complain of severe back discomfort; he passed the night screaming in pain. The following day the physician diagnosed an infection in the space between the vertebral disks and ordered antibiotics. The patient was hospitalized for several months to treat the infection.

Mr. Romero sued the hospital and the physicians who treated him, alleging that they failed to prepare and monitor proper medical records. The hospital didn't dispute the charge that nurses didn't supply the required notes; instead, it pointed out that they followed the hospital's official CBE policy.

The court ruled against the hospital on the grounds that Puerto Rico law requires qualitative nurses' notes for each nursing shift, and that violation of this regulation had caused Mr. Romero's injury. The court reasoned that a more complete picture of his evolving condition was unavailable because the hospital's CBE policy called for nurses to note qualitative observations only when needed to chronicle important clinical changes. Although objective aspects of the patient's care and condition (temperature, vital signs, medications) were charted regularly, important details, such as the changing condition of the surgical wound and the patient's reports of pain, weren't.

Playing it safe

Although CBE complies with legal principles, the system may be questioned in court until it becomes more widely known. If you believe your facility's CBE policy is unsafe or ambiguous, confer with your colleagues and supervisors, and then approach an administrator about clarifying it.

Using flow sheets

Flow sheets are record-keeping forms used for tracking information about the repetitive tasks you perform through the day, such as giving medication or monitoring your patient's vital signs or fluid balance. Using a flow sheet enables you to keep all routine measurements in one place and to compare data quickly. Flow sheets come in a variety of styles, including blank-ruled paper and graph paper, to suit various documenting needs.

Advantages

A flow sheet offers the following advantages:

- It displays a specific aspect of your patient's condition, such as his temperature, at a glance. You don't have to search through pages of notes to determine his temperature pattern over the past 48 hours.
- It saves you time. You can note the vital signs or medication given without having to write a full descriptive entry every time. You can use your nurses' notes to describe how the patient is responding to treatment.
- It documents that you're giving the patient continuous care.
- It provides a mechanism for non-licensed personnel to record their care and observations. Because nonlicensed personnel usually aren't permitted to chart in the nurses' notes, any information they have about patient care may be lost. Instead, you can ask them to describe their care and initial

each entry on a flow sheet. Then, if you have a question about the status of your patient's skin, for example, you can check the flow sheet to identify the nursing assistant who administered that day's bed bath.

Common errors

Flow sheets can create a legal tangle if you don't avoid two common mistakes:

- The first mistake is to treat flow sheets casually. For instance, some nurses will routinely check off whatever the previous shift checked off on the flow sheet, or make checks at the beginning of the shift before the care is provided, regardless of the care given, and then carefully chart the actual care in the nurses' notes. This creates an inconsistency. As part of the legal medical record, the flow sheet must accurately reflect the care provided.
- The second mistake is to depend too heavily on flow sheets. Flow sheets can help you document, quickly and accurately, what care was given and who provided it. However, don't neglect to record the patient's response to care in your nurses' notes. Like any other chart form, retain the flow sheet as part of the permanent chart so that you have a progressive picture of the patient's status and a record of your care.

meet the standard of care in fact caused the patient's injury, all the elements of negligence are met.

Sources of documentation duties and standards

Factors that influence nursing documentation standards include:

- Federal statutes and regulations
- state regulations and statutes, including licensing statutes and nurse practice acts
- custom
- accrediting bodies
- standards of practice issued by professional organizations
- facility *policies* and *procedures*.

Professional organizations and accrediting bodies have developed and refined recommendations and standards of practice for nursing documentation. Sometimes these standards are more stringent than those required by state law.

The American Nurses Association (ANA) has included documentation in its Standards of Nursing Practice. The ANA says documentation must be systematic, continuous, accessible, communicated, recorded, and readily available to all health care team members. The Joint Commission on Accreditation of Healthcare Organizations (JCAHO) also sets standards. Current standards stress a change from source-oriented documentation to a fully integrated, multidisciplinary approach.

Documentation should reflect the collaborative planning and provision of care and treatment. JCAHO doesn't specify a format for medical record documentation. Thus, patient care, treatment, and rehabilitation may involve many forms, from preprinted forms to handwritten reports to electronic formats,

which may include decision algorithms and care maps.

Many of the professional specialty societies, such as the American Association of Critical-Care Nurses, the Association of Operating Room Nurses, and the Emergency Department Nurses Association, have developed guidelines, standards, or recommendations concerning content and technique of nursing documentation.

Typically, a health care facility has integrated the appropriate laws, regulations, and standards into its own policy and procedure manual. Your best assurance of following the law may be to adhere to the facility's policy, which usually describes who is to maintain each portion of a patient's record and by which technique.

Hazards of improper nursing documentation

Nurses have made documentation errors that contribute substantially to the legal outcome.

Absence of information

In the previous case studies, nurses neglected to document pertinent information. Sections of a form weren't completed, complaints of a patient's pain and his responses to medication weren't documented, and pedal pulses, while they may have been assessed, weren't documented, implying that they weren't checked. (See *Omissions in documentation and nursing liability,* pages 78 and 79.)

Neglecting to document information about care given, assessments, and responses to medications forces the nurse, if she's ever called to testify, to rely on memory to recall

Omissions in documentation and nursing liability

The following cases show how neglecting to document information led to adverse legal outcomes.

In the case of *Tammy Derry v. Edward Peskin, MD, Saint Vincent Hospital, Arthur Curtis, MD, Susan Palmer, RN, American Medical Response, Lisa Lavoie, EMT, and David Wiggins, EMT* (1999), the plaintiff brought a wrongful death action against the defendants seeking monetary damages for the death of her unborn child.

In this Massachusetts case, Mrs. Derry had presented to the emergency department at Saint Vincent's in preterm labor. An ultrasound revealed no amniotic fluid remaining in the uterus and that the unborn child was in breech position. Dr. Curtis decided to have Mrs. Derry transferred to another medical center for management of delivery. The fetal heart rate was noted to show a significant increase in fetal distress.

Thirty minutes later Mrs. Derry received pain medication, and records reflect a prolonged variability of the fetal heart rate, indicating increasing fetal distress. Dr. Curtis discharged Mrs. Derry from Saint Vincent Hospital for transport to the labor and delivery unit at another hospital. Fifty minutes later she arrived at the other facility.

At the time of the pretrial motion, no documentation existed of an assessment of Mrs. Derry or her unborn child during transport. Upon arrival in the receiving labor and delivery unit, an immediate ultrasound was performed revealing a breech presentation and no amniotic fluid. The fetal heart rate was noted to be 40 beats per minute and the umbilical cord had prolapsed into Mrs. Derry's vagina. Mr. and Mrs. Derry were counseled about the grave prognosis for the baby, who was born 1 hour and 20 minutes later without a heartbeat.

Susan Palmer, the registered nurse who was assisting with Mrs. Derry's transfer, and the other defendants in this case would have had a stronger defense to the claims of negligence and wrongful death if she had presented documentation proving that she had monitored the condition of Mrs. Derry and her unborn child. Without documentation, her attorney couldn't argue that she had met the standard of care of monitoring the fetal heart rate during transport. The fact that the nurse was aware of the seriousness of Mrs. Derry's condition but didn't document an assessment of her or the unborn child during transport made a believable defense almost impossible. To further complicate this case, several consent forms were either missing from the chart or were present but not signed.

In *Stephen P. Flanagan v. John F. Kennedy Memorial Hospital* (Supreme Court of Pennsylvania (1995), Mr. Flanagan appealed an order of

Omissions in documentation and nursing liability *(continued)*

the court that granted summary judgment in favor of the defendant, John F. Kennedy Memorial Hospital. The court wouldn't allow Mr. Flanagan's expert witness' testimony to be admitted into evidence, and a summary judgment was granted 2 days after the trial began.

Mr. Flanagan's case was based on allegedly inadequate care that he received when he went to the hospital for treatment of a collapsed lung on December 2, 1991. Treatment involved the insertion of a chest tube. Mr. Flanagan claimed that he received substandard nursing care after the insertion of the tube, which led to "progressively worsening subcutaneous emphysema." Specifically, he asserts that the nursing staff failed to document his complaints of pain or his responses to medication, and that they also failed to monitor his breathing and palpate his chest. This case was initially brought against the facility and physicians responsible for Mr. Flanagan's care, but the actions against the physicians were subsequently discontinued, leaving the hospital (including its nursing staff) as the sole defendant.

Although the appellate court held that Mr. Flanagan had no case (since his only expert witness was not qualified to decide on causation of his injury), the nurses involved had to prepare and were expecting to go to trial. Then, a year later, another appeal was filed and heard by the court to determine whether there would be a trial after all. This second appeal was denied for the same reason (no qualified expert witness for the plaintiff).

It's better to document information accurately and according to standards and policies and procedures, rather than to live with the uncertainty of legal proceedings such as this.

---

crucial facts, such as specific times, treatments, and telephone or verbal conversations. As the *Woodward v. Nurse Dean* case demonstrates, the events leading to the lawsuit took place in September 1998, and the defense pretrial motion took place in May 2001. The actual trial didn't occur until after this time. Neglecting to document in this case required Nurse Dean to remember details and events that took place almost 3 years prior, relying solely on her memory and recollection.

Additionally, the more the nurse doesn't remember, the more likely a jury is to discredit the testimony. ●●▶ **LESSONS IN PRACTICE** You must document baseline assessment findings as well as any clinically significant changes thereafter. Remember, "If it wasn't documented, it wasn't done." Don't place yourself in the position of trying to remember the details of events that occurred years ago.

Charting after the fact

Generally, the medical record is considered accurate as long as there's no evidence of tampering. If there are signs of tampering, such as recopied portions of the record or other alterations, the record may not be admissible in court. In a suspected case of notes written after litigation, forensic experts are retained by the plaintiff's attorney to determine when portions where written. An alteration in the record can make a defensible case indefensible.

Many lawyers advise against keeping personal notes about a questionable patient care incident. Typically those notes are written when the nurse is less than objective and may convey a far different message than was intended. Personal notes you use at the time of an incident or to prepare for a deposition or trial can be obtained by the plaintiff's attorney in a subsequent trial. If you deny using them to refresh your memory, you're perjuring yourself. If you admit you did use personal notes, the notes may be used to incriminate you or other defendants. Simply put, avoid any written or oral statements without first consulting your attorney.

⬤⬤▶▶ **LESSONS IN PRACTICE** In the event of a legal challenge, or if the medical record has been requested for examination in a trial, avoid making changes, corrections, or additions. To do so would raise suspicion, even if you have legitimate reasons and the best intentions. The patient's attorney will likely have a copy of the record long before a suit is filed.

Missing records

The case of *Battocchi v. Washington Hospital Center* (1990) underscores the significance of missing records. In this case, parents brought a medical malpractice suit against the hospital and a physician for injury to their son during forceps delivery. The nurse had immediately documented the delivery and posted the record in the chart.

Later, the hospital's risk management personnel apparently lost the nurse's record. The court ruled in favor of the hospital and physician, saying the jury couldn't presume negligence and causation simply because the hospital lost the nurse's notes. The appeals court sent the case back to the trial court to determine whether loss of the record stemmed from negligence or impropriety.

Good charting, poor communication

Although thorough documentation is crucial, it isn't always enough. Unless you report any significant findings you document, exemplary charting can be worthless. In a 1995 Nebraska case, a couple sued a hospital, claiming that the staff's negligence caused brain damage to their newborn son. Jeffrey Critchfield was born at 7:30 a.m., weighing 4 lb 10 oz. According to the admission assessment, Jeffrey had chest wall retractions, cyanosis, pallor, a weak cry, and flaccid muscles. He was admitted to the neonatal intensive care unit, where nurses documented his grunting, pallor, and chest retractions. At about 7:45 p.m., a nurse documented that Jeffrey was lethargic.

At the trial, a pediatric neurologist testifying for the Critchfields stated that lethargy was a sign of neurologic changes, and that nursing observations recorded throughout the night indicated that Jeffrey had signs of acute brain damage from lack of oxygen and blood to the brain. He also said that the nurses should have reported these findings to the attending physician during the night and early morning hours. Another expert testified that the hospital should have had a policy requiring expert consultation, and that if nurses had reported Jeffrey's problems, his brain damage could have been ameliorated. The court ruled in favor of the Critchfields, reasoning that the hospital had a duty, through its nursing staff, to report medically significant changes in a patient's condition to the treating physician without delay.

INCIDENT REPORTS

An incident is an event that's inconsistent with the hospital's ordinary routine, regardless of whether injury occurs. In most health care facilities, any injury to a patient requires an incident report. Patient complaints, medication errors, and injuries to employees and visitors require incident reports as well.

An incident report serves two main purposes:

● to inform hospital administration of the incident so that it can monitor patterns and trends, thereby helping to prevent future similar incidents (risk management)

● to alert the administration and the hospital's insurance company to the possibility of liability claims and the need for further investigation (claims management).

Even when the incident isn't investigated, the report serves as a contemporary, factual statement of it. The report also helps identify witnesses if a lawsuit is started months or even years later. (See *Completing an incident report,* page 82.)

Using incident reports as courtroom evidence

Controversy exists over whether a patient's attorney may discover (request and receive a copy of) an incident report and introduce it into evidence in a malpractice lawsuit. *Rounds v. Jackson Park Hospital and Medical Center* (2001) illustrates that incident reports made after an incident occurs can become evidence to be submitted to a court of law for a jury to review.

Ms. Rounds asserted that as a result of the hospital's medical mismanagement in handling her symptoms of placental abruption, her fetus suffered fatal injuries. Ms. Rounds was seen and treated at Jackson Park Hospital before being transferred to St. Bernard's Hospital. She claimed that Jackson Park was negligent in discharging her after she presented with signs and symptoms of placental abruption, and in failing to notify the attending obstetrician of her signs and symptoms before transferring her to St. Bernard's Hospital. Jackson Park admitted that it provided nursing and medical care to Rounds, but denied all allegations of wrongdoing and negligence.

Completing an incident report

To be useful, an incident report must be filed promptly and must be thorough and factual.

What to include

An incident report should include only the following information:
- the names of the persons involved and any witnesses
- factual information about what happened and the consequences to the person involved (supply enough information so the hospital administration can decide whether the matter needs further investigation)
- any other relevant facts (such as your immediate actions in response to the incident; for example, notifying the patient's physician).

What not to include

Never include the following types of statements in an incident report:
- opinions (such as a reporter's opinion of the patient's prognosis or who's at fault)
- conclusions or assumptions (such as what caused the incident)
- suggestions of who was responsible for causing the incident
- suggestions to prevent the incident from happening again.

Including this type of information in an incident report could seriously hinder the defense in any lawsuit arising from the incident.

Remember, the incident report serves only to notify the administration that an incident has occurred. In effect, it says, "Administration: Note that this incident happened, and decide whether you want to investigate it further." Such items as detailed statements from witnesses and descriptions of remedial action are normally part of an investigative follow-up; don't include them in the incident report itself.

Potential pitfalls

Be especially careful that the hospital's reporting system doesn't lead to improper incident reporting. For example, some hospitals require nursing supervisors to correlate reports from witnesses and then file a single report. Also, some incident report forms invite inappropriate conclusions and assumptions by asking, "How can this incident be prevented in the future?" If your hospital's reporting system or forms contain such potential pitfalls, alert the administration to them.

Attorney-client privilege

The plaintiff's attorney requested nursing incident reports and another document prepared by Nurse Nwankwo regarding the sequence of events surrounding Rounds' transfer from Jackson Park to St.

Bernard's Hospital. Jackson Park responded that it had certain nursing incident reports and other related documents prepared by Nurse Edith Nwankwo, but asserted that these documents were prepared in anticipation of litigation and were otherwise protected by the state's Code of Civil Procedure (the Medical Studies Act), and therefore withheld from disclosing them based on attorney-client privilege and the state's Medical Studies Act.

To fall under the protection of privilege, the court held that an attorney-client privilege had to exist at the time the documents are prepared. Since neither Jackson Park Hospital nor Nurse Nwankwo could prove that her incident and special reports were made for and under direction of an attorney preparing for trial, no privilege existed. Without privilege, these documents had to be given to the court as evidence.

If the information contained in these reports doesn't match what was documented in the medical record at the time care was delivered to Ms. Rounds, the differences in these recordings will be questioned and could be harmful to the nurse's defense.

◗◗◗ LESSONS IN PRACTICE If you're asked to talk with the hospital's **insurance adjustor** or attorney about an incident, be cooperative, honest, and factual. If you have your own attorney, he should also be present. Fully disclosing what you know early on will help the hospital decide how to handle any legal consequences of an incident. It also preserves your testimony in case you're ever called to testify in court.

A*voiding litigation*

One of the best ways to avoid litigation is to document patient care objectively, accurately, and as completely as possible at the time care was delivered. (See *Documentation*

tips, page 84.) In addition to their potential impact on patient care, charting errors or omissions, even if seemingly harmless, will undermine your credibility in court. Especially avoid the following.

OMISSIONS
Include all significant facts that other nurses will need to assess the patient. Otherwise, a court may conclude that you failed to perform an action missing from the record or tried to hide evidence. Omissions, such as incomplete sections or blank answers on forms, can and will be construed in a court of law as substandard care and deliberate disregard for the patient's well-being. (See *What should this nurse have done?* page 85.)

PERSONAL OPINIONS
Don't record personal opinions. (See *Distinguishing between subjective and objective charting,* page 86.) Document only factual and objective observations and the patient's statements.

VAGUE ENTRIES
Imprecise or hurried charting is commonly interpreted as an indication that the care was also hurried and imprecise. Instead of "wound cleaned," chart "wound was cleaned and explored to its base."

LATE ENTRIES
If a late entry is necessary, identify it as such, sign, and date it. Reference to the date and time you're relating back to.

Documentation tips

If you're ever involved in a malpractice lawsuit, how you documented, what you documented, and what you didn't document will heavily influence the jury and the outcome of the trial. Following these important tips can ensure that your records don't tip the scales of justice against you.

How to document

- Use the appropriate form and document in ink.
- Record the patient's name and identification number on every page of his chart.
- Record the complete date and time of each entry.
- Be specific. Avoid general terms and vague expressions.
- Use only standard abbreviations.
- Use a medical term only if you're sure of its meaning.
- Document symptoms by using the patient's own words.
- Document objectively.
- Write legibly.

What to document

- Document any nursing action you take in response to a patient's problem. For example: "8 p.m. medicated for incision pain." Be sure to include the medication name, dose, route, and site.
- Document the patient's response to medications and other treatment.
- Document safeguards you use to protect the patient. For example: "raised side rails" or "applied safety belts."
- Document your conversation with the patient or family — in person, by facsimile, or by telephone.
- Document patient education.
- Document any incident in two places: in your progress notes and in an incident report. Don't mention the report in the patient's record unless your facility or state requires it.
- Document each observation. Failure to do so will produce gaps in the patient's records suggesting that you neglected the patient.
- Document procedures after you perform them, never in advance.
- Write on every line. Don't insert notes between lines or leave empty spaces for someone else to insert a note.
- Sign every entry with your full name and title.
- Chart an omission as a new entry. Never backdate or add to previously written entries. Within the body of the note, reference the time and date of omission.
- Draw a thin line through an error and write "error" above it, with the date and your full name. Never erase or obliterate an erroneous entry.
- Document only the care you provide. Never document for anyone else.
- Understand and follow the documentation standards of your facility and your state. These standards are usually defined in state nurse practice acts and in state or provincial administrative codes (the rules and regulations governing nurse practitioners and their practice).

What should this nurse have done?

To avoid litigation in the *Woodward* case, Nurse Dean should have completed all sections on the forms she was required to use to evaluate her patient, Mr. Farver. According to protocol, she would then have been required to report her findings to the shift commander, who, upon her summary and disposition recommendation, could have instituted the appropriate precautions for suicide monitoring. As the court concluded, she knew enough (demonstrated by what she did document)

to see that Farver had a level of risk for suicide. Had she completed the evaluation form properly and reported her findings to her supervisor, answers to questions about her deliberate indifference to Farver's medical and mental health needs would have been more favorable. Going one step further, to follow up and document her post-evaluation interventions, would have demonstrated Nurse Dean's compliance with the policies and procedures of the institution.

IMPROPER CORRECTIONS

Never erase or obliterate an error. Instead, draw a single line through it, label it "error," and sign and date it.

UNAUTHORIZED ENTRIES

You are the only person who should make entries into your nurse's record. Avoid using erroneous or vague abbreviations — use only standard abbreviations, and follow your facility's policies for which abbreviations to use. Beware of illegibility and lack of clarity — write so that others can read your entry. Use a dictionary if you're unsure of spelling or usage.

In addition, follow these tips:
● Be accurate and thorough when completing forms. Follow directions, such as seeking the review and signature of a supervisor if the

form requires it. Document your actions according to your facility's policies and procedures.
● Thoroughly review information documented before your shift. Neglecting to notice, follow through with, and document patient monitoring as recommended in the medical record by previous nurses or other health care providers can lead to an adverse outcome and litigation.
● Sections of a form that don't apply to a particular patient need to be completed with a "not applicable" response. If a patient refuses an examination, treatment, or procedure, or refuses or is unable to answer a question, document that information with an explanation. If your facility has a ***refusal of treatment form***, obtain the patient's signature according to policy and procedure.
● Know your facility's policies and procedures for how to document all

Distinguishing between subjective and objective charting

The most common error nurses make when they chart is writing value judgments and opinions — subjective information — rather than factual, or objective, information. Subjective information reflects how the nurse feels about the patient's condition, not the patient's condition. Here are some subjective entries, with their objective alternatives.

SUBJECTIVE CHARTING	OBJECTIVE CHARTING
Patient is drinking well.	Drank 1,500 ml fluids between 7 a.m. and noon.
Patient reported good relief from Demerol.	Pain in Ⓡ hip decreasing, now described as 2 on a scale of 1 to 10.
Dorsalis pedis pulse present. Good pedal pulses.	Peripheral pulses in legs 2+/4+ bilaterally.
Moves legs and feet well.	Leg strength 5+/5+ bilaterally all major muscle groups. Sensation intact to light touch, pin; denies numbness or tingling. Skin warm and dry. No edema.
Voiding qs.	Voided 350 ml clear yellow urine in bedpan.
Patient is nervous.	Patient repeatedly asks about length of hospitalization, expected discomfort, and time off from work.
Breath sounds normal.	Breath sounds clear to auscultation all lobes. Chest expansion symmetrical – no cough. Nail beds pink.
Bowel sounds normal.	Bowel sounds present in all quadrants – abdomen flat. NPO since 12:01 a.m.
Ate well.	Ate all of soft diet.

nursing functions in the medical record. Be familiar with all forms you deal with regularly and know how to complete them properly. Make sure you know your facility's policy on obtaining signed *informed consent* forms, where they go in the medical record, and who is responsible for seeing that they're complete and correctly filed in the chart. An unsigned consent form implies that there was no informed consent.

● With more emphasis on electronic documentation for medical records, the issue of failing to complete all sections of an electronic version of the record or form includes consideration of computer functions and software designs. Proper design and programming of forms in the development of electronic software becomes extremely important. The scope of review and design of the form needs to encompass which documentation elements are absolute and require the field to be completed before allowing the user to continue. Input by an interdisciplinary team including nurses, physicians, pharmacists, and administrators knowledgeable in standards and regulations is important to ensure that all details and requirements are included in an electronic medical record.

● Know the standards of care for your area of nursing, and follow them. Document accurately and completely any variances from the norm. Report all variances and document who you notified and when you did so. Accurately and completely document any responses you receive regarding this notification.

● Know your department and facility policies and procedures. Absence of policies and procedures as well as not following established policies and procedures, can become very problematic for the nurse. Deviation from established policies and procedures can lead to a claim of not meeting the standards of care, which may lead to a finding of negligence in a court of law.

S*elected references*

Baker, S.K. "Minimizing Litigation Risk. Documentation Strategies in the Occupational Health Setting," *AAOHN Journal* 48(2):100-105, February 2000.

Brown, S. "The Legal Pitfalls of Home Care," *RN* 63(11): 5-80, November 2000.

Burke, L.J. and Murphy, J. "Patient Documentation," *Journal of Nursing Administration* 30(7-8):342, July-August 2000.

Carelock, J., and Innerarity, S. "Critical Incidents: Effective Communication and Documentation," *Critical Care Nursing Quarterly* 23(4):59-66, February 2001.

Frank-Stromborg, et al. "Nurse Documentation: Not Done or Worse, Done the Wrong Way — Part II," *Oncology Nursing Forum* 28(5):841-46, June 2001.

Jacobsen, K.A. "The Critical Care Nurse's Documentation: A Liability Perspective," *QRC Advisor* 16(9):4-8, July 2000.

Koniak-Griffin, D. "Strategies for Reducing the Risk of Malpractice Litigation in Perinatal Nursing," *Journal of Obstetric, Gynecologic, and Neonatal Nursing* 28(3):291-99, May-June 1999.

Kurtz, C.A. "Accurate Documentation Equals Quality Patient Care," *Insight* 27(1):8-10, January-March 2002.

Mahler, C.L. "Just the Facts, Please: A Guide to Effective Documentation," *Home Care Provider* 6(4):120-25, August 2001.

Noone, J.M. "Charting by Exception," *Journal of Nursing Administration* 30(7-8):342-43, July-August 2000.

Sullivan, G.H. "Keep Your Charting on Course," *RN* 63(5):75-79, May 2000.

"Things You Can Do to Protect Your Facility Against Lawsuits. Part III: Avoiding Documentation Risks," *LTC Regulatory Risk & Liability Advisor* 9(2):1-4, January 2001.

Chapter Five

FAILURE TO PERFORM A PROPER ASSESSMENT

FAILURE TO PERFORM a proper patient assessment is a common allegation in professional **negligence** cases. An assessment is the continuous collection of data used to identify a patient's actual — and potential — health needs. It includes data from a patient history, a physical examination, and a review of pertinent laboratory and medical information.

Simply knowing what information to include in an assessment isn't enough, however. You must also know what constitutes a proper assessment. Whether the assessment is proper depends on how well it meets the **standards of care.** A nursing standard of care will be held as the degree of care deemed "adequate" by the nursing profession. In other words, the standards are the minimal requirements that define an acceptable or satisfactory level of care. Over time, standards have evolved to ensure that patients receive quality care. An assessment won't be considered proper if it falls below or deviates from the standards of care.

The standards of care applied in a professional liability case are typically derived from sources such as state statutes, **nurse practice acts,** professional associations and their annual meetings, professional literature, and the interaction of nursing leaders. If a certain practice becomes generally accepted, it will be recognized as a "standard practice." For example, because it's generally accepted that a nurse should repeat assessment of an abnormal vital sign, this is considered to be a standard of care. A nurse is also required to notify a physician if a patient's status worsens in any way. Both of these actions by the nurse have been generally accepted as "standard practice" by the nursing community.

Be aware, too, that what's recognized as an "accepted standard practice" may not always prove to be the safest or best practice. It will, however, be used as the minimum standard to which a nurse will be compared in a professional **liability** issue.

Case studies

The following court cases illustrate the use of standards in determining whether an adequate assessment has been performed.

CASE 1

The issue of proper assessment is frequently scrutinized by the courts. Consider, for example, the court's conclusions in the case of *Goff v. Physicians General Hospital of San Jose* (1958). A woman was admitted to the hospital for delivery of her baby. Her physician ordered administration of medication to induce labor. In the delivery room, the physician made an incision just to the left of the 12 o'clock position of the uterus to "relieve the constrictive band of muscle." He didn't suture the incision but instead, inserted pelvic packs to control bleeding.

After the patient returned to her room, the nurse (who was also in attendance in the delivery room) told the physician that the patient was "bleeding too much." He stated that the bleeding was normal and instructed the nurse to observe the rate of bleeding by timing the period it took for the perineal pads to become soaked.

The first time that the nurse checked the pads, she found "some" blood. Thirty minutes later, the pads were "approaching the saturation point." In another 15 minutes, the pads were found to be soaked and the nurse changed them. During her care, the nurse didn't take the patient's blood pressure, temperature, heart rate, or respiratory rate. She didn't call the physician because, in her opinion, "he would not have come anyway." In retrospect, the nurse testified that she believed that an emergency existed when the pads had approached the saturation point. She also believed that the patient was in a serious condition when the pads were soaked.

At the end of the evening shift, the night nurse came on duty. The night nurse assessed the patient to be cold and clammy, pulseless, and "going into shock." She called the physician, who arrived 10 minutes later and took the patient back to the delivery room where oxygen and adrenalin were administered. A blood transfusion was to be started but the physician was unable to locate a vein. The patient died of hemorrhage from laceration of the cervix. The court concluded that the nurse's negligence in failing to properly assess the patient contributed to her death. (See *Importance of a timely assessment,* page 90.)

CASE 2

In another case addressing nursing assessment issues, *Thomas et al. v. Corson et al.* (1972), the **decedent** was struck by a vehicle when he was standing on the road wiping the freezing rain from his windshield. He was taken to the local hospital at 11:10 p.m., at which time the admitting nurse documented as part of her assessment that the patient was hit by an automobile and complained of numbness in the right anterior thigh.

The patient's leg didn't appear to be deformed and the patient was

Importance of a timely assessment

Nesbitt v. Georgia Baptist Medical Center illustrates the potential for catastrophic outcome and financial risk to hospitals when assessments aren't performed in a timely manner. The patient underwent routine neck surgery to repair a pinched nerve in his neck. The attending neurosurgeon ordered the nursing staff of the defendant hospital to contact him immediately if the patient's pulse dropped below 60 or his systolic blood pressure dropped below 90.

The patient was placed on a pain-management program by which he could push a button and receive a certain dose of narcotic medication for pain. He pushed the button each of the first 25 hours following surgery. On the following morning at 8:00 a.m., the nurse noted that the patient's pulse was 78 and his systolic blood pressure was 130. At 12 noon, his pulse was 60 and systolic pressure was 100. The nurse didn't contact the neurosurgeon, nor did she recheck the vital signs.

At 1:40 p.m., the patient's family called for a nurse repeatedly because they couldn't awaken him. Finally, a nurse responded 30 minutes after the family's first call and notified the neurosurgeon. The patient suffered respiratory depression resulting in brain damage.

The lawsuit filed by the patient and his wife contained these complaints:

- The nurses should have contacted the neurosurgeon when they found the pulse to be 60.
- The nurses were negligent in failing to check the patient's pulse and blood pressure more frequently after noting that both vital signs had decreased and his pulse was at the rate the neurosurgeon had specified for notification.
- Had the nurses acted appropriately and followed the physician's orders, the patient wouldn't have suffered brain damage.

The jury awarded $1.5 million to the patient and his wife. Was the nurse's assessment timely? How could the assessment have been done differently?

In answering these questions, keep in mind that assessment isn't limited to the collection of numerical values of measurement, such as temperature, pulse, and respiratory rate. Assessment is multifaceted and consists of several components, including reassessment after abnormal findings, intervening as appropriate, and clear and timely communication and documentation of this data. Identifying abnormal assessment findings alone isn't enough.

able to move it. The nurse telephoned the physician at 11:30 p.m. and reported the patient's vital signs, including a blood pressure reading of 80/60 at 11:15 p.m. and 90/60 at 11:25 p.m.

The physician was located 10 minutes away from the hospital, but didn't arrive to assess the patient until 2:00 a.m. Between 12 midnight and the physician's arrival, the nurses attending the patient continued to assess him. At approximately 12:05 a.m., his blood pressure was measured to be as low as 70/50 and the patient continued to feel numbness in his leg. At 2:00 a.m., the nurse found the patient breathing very poorly, in a Cheyne-Stokes pattern with no pulse. When the physician arrived at the hospital, he pronounced the patient dead.

On autopsy, the decedent was found to have a "badly comminuted" fracture of the left femoral neck in the hip area with overriding external rotation and hemorrhage. It also showed badly comminuted fractures in the pelvic area with jagged fragments penetrating the peritoneal cavity as well as fracture and separation of the coccyx from the sacrum with extensive hemorrhage around these fractures. The medical examiner certified that the cause of the decedent's death was "traumatic shock, fractured femur and pelvis."

The court concluded that the nurses were negligent in that they failed to notify the physician on call at 12:05 am and communicate the patient's vital signs.

Components of an assessment

To understand how a nurse might fail to properly assess her patient, it might be helpful to revisit the elements comprising an assessment and why assessment is considered such a pertinent part of nursing care.

The basic components of a nursing assessment include the nursing history, physical examination (inspection, palpation, percussion, and auscultation), review of study results (laboratory, radiology, and other results), review of previous health records, and interviews with family members and significant others.

Once the data is gathered, analysis of that data completes the assessment phase. (See *Analyzing assessment data,* page 92.) The overall purpose of the nursing assessment is to determine the patient's current status of wellness versus illness.

PATIENT HISTORY

Performing an assessment usually begins with obtaining a history from the patient. It's an opportunity to collect data directly from the patient and fully explore the information contained within his answers. (See *Patient history,* page 93.) When possible, you should quantify any complaints the patient reports. For example, "headaches one to two times a week" is more specific than "frequent" headaches; "abdominal discomfort following every meal" is better than "often experiences discomfort following meals." Most important, don't forget to document the information collected during the history in the medical record in a succinct, complete manner.

The history plays an important role in assessing a patient. Take, for example, the history obtained by the nurse in *Ramsey et al. v. Physicians Memorial Hospital, Inc., et al.* (1977). A mother took her sons to the local emergency department (ED) after noting that they had a chest and head rash accompanied

Analyzing assessment data

The final step in patient assessment is analyzing the data you've compiled. These tips will help you organize the data:

- *Group significant data into logical clusters.* You'll base your nursing diagnosis not on a single sign or symptom, but on a cluster of assessment findings. By analyzing the clustered data and identifying patterns of illness-related behavior, you can begin to perceive the patient's problem or risks for developing other problems.
- *Identify data gaps.* Signs, symptoms, and isolated incidents that don't fit into consistent patterns can provide the missing facts you need to determine the overall pattern of your patient's problem.
- *Identify conflicting or inconsistent data.* Clarify information that conflicts with other assessment findings, and determine what's causing the inconsistency. For example, a patient with diabetes who says that she complies with her

prescribed diet and insulin administration schedule, but whose serum glucose is greatly elevated, may need to have her treatment regimen reviewed or revised.

- *Determine the patient's perception of normal health.* A patient may find it harder to comply with the treatment regimen when his idea of normality doesn't agree with yours.
- *Determine how the patient handles his health problem.* For instance, is the patient coping with his health problem successfully, or does he need help? Does he deny that he has a problem, or does he admit it but lack solutions to the problem?
- *Form an opinion about the patient's health status.* Base your opinion on actual, potential, or possible concerns reflected by the patient's responses to his condition, and use this to formulate your nursing diagnosis.

---

by a high fever. The mother reported to the nurse attending to the boys that she removed two ticks from the head and stomach of one of the boys. The nurse didn't communicate this part of the history to the physician. The physician, deciding that the boys had measles, prescribed aspirin and instructed that the boys be kept in a dark room.

Following the boys' release from the ED, the rash spread to the arms

and the legs and the fever didn't subside. The parents returned to the ED with their sons, where they were assessed by a different physician. The second physician was unsure of the previous physician's diagnosis of measles and referred the parents and their sons to their pediatrician. When that physician examined the boys, he advised to keep the boys in a dark room and notify him of any change. The following day, one of the boys was found dead and the second boy was subsequently successfully treated for Rocky Mountain spotted fever. An autopsy confirmed that the first boy died of Rocky Mountain spotted fever.

In its findings, the court stated, "Evidence supported finding that the failure of the nurse to notify physician of patient history involving removal of ticks from one of the boys constituted a violation of her duties as a nurse, and failure to relate the information to the physician was a contributing **proximate cause** of death in one child and of serious illness in the other." Here, while the nurse did an excellent job of obtaining pertinent information from the mother of the patients, she failed to communicate it to the physician. This pertinent information, critical to diagnosis, was lost in the care and treatment of the decedent.

PHYSICAL EXAMINATION

The physical examination includes objective data that you can see, hear, feel, or smell. Gather this information through inspection, percussion, palpation, and auscultation. Use it to verify symptoms related in the history. Not having the appropriate equipment or **nursing skills** isn't an excuse for an incomplete physical examination. If you lack the skills necessary to perform a task, you're obligated to obtain assistance from a nurse who possesses those skills.

The information you collect in the physical examination must be documented in objective terms so that it can be easily understood by

> ## Patient history
>
> A patient history consists primarily of subjective data. It focuses on many aspects of the patient's health history, such as his perception of normal levels of function, his current levels of physical, mental, and emotional function, and his response to illness, hospitalization, and therapy. The patient history also explores the patient's past coping patterns and their effectiveness, activities of daily living, preventive health practices, lifestyle, and compliance with medical recommendations. Information may come from the patient himself, from the patient's family, or from other health care professionals.

other members of the health care team. Physical examination findings should be documented in the record in a chronological approach.

Prone to lawsuits

Physical examination is probably the one aspect of nursing assessment mostly likely to result in a lawsuit. Because the nurse maintains a near-constant presence at the patient's bedside, it's expected that she'll repeatedly assess him and report any changes — or consistently poor clinical status — to the physician. Failure to monitor a patient constantly, and report your findings to the attending physician, can have serious consequences. The nurse in the *Goff* case was aware of the patient's excess bleed-

RELATED CASES

Performing a thorough assessment

Standards for assessment don't stop with vital signs. In the case of *Minster v. Pohl* (1992), the defendant nurse improperly placed a feeding tube and failed to verify its placement. The failure to assess proper placement resulted in the tube remaining where the nurse originally placed it — in the lung, not the stomach — leading to pneumothorax. Evidence supported that the pneumothorax eventually led to the patient's death.

Similarly, the court in *Cooper v. National Motor Bearing Company* (1955) concluded that the defendant nurse was negligent in her assessment of a puncture wound sustained by the patient. The nurse, who worked in an industrial setting, was in charge of the company's first aid room. In inspecting the puncture wound on the patient's forehead, the nurse failed to identify the presence of foreign bodies, which remained in the wound and contributed to the formation of a cancer.

Other cases have resulted from failure to assess circulation during a procedure. In *Palmer v. Clarksdale Hospital* (1952), the patient ultimately developed gangrenous sores on her feet following the application of straps to the lower extremities during an operation. The patient alleged that during the 45-minute procedure, leg straps were applied too tightly, and that the nurse failed to loosen the straps or assess the condition of the extremities. In the care and treatment of such patients in which a strap, restraint, or other device is applied, the standard of care requires a regular assessment of the affected area's circulation.

ing but failed to report the information to her supervisor, failed to call the physician, and didn't regularly assess the patient's vital signs. (See *Performing a thorough assessment*.)

The scope of an assessment can be more stringent in specialty areas. For example, assessment of a trauma patient requires the quick, accurate, coordinated efforts of a multidisciplinary team. The nurse's assessment skills must be sharp, accurate, and timely. The physical assessment should include a primary survey of airway, breathing, and circulation; an examination of the cervical spine; and a neurologic review.

The primary physical assessment is typically performed at the time the patient history is taken. A secondary assessment is done later, for a more thorough, head-to-toe examination to detect injuries that could have been missed in the quick, urgent, primary survey. Assessment plays a valuable role in obtaining prompt intervention to correct or prevent any clinical deterioration to the patient.

An ongoing process

Always keep in mind that assessment doesn't end after your initial physical examination of the patient. Remember to reassess the patient after any treatment. It's both sound nursing care and a requirement of the Joint Commission on Accreditation of Healthcare Organizations to note and document a patient's response to care. If the patient hasn't had the expected response to treatment, you'll also need to document your subsequent intervention.

REVIEW OF TEST RESULTS

Diagnostic and laboratory test findings complete the objective database. Together with the patient history and physical examination, they form a significant profile of the patient's condition.

REVIEW OF PREVIOUS HEALTH RECORDS

Your assessment must also include a review of any health records that accompany the patient. This may include lists of medications the patient routinely takes or any record that arrives with a patient who has been transferred from another health care facility. Transfer documents are a vehicle of communication between the transferring facility and the receiving facility. It isn't acceptable to simply place these papers in the chart. You're obligated to review the record and consider all information documented within it. If the records are unclear or information appears to be inconsistent, you're expected to contact the transferring facility or confer with the patient or his family to clarify the information.

INTERVIEWS WITH FAMILY MEMBERS

In your assessment, you should consider including interviews with or information provided by the patient's family members or significant other. Depending on the patient's level of consciousness, or his reliability as a source, the family may be the only source of information available to you and the rest of the health care team.

Consider the nurse's decision to ignore the family's input in the case of *Manning v. Twin Falls Clinic & Hospital, Inc.* (1992). The nurse disconnected the patient's supplemental oxygen during his transfer to another room despite the family's statements that the patient couldn't survive without his oxygen and their request that a portable oxygen unit be used during the move. Expert testimony presented in court on behalf of the patient supported that the nurse's conduct in disconnecting the supplemental oxygen to the patient during the transfer was an extreme deviation from the required standard of care.

Legal issues

In examining assessment from a legal perspective, several issues arise: the nurse-patient relationship, the expectation of continuous assessment, communication and documentation of assessment findings, implementation of nursing actions, and identification of nursing diagnoses.

NURSE-PATIENT RELATIONSHIP

The first issue is the nurse-patient relationship: Have you established a relationship with the patient? Even if you're only watching a patient while your colleague, his regular nurse, is off the unit for a lunch break, you've entered into a relationship. Once this relationship is initiated, **duty** is established — that is, you have a legal obligation to the patient to act as any reasonable and prudent nurse at the same level of training would do. For nurses, courts have determined that this relationship may be established easily, even through a single telephone conversation.

Consider another scenario: you have just arrived for your shift in the ED and you've been assigned to admit a patient to a medical-surgical unit. The patient is ready to be transported. You spend only 10 minutes with the patient, but you have entered into a nurse-patient relationship. The same applies to a patient who is transferred to your unit and decides after 30 minutes that he wants to leave, against medical advice. Legally speaking, even the briefest of contact establishes a nurse-patient relationship.

CONTINUOUS ASSESSMENT

Another issue you must consider is continuous assessment, which is based on the standards of care that govern the nursing process. Your responsibility to the patient doesn't end once you've completed the initial, thorough assessment. Once-a-shift assessment typically isn't enough, either — nor is simply following the physician's orders regarding how often to assess the patient's vital signs. If the patient's

clinical status warrants, you should check vital signs more frequently.

COMMUNICATING AND DOCUMENTING ASSESSMENT FINDINGS

Once you've performed the assessment, you need to communicate it, when appropriate, to other health care providers. If the assessment changes (whether improvement or deterioration), you need to decide whether you should communicate your findings to the physician or other members of the health care team, and do so if it's warranted. (See chapter 3, Failure to communicate information.)

Documentation, once done for the sole purpose of communicating care and treatment from one provider to the next, has evolved into a means of avoiding malpractice allegations and meeting requirements for regulatory agencies and third-party payers. (See chapter 4, Failure to document information.)

IMPLEMENTING NURSING ACTIONS

You also must consider whether your findings indicate the need for some change from the physician's standard orders. For example, your findings might suggest the need for nursing action, such as more frequent assessment, changing or reinforcing a dressing, or the use of modalities to prevent skin breakdown. Nursing care and treatment require more than following a physician's orders. Independent judgments by the nurse as to the patient's needs are necessary and expected when the patient's status changes, or when abnormal findings appear during assessment. Bad nursing judgment opens the doors to lawsuits.

IDENTIFYING NURSING DIAGNOSES

Another issue involving assessment concerns the identification of nursing diagnoses. In 1990, the North American Nursing Diagnosis Association adopted the following definition of a nursing diagnosis: "A nursing diagnosis is a clinical judgment about individual, family, or community responses to actual or potential health problems or life processes. Nursing diagnoses provide the basis for the selection of nursing interventions to achieve outcomes for which the nurse is accountable."

After clustering significant assessment data and analyzing the pattern, your next step is to identify the patient's actual and potential health problems. In forming a nursing diagnosis, you'll identify the patient's problem, write a diagnostic statement, and validate the diagnosis. You'll establish several nursing diagnoses, derived from the information obtained during your assessment. These diagnoses, arranged according to priority to address the patient's most crucial problems first, will direct the rest of your nursing care plan. (See *Legal issues involving assessment*.)

LEGAL RISKS IN SPECIAL CARE UNITS

In special care units, such as the ED, operating room, postanesthesia

> ## Legal issues involving assessment
>
> When assessing your patients, keep these legal issues in mind to safeguard your practice.
>
> - Have you entered into a nurse-patient relationship?
> - Is your assessment continual?
> - Have you communicated your assessment findings to the appropriate personnel and documented accordingly?
> - Have you implemented the appropriate nursing orders?
> - Have you identified the appropriate nursing diagnoses?

care unit (PACU), intensive care unit (ICU), and other critical care areas, nurses regularly perform tasks that only physicians used to perform. Here, patient care offers exciting nursing challenges, increased nursing responsibilities — and extra risk of liability. For example, if you're an ED nurse, you'll have to employ triage; that is, classifying patients according to the seriousness of their medical problems. If you make a mistake and a patient's treatment is needlessly delayed, you may be liable.

If you're assigned to the PACU, ICU, or other critical care area, you're already aware that you must watch your patients for signs and symptoms of adverse anesthetic effects, postoperative cardiac and pulmonary complications, and shock caused by hypoxia, hemorrhage, or infection. In any of these special care units, the patient's survival may depend on your judgment.

Where you stand legally

If you work in a special care unit, take your increased liability seriously. Remember, even though hospital policy requires that you perform certain tasks, or you perform them under physician's orders as a physician's **borrowed servant** or ostensible agent, your individual liability continues. If a patient sues for malpractice, all the persons involved can be held separately and jointly liable. For this reason, you should always carefully evaluate the jobs you're asked to do, and if you feel that any task is beyond your training and expertise, don't attempt it. Even if you can do it, make sure you're permitted by hospital policy and your state or jurisdictional nurse practice act. (See *Self-protection in special care units.*)

How nursing standards apply

A nurse working in a special care unit is typically subject to the same general rule of law as her staff nurse colleagues: She must meet the standard of care that a reasonably well-qualified and prudent nurse would meet in the same or similar circumstances. However, in a malpractice lawsuit, when deciding whether a specialty nurse has acted reasonably, the court won't consider what the average licensed practical nurse (LPN) or registered nurse would have done. Instead, the court will seek to determine the standard of care that an LPN or a registered nurse specifically trained to work in the special care unit would have met. Thus, the law imposes a higher standard of conduct on persons with superior knowledge, skill, or training.

Assessment in special care situations

Hunt v. Palm Springs General Hospital (1977) illustrates how the courts evaluate the reasonable nurse standard in light of prevailing practices. The patient, Mr. Hunt, was taken to the ED with seizures. When he was examined, his physician concluded that Mr. Hunt, a known drug addict, was experiencing seizures because he had gone without drugs for several days. The physician advised the hospital administration that the patient's condition wasn't critical, but he nevertheless required hospitalization.

The hospital refused to admit Mr. Hunt because of a history of unpaid bills. During the next 4 hours, Mr. Hunt waited in the ED while the physician tried to find hospitalization for him elsewhere in the city. Eventually, Mr. Hunt was admitted to a neighboring hospital. He lived for 26 hours before dying of brain damage caused by prolonged seizures.

The court examined the practice of ED nurses elsewhere and found that the Palm Springs General Hospital nurses had acted unreasonably. Their duty was to monitor Mr. Hunt's condition periodically while he awaited transfer to another hospital. If this duty had been carried out, the court concluded, the nurses would have noted his elevated temperature — a clear indication that he needed immediate hospitalization.

Similarly, in *Cline v. Lund* (1973), the patient, Ms. Cline, was sent to a

EXPERT OPINION

Self-protection in special care units

If you're working in a special care unit of a hospital — the emergency department, intensive care unit, operating room, or postanesthesia care unit — your expanded responsibilities make you especially vulnerable to malpractice lawsuits. To protect yourself, take these precautions.

Know your role

Request a clear, written definition of your role in the hospital. Your hospital should have an overall policy and an individual, written job description for you that specifies the limits of your nursing role. You'll be better protected if guidelines for advanced nursing competencies are formally established.

Document thoroughly

Document everything you do, so there's no question later about your actions. Your nurses' notes, of course, should reflect the nursing process: document your assessment of the patient, your care plan, your actual care, and your evaluation of the plan's effectiveness.

Maintain skills

Make sure of your own competence. If your role expands, your skills have to grow, too. If that requires advanced courses and supervised clinical experience, make sure you get both.

Insure yourself

Damages awarded to patients can be very high, and high legal fees may mean you can't afford even to defend yourself in a lawsuit. If you don't have your own professional liability insurance, and your hospital doesn't help defend you against a lawsuit, you could face a startling bill even after all claims against you are proven groundless and dropped. (You might never even get to court — but you could still find yourself with a large bill for legal consultation.)

---

coronary care stepdown unit when problems developed after she underwent a hysterectomy. Except for one bout with nausea, she appeared to be making satisfactory progress. At about 2:30 p.m. the next day, a nurse dangled Ms. Cline's legs from the side of her bed. The nurse charted that the patient tolerated the dangling well. However, by 3:30 p.m., Ms. Cline was unresponsive,

her blood pressure was rising, and she was vomiting.

At 9:00 p.m., when Ms. Cline's blood pressure reached 142/90 mm Hg, the attending nurse notified her supervisor, who at 9:40 p.m. notified the attending physician. He came to the hospital, examined the patient, and — suspecting an internal hemorrhage — ordered blood work and vital signs taken every 30 minutes. At 11:45 p.m., the patient's blood pressure was 160/90 mm Hg. Her arms and legs were stiff and her fists were clenched. Instead of summoning the physician again, the attending nurse once more notified her supervisor. A half-hour later, at 12:15 a.m., when Ms. Cline's blood pressure had reached 230/130 mm Hg, the physician was called. The patient stopped breathing at 12:40 a.m., suffered a cardiac arrest at 12:45 a.m., and died at 4:45 a.m.

In the ensuing lawsuit, the court found the nurse liable, stating that her care had fallen below that of a ***reasonably prudent nurse*** in the same or similar circumstances. "Nurses," the court decision said, "should notify the physician of any significant change or unresponsiveness."

Other practice settings that aren't immune to malpractice cases involving failure to assess are obstetric and pediatric departments. Obstetric nursing carries a double duty, in a sense, because the nurse cares for both the patient and the fetus. Because courts recognize a legal duty to the fetus, the nurse may be found liable to both the patient and her unborn child. Numerous assessment issues in this practice area can present risk for lawsuits, including failure to recognize Rh incompatibility, failure to monitor the patient through labor, failure to monitor contractions and fetal heart rate, and failure to recognize signs of preeclampsia or other labor complications.

For example, in *O'Neal v. Annapolis Hospital* (1990), the patient's family asserted that the nurses were negligent in failing to take and record fetal heart tones periodically during labor. The baby sustained

permanent brain damage as a result.

Pediatric medicine can also present legal challenges. In *Duling v. Bluefield Sanitarium, Inc.* (1965), a 13-year-old patient with known rheumatic fever was coughing incessantly, her nails turning blue, and her heart pounding. The patient's mother pleaded with the nurse to pay attention to these findings. Eventually, a nursing supervisor came upon the distraught mother in a corridor and hurried to the patient's room. The supervisor called a physician to assess the patient. Despite intensive, extraordinary care and the efforts of the physician, the child died the following day.

Staying within nursing practice limits

You must not presume, because you work in a special care unit, that your increased training and broadened authority permit you to exceed nursing's legal limits. This is especially important in an area, such as medical diagnosis, in which you can easily cross the legal boundary between acting with the authority of a nurse and that of a physician.

Overstepping the boundaries of the nursing profession is especially likely to happen in the ED, where an on-call physician may refuse to see a patient himself, instead ordering care based on a nurse's observations. In another common ED situation, a patient may ask an ED nurse for advice over the telephone. In such a case, she should respond carefully, telling the patient to come to the ED or to see his physician if he has questions or his symptoms persist.

Similar situations may occur in other special care units, where split-second patient care decisions are sometimes made on the basis of nurses' phone calls to attending physicians.

Keep in mind that all state and jurisdictional nurse practice acts prohibit you from medically diagnosing a patient's condition. You can tell the physician about signs and symptoms you've observed, but you can't decide which medical treatments to administer. If you do, you'll be *practicing medicine without a license,* and you'll be held at least partly liable for any resulting harm to the patient.

In *Methodist Hospital v. Ball* (1961), a young man, Mr. Ball, was brought to the ED with injuries sustained in an automobile accident. Because of a sudden influx of critically ill patients, the ED staff was unable to care for him immediately.

While lying on a stretcher in the hospital hallway, Mr. Ball became boisterous and demanded care. Apparently, the attending nurse decided he was drunk. Instead of being treated, Mr. Ball was put into restraints and transported by ambulance to another local hospital. There, 15 minutes after arriving, he died from internal bleeding.

An autopsy revealed no evidence of alcohol in Mr. Ball's system. In the resulting lawsuit, the court found the attending nurse and medical resident negligent because they failed to diagnose Mr. Ball's condition properly, to give supportive treatment, and to alert personnel at the second hospital about Mr. Ball's critical condition.

When assessment can turn into a lawsuit

Failure to perform a proper assessment can turn into a lawsuit when all four elements of *malpractice* or *professional negligence* are met. Professional negligence or malpractice occurs when a nurse fails to do what a reasonably prudent nurse would have done in similar circumstances. This is premised on the four elements of professional negligence or malpractice: existence of a duty, breach of the duty, proximate cause, and damages. In examining the legal issues surrounding nursing assessment, the discussion must begin with the first element, duty.

DUTY

What creates the nurse's duty to assess? An individual who sets out to perform the professional services of a nurse has a legal duty to use the reasonable degree of skill, knowledge, and care ordinarily used by similarly trained nurses acting under similar circumstances. The California Appellate Court in the case of *Fraijo v. Hartland Hospital* (1979) acknowledged the following instruction setting forth the duty of a professional nurse with respect to the care of a patient: "It is the duty of one who undertakes to perform the service of a trained or graduate nurse to have the knowledge and skill ordinarily possessed, and to ex-

Sources of standards of care

There are many sources that create standards of care, including:

- Professional organizations, such as the American Nurses Association, the National League for Nursing, the American Association of Critical Care Nurses, and the Association of Perioperative Registered Nurses
- Federal organizations such as the Centers for Medicare and Medicaid Services
- Other external agencies such as the Joint Commission for the Accreditation of Healthcare Organizations
- Hospital policies and procedures
- Professional literature and textbooks
- Equipment inserts and manuals

---

ercise the care and skill ordinarily used in like situations, by trained and skilled members of the nursing profession practicing their profession in the same or similar circumstances." Who or what establishes these standards of care? There are many sources. (See *Sources of standards of care.*) Keep in mind that duty can be established when you're volunteering as a nurse or even giving advice to a family member or neighbor.

BREACH OF DUTY

The second element, **breach of duty,** is the nurse's failure to carry out her duty to the patient. Accordingly, either an omission or commission can constitute a breach of the standard of care. In other words, failure to assess — or inaccurate assessment — may constitute a breach of duty. For example, the nurse in the *Goff* case conducted a portion of her assessment of the patient by changing the perineal pads and examining them for the degree of blood saturation. The defendant

physician testified that the nurses should have notified him at 12:05 a.m. of the change in the patient's vital signs and that those changes were, in fact, signs of shock, which required his immediate care and attention. He further contended that to a trained nurse, the findings at 12:01 a.m. would indicate a critical condition and that the patient's life was in jeopardy, even though she may not have been in danger of immediate death. It's standard procedure and customary practice for nurses, as part of the health care team, to advise the physician of any significant changes in vital signs.

CAUSATION

In testing for a **causal connection** between a nurse's alleged negligence and a patient's injury, the court usually utilizes the "but for" test; that is, but for the nurse's conduct, the patient wouldn't have suffered injury. The patient's counsel will have to prove that more likely than not, the nurse's action — or failure to act — resulted in the patient's injury. In some cases — for example, those involving multiple defendants (or **tortfeasors**) or missed diagnoses — the "but for" test won't be applied due to lack of sufficient guidance. In such cases other, less common, tests will be employed.

In proving a negligence case involving the duty to assess, the **plaintiff** must also prove that the alleged negligent conduct was the **proximate cause** of the injury. Essentially, establishing proximate cause involves determining whether the act of negligence was, in fact, the cause of the injury, and determining if the act of negligence was so closely related to the injury that there's justification for imposing liability. For example, in *Rampe v. Community General Hospital of Sullivan County* (1997), evidence before the court didn't establish that an obstetrical nurse's negligence in failing to notify the obstetrician of changes in fetal heart rate was the proximate cause of the infant's injuries. In addition, there was no proof that an additional phone call to the obstetrician from the nurse would have prompted the obstetrician to order a cesarean delivery to be performed an earlier time.

DAMAGES

The fourth element of negligence, **damages,** requires proof of actual physical loss or damage that's proximately caused by the defendant's negligent conduct. For a plaintiff to prevail in a question of negligence, it's essential that there be damage to the patient. A nurse may have a duty to perform an assessment and she may fail to do that assessment,

but if there's no damage to the patient as a result of that failure, a lawsuit can't be brought. There may have been negligence, but no harm resulted. For example, a patient at risk for falling may, in fact, fall while in the health care facility. If the patient sustains absolutely no damages, the failure to protect the patient from falling won't constitute malpractice.

When a nurse realizes that she has failed in her assessment, it's critical for her to communicate to the risk manager the exact extent of the patient's injury, if any. Consider, for example, a case in which the nurse fails to assess that a patient is at risk for falling. Consequently, the nurse fails to institute the proper safeguards and the patient falls. It's crucial that the nurse conduct a continuous assessment and document the patient's condition. If a lawsuit follows, the nurse's documentation might help to determine what, if any, damage was directly related to the patient's fall. If the patient doesn't sustain injuries because of the fall in the health care facility, but falls again at home and becomes injured, the nurse and facility will limit liability if thorough documentation was completed at the time of the first fall.

A*voiding litigation*

Critical thinking is required during your ongoing assessment of a patient. Once you have collected data, you need to synthesize that data and plan the necessary care. Do you need to implement some standard physician's orders? Call the physician? Implement standard

Limiting your liability

When it comes to assessment, using these tips may help to keep you out of the courtroom.
- Conduct a thorough assessment of your patient.
- Listen to your patient.
- Continue to assess and reassess your patient throughout your

shift, especially after medications are administered or procedures are performed.
- Don't stop with assessment; follow up appropriately with your findings. Communication and documentation are essential.

nursing orders? Administer medication?

Physician's orders, whether one-time orders or standing orders, can get nurses into a lot of legal trouble. If the physician ordered vital signs to be taken as frequently as every 10 minutes, the nurse generally will be held to that order.

To limit your liability, don't perform an assessment in haste. Consider, for example, the nurse who cared for the patient who sustained an incomplete spontaneous abortion. The nurse knew the patient's history and observed the aborted tissue. In preparation for a dilatation and curettage, the nurse carried out the physician's order for pitocin; in starting the infusion, the nurse palpated the patient's uterus and noted a very firm umbilicus. The nurse stopped the infusion to listen for fetal heart tones, which were present. Additional assessment revealed that the patient was pregnant with twins and only one fetus had been aborted. Thus, failing to continue to assess the patient can result in missing pieces of critical information.

There are a variety of ways for the nurse to limit her liability when it comes to conducting a proper assessment. (See *Limiting your liability*.) For example, conduct a thorough assessment of your patient. If your patient is unconscious or otherwise unable to answer your questions, don't skip the nursing history; turn to other sources of information — such as family members — to collect as much data as possible.

Listen to your patient and his family members. Remember, too, that assessment shouldn't end after the most critical portion of your patient's illness; it should be continued until discharge to establish what your patient's needs will be once he's at home.

Once you've assessed the patient, follow up with appropriate actions regarding the data collected. Perform additional interventions or assessments as necessary, communicate your findings to the appropriate personnel, and document your assessment findings, your interventions, who you contacted, and the people you notified.

When documenting, use language that's quantifying and succinct. Remember that from a legal perspective, if it wasn't documented, it wasn't done; if it was poorly documented, it was poorly done; and if it was incorrectly documented, it was fraudulent. Quality writing inspires quality performance. Aim to document contemporaneously (or as close to it as possible), accurately, appropriately, and completely.

Follow any policy or order regarding assessment and documentation of the assessment. While policies aren't considered "laws," courts generally will rule against a nurse for not following a policy. Likewise, orders are meant to be followed. Be sure to comply with the details as outlined by an order.

Ultimately, a complete record can demonstrate to the Board of Nursing and the court that you're a competent nurse. It can keep you from being named as a defendant in a lawsuit, keep you out of court if you are named in a lawsuit, and help you win if you do go to court.

Selected references

Assessment Made Incredibly Easy, 2nd ed. Springhouse, Pa.: Springhouse Corp., 2002.

Collins, S.E. "Litigation Risks for Infusion Specialists. Understanding the Issues," *Journal of Infusion Nursing* 24(6):375-80, November-December 2001.

Higgs, J., et al. "Integrating Clinical Reasoning and Evidence-Based Practice," *AACN Clinical Issues* 12(4):482-90, November 2001.

Klein, C.A. "Acute Signs and Symptoms Require Prompt Follow-Up," *The Nurse Practitioner* 26(11):57-58, November 2001.

Langslow, A. "Nursing Observations Prove Critical," *Australian Nursing Journal* 8(1):37-38, July 2000.

Mahlmeister, L., and Van Mullem, C. "The Process of Triage in Perinatal Settings: Clinical and Legal Issues," *Journal of Perinatal and Neonatal Nursing* 13(4):13-30, March 2000.

Selbst, S.M., and Osterhoudt, K. "Pediatric Emergency Medicine: Legal Briefs," *Pediatric Emergency Care* 16(2):116-18, April 2000.

Smith-Blair, N., and Neighbors, M. "Use of Critical Thinking Disposition Inventory in Critical Care Orientation," *Journal of Continuing Education in Nursing* 31(6):251-56, November-December 2000.

Thomas, D.O. "Special Considerations for Pediatric Triage in the Emergency Department," *Nursing Clinics of North America* 37(1):145-59, March 2002.

Thompson, C., and Dowding, D. "Responding to Uncertainty in Nursing Practice," *International Journal of Nursing Studies* 38(5):609-15, October 2001.

Waitman, J. and McCaffery, M. "Meperidine — A Liability," *AJN* 101(1):57-58, January 2001.

Chapter Six

FAILURE TO PROTECT

O␣NE OF YOUR most important responsibilities is your patient's physical safety. To prevent falls, for example, you have to make sure bed rails are up for a debilitated, confused, or medicated patient. Because bed rails may also be safety hazards, you should weigh their use in each case. You also need to help a weak patient walk, use proper transfer techniques, and sometimes use restraints to immobilize a patient.

In the interest of patient safety, you also must keep an eye on your facility and its equipment. If you see loose bed rails, a wet spot on the floor, or improperly functioning equipment, you have a duty to report the problem.

Case studies

The following court cases illustrate how inattention to the safety of your patient and the environment may not only endanger patients, but also make you — and the facility — liable for injuries.

CASE 1

Vincent McDonald and Nancy McDonald, Appellants v. Aliquippa Hospital, Appellee (1992) illustrates the responsibility of the hospital and its nursing employees for the safety and well-being of a patient. Mr. McDonald filed a lawsuit against the hospital to recover damages for injuries caused by the unexpected closing of automatic hospital doors on his extended right foot.

Mr. McDonald testified that the automatic doors in the hospital corridor were open as he was being transported by wheelchair from the radiology department to his room. As the nurse was pushing him through the doorway, the doors unexpectedly closed tightly on his right foot, which was extended in a position parallel to the floor. The nurse apparently momentarily panicked and pulled on his foot, causing the doors to close more tightly, rather than acting immediately to manually release the doors, which she ultimately had to do. The McDonalds alleged in their lawsuit that the doors had been improperly maintained and that the nurse was negligent in failing to exercise due care for the safety of her patient.

The original trial court, after hearing the McDonalds' evidence, entered a **compulsory non-suit** — essentially meaning that there wasn't sufficient evidence to proceed with a case. A compulsory non-suit indicates that, after hearing the evidence, the trial judge finds as a matter of law that the verdict must be in favor of the hospital defendant and removes the matter from a jury's decision. The Superior Court reversed the trial court's decision on the basis that the patient's testimony established a **prima facie** case of negligence, and a jury could infer that the injuries that the automatic doors caused to the patient resulted from negligence on the part of the hospital and the hospital employee.

Prima facie is a fact presumed to be true unless disproved by some evidence to the contrary. A prima facie case of negligence infers that there was proof of:

● a duty on the part of the hospital and hospital employee to the patient.
● a breach of that duty by omission (failing to do something that should have been done) or commission (doing an act which shouldn't have been done).
● legal and proximate harm to the patient caused by the breach.

Accordingly, the Superior Court reversed and remanded the case for a new trial.

CASE 2

Patient falls represent a major concern for health care facilities. (See *Assessing a patient's fall risk,* page 108.)

In *Cooper v. Rehabilitation Facility at Austin* (1998), the plaintiff, Ms. Cooper, age 71, had a history of rheumatoid arthritis but was found to be a good candidate for knee replacement. In anticipation of the operation, she was admitted to a rehabilitation hospital to increase her mobility in preparation for surgery. While nurses attempted to transfer Ms. Cooper from a wheelchair to a bed, the patient complained of pain, became nauseous, and fainted. Eventually, she was transferred to a bed. The nurses administered oxygen, gave pain medication, and called her physician. Later that day, it was determined that the plaintiff had a fractured right tibia and fibula. The next day, after she continued to complain of pain in her left leg, her left tibia and fibula were determined to be fractured as well. The patient sued the hospital, the nurses, and the physician.

Ms. Cooper settled her case against the physician and agreed to a non-suit regarding her claim against the nurses, but went to trial against the hospital alone on a charge of negligence. The jury found the hospital vicariously liable for the nurses' negligence in transferring the patient to the bed, as well as for the other health care workers who failed to diagnose and treat her injuries in a timely manner. The $1,250,000 verdict was reduced to $1,235,000, taking into consideration the physician's previous settlement of $15,000. The hospital appealed but the verdict was upheld. The considerable sum of damages was based on the pain and suffering that Ms. Cooper experi-

Assessing a patient's fall risk

In conjunction with providing a safe environment, the assessment of a patient as a fall risk has to be considered by the nurse assigned to the patient. In the case of Northport New York Veterans Administration Hospital, a fall risk program was in effect but was ignored, ultimately resulting in the death of a patient. The case of *Lamarca v. United States* (1998) involved a federal tort claim against the United States. When a veterans' hospital and its employees are believed to have caused injury through malpractice, an action can only be brought against the United States as a party in interest.

Mr. Lamarca had a long history of arthritis and heart disease. While visiting the arthritis clinic, he became dizzy and was later admitted from the emergency department to the cardiac intensive care unit. In the hospital he received not only his cardiac medication, but also several sedating medications, including an antianxiety medication.

On April 12, the day after admission, the patient's wife found him in bed unconscious. She was given no explanation, except from a roommate who explained that there had been an accident. Mr. Lamarca's wife later learned that the nurse had found him on the floor around 11:30 a.m. Nurse Adams completed the incident report, which stated that the patient had fallen out of bed, but it was unclear whether he had been trying to get out of bed or had slipped off the side as the side rails were down. The patient fractured his hip and subsequently developed deep venous thrombosis, became malnourished, and suffered from decubitus ulcers stages I through IV, all of which contributed to his death.

The U.S. District Court for the Eastern District of New York held that the hospital breached its duty of care by failing to place the patient on "full fall risk," thereby causing the fractured hip. The breach of duty also involved failing to assist the patient with meals and not providing appropriate skin care, thereby allowing the progression of his decubitus ulcers. The Court awarded damages to the widow for the patient's pain and suffering, funeral expenses, loss of consortium (the monetary value for the loss of her husband's services), and lost income.

What's particularly interesting about this case is that during testimony there was an inconsistency as to whether the bed rails were up or down. According to the incident report they were down. However, at trial, it was determined that a later written note attempted to place the fall as occurring later in the day and indicated that the side rails were allegedly in the up position. It was also discovered that the nursing flow sheets for the 11th and 12th of April were missing from the patient's chart.

enced as well as the change in her circumstances. Prior to the fractures, she had still had the ability to perform some activities for herself and had hoped by having the surgery to be able to do more. It was obvious from the records that she had been making progress before the fractures occurred. The court found that she had entered the hospital to gain mobility and independence, not to lose it.

Legal issues

In your practice, you should be alert for special safety concerns, such as premises liability, patient falls, the safety of equipment, the prospect of suicide attempts, the use of restraints, and the risk of transmitting disease.

PREMISES LIABILITY

A health care facility is either a property owner or a tenant in possession of rental property and, as such, is responsible for the maintenance of the property. The facility can incur liability for acts that occur on the premises, even if the acts have no direct relationship to medical treatment.

Facility's responsibility for patient safety

A health care facility has a duty to make its premises safe for patients and visitors, who are entitled to rely on the assumption that the facility has exercised reasonable care for their safety. In the *McDonald* case, the court found that patients are es-

pecially vulnerable to faulty doors and other faulty equipment. The facility has a duty to inspect such equipment and maintain it in good operating order. The failure of the doors to sense an object in their path and remain open or to release when hitting an object are malfunctions that wouldn't occur if the doors were inspected regularly and properly maintained.

This type of case falls under a legal doctrine that's known as ***corporate liability,*** which holds the health care facility liable for its own wrongful conduct, including failure to keep the physical plant reasonably safe. If a patient is injured because the facility alone breached one of its duties, the facility is responsible for the injury. The second doctrine of institutional malpractice liability is ***respondeat superior,*** which means a facility is liable for an employee's wrongful conduct. Under this doctrine, both the employee and the health care facility can be found liable for a breach of duty to the patient — including the duty of ensuring his safety.

Even if the doors weren't malfunctioning, then the nurse, who was a hospital employee, had a duty to be alert and to exercise care to move her patient through the doors safely instead of allowing them to close upon and do injury to the plaintiff's extended leg. (See *When an accident becomes negligence,* page 110.)

Slips and falls

Both the *Cooper* and *Lamarca* cases illustrate failure of nurses to protect

When an accident becomes negligence

The nurse in *Vincent McDonald and Nancy McDonald, Appellants v. Aliquippa Hospital, Appellee* (1992) had a duty to her patient to transport him safely to his room. The failure of the hospital to maintain the automatic doors compounded the nurse's negligence in attempting to pull the patient's foot through the doors instead of immediately forcing the doors open. Had the nurse acted expeditiously to open the doors, more likely than not, she wouldn't have been responsible for equipment failure that wasn't within her purview to maintain.

If a piece of equipment or a dangerous condition exists, a hospital employee with knowledge of the dangerous condition should report the situation to the appropriate supervisor. In the *McDonald* case, the nurse wouldn't have known about the dangerous nature of the door until the unexpected door closing occurred. However, using a different scenario, if there had been a previous report of this door closing unexpectedly or precipitously and injuring or almost injuring other patients or visitors, then the failure of the hospital to correct the situation and the failure of nurses who were aware of this situation to stop using the doors would then cause liability to fall upon both the hospital and the nurse.

their patients either by being involved in a patient's fall or by failing to assess a fall risk. Falls are a frequent basis for suits involving nurses. Falls can also be caused by debris or a cord on the floor, pieces of equipment that are out of place, poor transfer technique by the staff, or too few staff doing the transfer. Generally, the lawsuit is brought when the fall results in a serious injury such as a fracture, including a fractured hip in an elderly person, or a head injury. Because the health care facility is generally a property owner, there will be a question as to whether the facility had actual or constructive notice of a dangerous condition and whether that condition had a *causal connec-*

tion (proximate or legal cause) to the fall. *Actual notice* is oral or written notice concerning a dangerous condition or a defective condition. In cases in which actual notice existed, the court must determine whether the facility (acting through its employees) had enough time between the notice and the accident to have remedied the situation. *Constructive notice* implies that the defect or dangerous condition was visible and apparent and had existed for a sufficient length of time prior to the accident to allow for its discovery and correction. How often are floors mopped? Are signs placed in an area that's slippery? Is debris removed from the floors following a procedure? Has equip-

Preventing falls

Almost anything can cause a patient to fall, particularly if he's elderly or receiving medication. Here are some ways you can protect your patient from falls:

- Make sure his bed's side rails are kept up, when indicated.
- Orient him to his surroundings and to the time, and reorient him as necessary.
- Provide adequate lighting and a clean, clutter-free area.
- Review the medications he's taking, and be aware that certain medications, such as diuretics, may increase his risk for falling.
- Monitor him regularly — con-

stantly, if his condition makes this necessary.
- Offer a bedpan or commode regularly.
- Ensure that adequate staff is available to perform safe patient transfers to or from bed or to assist the patient as needed.
- Ensure that the patient wears proper shoes for walking.
- See that the call light is within easy reach and is in working condition.
- Supervise the patient when he's in a chair. A patient can fall out of a chair just as easily as out of a bed and be just as seriously injured.

---

ment been moved from an area where people would trip or fall or be hurt by it? These are the types of questions that are asked to determine whether there was actual or constructive notice.

●●● **LESSONS IN PRACTICE** Patient safety, like good care, is paramount to preventing litigation. Because almost anything can cause a fall — improper transfer, medication, bed rails down on a confused or weak patient, debris on the floor, or equipment out of place — be vigilant and protective of your patients as well as visitors. (See *Preventing falls.*)

Other considerations in preventing falls include:
- What medication is the patient taking? Does it have a sedative or

an agitating effect? (See *Drugs associated with falls,* page 112.)
- Is the patient elderly, weak, or in a new environment? Does he have impaired vision or hearing, mental confusion, or dizziness?
- Does the staff respond in a timely manner when a patient calls or rings for the nurse?
- Are meal trays left where the patient can't reach them?

Once you're aware, preventing injury to the patient should become second nature. However, nothing is foolproof. Be sure to document all interventions as a safeguard against litigation.

The decision to raise or lower side rails should be part of a patient's fall risk assessment. At times, a raised side rail may increase the severity of the injury if

Drugs associated with falls

This list highlights some classes of commonly prescribed drugs and the possible adverse effects of each that may increase a patient's risk for falling.

Diuretics
Hypovolemia, orthostatic hypotension, electrolyte imbalance, urinary incontinence

Antihypertensives
Hypotension

Tricyclic antidepressants
Orthostatic hypotension

Antipsychotics
Orthostatic hypotension, muscle rigidity, sedation

Benzodiazepines and antihistamines
Excessive sedation, confusion, paradoxical agitation, loss of balance

Narcotics
Hypotension, sedation, motor incoordination, agitation

Hypnotics
Excessive sedation, ataxia, poor balance, confusion, paradoxical agitation

Antidiabetic drugs
Acute hypoglycemia

Alcohol
Intoxication, motor incoordination, agitation, sedation, confusion

the patient falls over the rails. Side rails may also be considered a type of restraint and, therefore, routinely raising them may not be recommended. You should always document your assessment of a patient's risk of falling. Check with your facility to see if they have a fall risk assessment program. In addition, always keep a patient's bed in the lowest possible position.

Observing your patient's gait may help you assess his risk for falling. See if he's steady on his feet. Have him walk away from you, so you can assess his ability to walk without assistance. Note whether your patient has a wide base for walking, seems to lose his balance when standing, doesn't appear to be well coordinated, sways or lurches when walking, attempts to hold on to furniture for support, or needs an assistive device, such as a walker or a cane.

Defective or dangerous equipment
Salter v. Deaconess Family Medical Center (1999) involved nursing negligence in the care of a 4-day-old infant, Demitrius Hawkins. Katherine Battaglia, a nurse at Deaconess, heated a wet washcloth in a microwave for one minute. She placed the heated washcloth on the baby's heel to facilitate drawing blood. Prior to placing the heated washcloth, she allegedly touched it to her arm to test the temperature, and apparently it felt satisfactory. However, a temperature that's safe for an adult probably isn't safe for a newborn. The infant suffered second-degree burns that required various treat-

ments, including debridement over a 3-month period.

A lawsuit commenced and after *discovery* (*depositions*, which are questions answered under oath) was completed and expert reports submitted, the parent plaintiff filed a motion for partial **summary judgment.** The Supreme Court of Erie County entered a partial summary judgment in favor of the parent and against the nurse and hospital defendants. The defendants appealed. The Supreme Court of New York, Appellate Division, affirmed the judgment of the lower Court, holding the nurse and hospital legally responsible for the infant's injury, and ruled that the evidence supported the granting of the motion for summary judgment.

In support of the motion for summary judgment, the plaintiff submitted a nursing expert opinion indicating that Nurse Battaglia deviated from the standard of care by applying a heated washcloth that was too hot for its intended use to an infant's heel. Nurse Battaglia admitted, in her deposition, that the child's burns were due to the application of the washcloth. A prima facie case was established that the nurse's deviation from an acceptable practice was a proximate cause of the infant's burns.

The court entered a summary judgment in the plaintiff's favor not only for negligence but also under the doctrine of *res ipsa loquitur* (the thing speaks for itself). Res ipsa loquitur is a legal doctrine of **circumstantial evidence** that's applied when a defendant is solely and exclusively in control at the time of injury, the injury is of a type that wouldn't occur without

negligence, and the injured party couldn't have contributed to his or her injury. In effect, the doctrine places the burden on the defendant to prove that he or she isn't negligent. (See *Whose negligence?*, page 114.)

In both cases previously discussed, failure to safeguard the patient while providing care resulted in injury. All patients require careful observation, but certain patient populations require particular care and scrutiny. Some of the most vulnerable patients are the very young, who can't indicate verbally that they're being injured, or the very old or mentally infirm such as an elderly patient with Alzheimer's disease.

While there was no defect in the equipment being used in the *Salter* and *Grant* cases, the failure of the nurses to determine the appropriate equipment to use for a specific patient, or the appropriate use of the equipment, was just as negligent as using a piece of defective equipment that caused an injury.

You're responsible for ensuring that the equipment used for patient care is free from defects. You should also exercise reasonable care in selecting equipment for a specific procedure and patient and then helping to maintain the equipment. Here again, your patient care must reflect what the reasonably well-qualified and prudent nurse would do in the same or similar circumstances. This means that if you know a specific piece of equipment isn't functioning properly, you must take steps to correct the defect and document the steps you took. If you don't, and a patient is injured because of the defective

Whose negligence?

The disputed facts in the case of *Terry Grant, Administratrix of the Estate of Robert Burkhardt, Deceased v. Victory Park Nursing Home, CCP of Hamilton County, Ohio,* No. A-9400115 (1994), indicate that Mr. Burkhardt was age 70 at the time of the incident and was suffering from Alzheimer's disease and diabetes. He was a patient in the defendant nursing home. His daughter left a heating pad on her father's nightstand; the heating pad was subsequently used on his foot and caused severe burns. The burns became infected and led to the leg being amputated below the knee.

Mr. Burkhardt died shortly after the amputation. The lawsuit claimed the nursing staff either helped the decedent to apply the heating pad or failed to properly monitor him.

The nursing home claimed that the burn wasn't the proximate cause of his death, that the nursing staff wasn't aware of or on notice of a heating pad, and that, in any event, decedent's daughter was negligent in leaving it with the decedent. The ultimate outcome of this lawsuit was a settlement in favor of the plaintiff in the amount of $100,000.

---

equipment, you may be sued for malpractice.

Selecting proper equipment and maintaining it also means making sure it isn't contaminated. When cleaning equipment, always follow facility procedures strictly and document your actions carefully to decrease the risk of being held liable for using contaminated equipment.

You can also be held liable for improper use of equipment that's functioning properly, as in the cases detailed previously. This liability frequently occurs with equipment that can cause burns — for example, diathermy machines, electrosurgical equipment, and hot-water bottles.

▶▶ LESSONS IN PRACTICE When using equipment, carry out the procedure or therapy carefully, observe the patient continually un-

til finished, and frequently ask the patient (if he's awake) whether he's experiencing any pain or discomfort.

Nurses aren't usually responsible for detecting equipment defects that aren't open and obvious. However, you should be familiar with the manufacturer's recommendations and current nursing procedure on equipment checks. Read all cautionary labels on equipment and follow the instructions. Don't modify or change a device or use it for anything other than its intended use.

SUICIDE PREVENTION

Harnish vs. Lancaster General Hospital and Kurtis Jens, M.D., CCP of Lancaster County (1999), illustrates the alleged failure of hospital personnel to observe and protect. Mr. Harnish, age 19, was admitted to the psychiatric floor of a general hospital with the diagnosis of major depression associated with religious obsessionality. During his admission he was observed superficially slashing his wrists with a razor, despite hospital policy that didn't allow patients to have razors or other sharp implements in the room without supervision. Despite this event, associated with talk about suicide and writing notes evidencing his deep depression, the nursing staff made no attempt to provide closer observation.

Two days later, the patient was found hanging from a hook in his bathroom by his pajamas, which were tied around his neck. He was resuscitated, but died three days later from brain damage suffered as a result of hypoxia. A lawsuit was brought against the hospital for the negligence of the nursing staff in failing to monitor and protect the decedent, especially after he slashed his wrists and talked of committing suicide.

This case was tried before a jury and the verdict was in favor of the hospital and psychiatrist. Although the jury found the defendants negligent for failure to properly monitor and anticipate what resulted ultimately in a successful suicide act, this negligence didn't rise to the level of ***gross negligence*** — a very difficult legal standard almost implying a reckless disregard for a patient's well-being, which is required in Pennsylvania in order to prove a psychiatric malpractice case.

Whether the patient is in a medical or psychiatric unit, the nurse may be held responsible for a patient's suicide or suicide attempt if the court finds that the nurse knew or should have known that the patient was likely to harm himself. The court will also consider whether the nurse acted appropriately, with knowledge of the patient's risk; that is, whether she acted reasonably to prevent patient injury or death. For your legal protection, thoroughly document your assessment of the patient's risk for suicide, your actions based on that assessment, and the patient's response.

RESTRAINTS

Usually prescribed to ensure a patient's safety, restraints can also endanger the patient. When a physician prescribes a restraining device, keep in mind that such devices don't remove your responsibility for the patient's safety — in fact, they increase it.

Restraints may be used only to prevent a patient from seriously injuring himself or others — and only when all other physical and psychological therapies would likely fail to prevent such injuries. Whenever possible, use minimal restraint — only the amount necessary to protect the patient and safeguard the staff and others is required. Use of restraints is usually limited to a specific period of time. (See *Caring for a patient in restraints,* page 116.)

If you make a decision to apply restraints, you should immediately request that a physician examine the patient and write an order for restraints. In an emergency situation — such as a violent outburst with actual or potential harm to

Caring for a patient in restraints

The Joint Commission on Accreditation of Healthcare Organizations (JCAHO) standards are specific regarding restraint.

Authorization

JCAHO requires that before restraints are used:

- documentation shows that such interventions are clinically justified
- less restrictive interventions have been attempted
- the patient's current condition is considered and a physician is consulted for an order.

Orders are to be time-limited; that is, written for a specific episode, with start and end times, rather than for an unspecified event or duration. Your facility should have an established policy specifying the maximum length of time that each intervention may be used.

In an emergency, specially trained staff may initiate the use of restraints or seclusion and obtain the physician's order within a specified time (as established by the facility's policy).

Care requirements

When you're caring for a patient in restraints, periodic monitoring and observation is essential (as required by your facility's policy).

For patients who require frequent or prolonged restraint or seclusion, the treatment team should meet to consider alternatives and changes in the care plan. Generally, 72 hours of continuous restraint or more than four episodes in 7 days is considered prolonged or frequent.

While a patient is in restraints, document such items as his hydration, feeding, toileting, and range of motion and condition of limbs.

---

persons or property — any person may apply restraints to the patient. But obtain an order for the restraint as soon as possible, and document the incident carefully.

Potential liability

You should make sure you know how to use restraining devices safely and effectively. You may be held liable if your restraints don't prove effective and the patient is injured as a result. (See *How to use restraints.*)

Be aware that neglecting to use restraints when they may have been necessary also can leave you open for liability. (See *Failure to use restraints,* page 118.)

If a competent patient makes an informed decision to refuse restraint, a facility may require the patient to sign a release absolving the facility of liability should injury result from the patient's refusal to be restrained.

As a nurse, you may also be held liable in a lawsuit if you can't verify that, in your judgment, a patient needed to be restrained and that he

How to use restraints

When applying restraints, follow these guidelines:

- Restraint is a form of imprisonment, so it should be used only as a last resort. Before restraining a patient, consider alternatives such as constant observation.
- Take care to avoid undue force; otherwise, you may invite a lawsuit for **battery.** Even threatening to use force may be sufficient cause for legal action; for a charge of **assault,** no touching is required.
- When restraints must be used, contact the patient's physician as soon as possible.
- When a physician isn't immediately available, you're responsible for ensuring that restraints (and seclusion) are used only to the extent necessary to prevent injury.
- Most states follow the least restrictive principle, which holds that no more restraint should be used than necessary. For example,

a restraining vest shouldn't be used when simple wrist restraints will suffice.

- To avoid allegations of false imprisonment, carefully document the decision-making process that led to the use of restraints, and review the continuing need for restraints on a regular basis.
- Bed side rails are a form of restraint, and shouldn't be raised indiscriminately. The patient's age alone isn't a justification for raising the side rails.
- Tranquilizing drugs, or chemical restraints, may provide alternatives to physical restraints. However, use them sparingly, with caution, and only with a physician's order. The patient's right to the least restrictive treatment or to an open-door policy that allows patients to move about freely means little if accompanied by indiscriminate drug use as a substitute for restraints.

was restrained only as long as necessary. If you restrain a patient simply for shouting obscenities, for example, you risk a lawsuit for *false imprisonment.* The general practice is to use the least restrictive form of restraint.

In addition, restraints should never be used for punishment, staff convenience, or as a substitute for treatment. The case of *Alt v. John Umstead Hospital* (1997) demonstrates this principle. In this case, a

patient in a psychiatric hospital threw his dinner tray and yelled obscenities at a nurse. The nurse, who was later named as a defendant, placed the patient in seclusion and four-point restraints. She called the physician, also an employee of the hospital, and reported the patient's behavior and received a verbal order for seclusion and restraints for up to 8 hours. However, the physician visited the patient 6 hours later and allowed the patient to re-

Failure to use restraints

Busta v. Columbus Hospital Corp. (1996) involved a situation in which restraints weren't used, but perhaps should have been. Delbert Busta was admitted to Columbus Hospital on November 26, 1991, to a room on the third floor. During the early morning hours of December 1, 1991, the patient took a makeshift rope, attached it to a clothing hook, used it to climb out the window, and fell. He was found on the ground with serious injuries related to the fall, and died within 24 hours.

Kathy Fitzgerald, the nurse assigned to the patient, noted that previously Mr. Busta had been a very cooperative patient, but on her last rounds with him he had refused medication, refused repositioning, requested that the compression devices be removed from his legs and that he be "left alone." His pulse rate was tachycardic and his blood pressure was elevated. None of these changes in demeanor or vital signs were reported to his physician. Additionally, the patient was on several medications known to cause confusion, psychosis, and anxiety.

A judgment was entered on a jury verdict awarding $805,000, apportioning fault of the incident at 70% to the hospital and 30% to the patient. This case illustrates that a nurse may be held liable if there's an inability to verify that a patient needed to be restrained.

However, a court may find that reasonable care and skill were used in determining that restraints were no longer necessary, absolving the nurse of liability. In *Gerard v. Sacred Heart Medical Center* (1997), the plaintiff, Donovan Gerard, was admitted to Sacred Heart Medical Center after an automobile accident resulting in head injuries. He was intermittently agitated, confused, and difficult to manage. Against his family's wishes, soft restraints were used. Nurse Young was assigned to the patient and, after assessing his condition, she determined that he didn't need to be restrained. The restraints were removed; as he was transferring to a chair, he fell out of bed.

The patient sued the hospital, alleging nursing negligence for not having him restrained. The jury returned a verdict in favor of the hospital and the patient appealed. The Appellate Court affirmed the judgment of the lower court, maintaining that health care personnel aren't liable for an error in judgment, if in arriving at that judgment, reasonable care and skill were exercised.

main in four-point leather restraints throughout the night. The patient filed a lawsuit against the hospital.

The court found that throwing a tray and shouting obscenities didn't constitute imminent danger to the patient or others and therefore did not justify the use of seclusion and restraints. The court further held that the failure of the nurse and physician to release the patient from four-point restraints during the first 3 hours of seclusion was a violation of acceptable professional standards and was motivated by a desire, in this particular case, to punish the patient.

DISEASE TRANSMISSION
Be careful not to cause contamination or cross-infection of patients. In *Widman v. Paoli Memorial Hospital* (1989), the hospital was found negligent because a preoperative patient was assigned to the same room as a patient infected with the *Klebsiella* organism. The court found that the hospital didn't ensure that personnel assigned to care for the patient followed established infection-control procedures.

Avoiding litigation

A nurse involved in a malpractice lawsuit is judged on how well she performed her duty as measured against the appropriate standards of care. The court will analyze whether the defendant nurse gave the plaintiff patient care equal to that given by a reasonably well-qualified and prudent nurse in the same or similar circumstances.

With regard to patient safety, your duty includes anticipating foreseeable risks. For example, if you're aware that the floor in a patient's room is dangerously slippery, you must report the condition to the appropriate department and place caution signs on the floor to warn of the danger. If you don't, and a patient or visitor falls and is injured, you could be held liable. In fact, you might be held liable even if you didn't know the floor was slippery. Using accepted standards of care, a court might reason that part of your duty as a reasonable and prudent nurse was to check the floor of your unit regularly and report any patient hazard immediately.

The standards of care that you meet will vary with your job and the training you've had. A staff nurse's actions, for example, will be measured against staff nurse standards, and a gerontologic nurse's actions will be measured against standards that gerontologic nurses must meet.

Being familiar with and practicing according to the standards you would be held against are the best ways to keep yourself out of the courtroom. Keep in mind the following suggestions.

PATIENT AND VISITOR SAFETY
The responsibility for patient and visitor safety rests with all employees. A patient assigned to a nurse becomes her immediate responsibility. The nurse's observation of the patient's condition, whether debilitated, elderly, confused, sedated, or postoperative, will dictate what safety precautions should be employed. However, the nurse's responsibility doesn't end there. If a nurse observes an object on the floor or defective equipment, it's her responsibility to either take care of the problem herself (for example, by removing the object from the floor) or report the problem so that corrective action can be taken. Failing to do so may lead to injury

to patients, facility staff, or visitors, resulting in liability for the nurse, as well as her employer.

EQUIPMENT SAFETY

Always understand the equipment you're using. If you aren't familiar with it, seek a demonstration of the proper way to use it or ask your supervisor for an update or refresher course regarding the use of equipment. You should do this before you need to use the equipment.

Make sure the equipment you use is recalibrated as necessary to assure accuracy. Test results that don't seem consistent with a patient's condition may result from equipment that isn't regularly calibrated. Blood glucose monitoring machines are a good example of such equipment.

If a piece of equipment malfunctions or is misused, resulting in a patient's injury, care for the patient first. Then notify the physician, your supervisor, and, if your facility has such, the engineering or biomedical department. Don't throw the equipment away. Document the incident, your actions, and who you notified, and complete an incident report. If the equipment caused or contributed to a serious injury or death, the Safe Medical Device Act requires the facility to report the incident to the Food and Drug Administration and to the manufacturer. There's also a voluntary program called MedWatch for reporting adverse events resulting from medical devices and drugs.

PREVENTING SUICIDES

Preventing suicides is another important aspect of patient safety. Keep in mind that self-destructive, suicidal patients are found in medical as well as psychiatric units. (See *Suicide prevention.*)

USE OF RESTRAINTS

As mentioned previously, patients have won lawsuits against hospitals and nurses for using restraints that caused injury, and for not using restraints when they may have been necessary for the patient's safety. Considerations for determining the appropriate use of restraints include the patient's condition, his medications, and his ability or opportunity to harm himself either by flight, fall, or some other means.

Document attempts to safeguard the patient without the use of restraints. If the patient's condition declines and a restraint becomes necessary, document your findings and communicate them to the physician. Follow your facility's policies and procedures at all times; these policies should include guidelines about the frequency of patient checks, the length of time restraints can be applied before having to be removed, how often the patient's skin and circulation should be assessed, and how often range of motion exercises should be performed. If a patient is restrained for longer than 2 hours, chart each time he's released, taken to the bathroom or placed on a bedpan, and monitored for skin breakdown. The prolonged use of restraints leading to immobility can be associated with dehydration, pressure sores, infection, incontinence, and depression.

Suicide prevention

Your first obligation to prevent suicide is to closely supervise the patient. A suicidal patient may require one-on-one, 24-hour-a-day supervision until the immediate threat of self-harm is over. Take from him all potentially dangerous objects, such as belts, bed linens, glassware, and eating utensils. Be sure he swallows pills when you give them; otherwise, he may retain them in his mouth to save them for later.

Assess the hospital environment carefully for possible dangers. If the patient can easily open or break his room windows, or if escape from your unit would be easy, you may have to transfer him to a safer, more secure place — if necessary, to a seclusion room.

Remember, whether you work on a psychiatric unit or a medical unit, you'll be held responsible for the decisions you make about a suicidal patient's care. If you're sued because he's harmed himself while in your care, the court will judge you on the basis of:

- whether you knew (or should have known) that the patient was likely to harm himself
- whether, knowing he was likely to harm himself, you exercised reasonable care in helping him avoid injury or death.

Carefully choose the appropriate restraint device for the patient's condition. Check height and weight requirements to be sure that the restraining device is the correct size. Check the positioning of the restraint, particularly in the front and in the back to make sure it's applied correctly. Tie knots that will release easily to ensure quick access if necessary. Apply and adjust restraints as needed for the patient's comfort. To avoid constriction, tie bed restraints to the part of the bed that moves with the patient when the bed controls are used.

When a patient wears a restraining belt, make sure he doesn't undo it or inadvertently readjust it; if he does, it could choke or otherwise injure him. Also make sure the belt fits properly; if it's too tight, it could restrict the patient's breathing or irritate his skin. You may have to decide when the belt is no longer necessary.

Check the governing laws and protocols for an automatic expiration of restraint orders. If you fail to handle patient restraints properly, you may be accused of false imprisonment. Try to keep the use of restraints as the exception, not the rule. Use the least restrictive device that will keep the patient safe.

DECREASING YOUR LIABILITY

As a nurse, you have an important duty to ensure your patient's safety. Remember, all your actions directed toward patient safety must be in line with your facility's policies and procedures, so be sure you know what these are. If no policies exist, or if they're outdated or poorly drafted, bring this to your supervisor's or nurse manager's attention. Consider volunteering to help write or rewrite the policies. By getting involved in efforts to improve patient's safety, you may decrease your potential liability and, at the same time, improve the quality of patient care.

Selected references

Better ElderCare: A Nurse's Guide to Caring for Older Adults. Springhouse, Pa.: Springhouse Corp., 2002.

Ellerton, M.L. "Client Restraints More Than a Safety Issue," *Canadian Nurse* 98(2):32-33, February 2002.

Evans, D., et al. "Falls Risk Factors in the Hospital Setting: A Systematic Review," *International Journal of Nursing Practice* 7(1):38-45, February 2001.

"Fatal Falls: Lessons for the Future," *Sentinel Event Alert* (14):1-3, July 2000.

Holley, S. "A Look at the Problem of Falls Among People with Cancer," *Clinical Journal of Oncology Nursing* 6(4):193-97, July-August 2002.

"Infusion Pumps: Preventing Future Adverse Events," *Sentinel Event Alert/Joint Commission on the Accreditation of Healthcare Organizations* (15):1-3, 30, November 2002.

Lewis, D.M. "Responding to a Violent Incident: Physical Restraint or Anger Management as Therapeutic Interventions," *Journal of Psychiatric and Mental Health Nursing* 9(1):57-63, February 2002.

Nurse's Legal Handbook, 4th ed. Springhouse, Pa: Springhouse Corp., 2000.

Oliver, D., et al. "Preventing Patient Falls," *Age and Ageing* 31(1):75-76, January 2002.

Owens, M.F. "Patient Restraints. Protection for Whom?" *JONA'S Healthcare Law, Ethics and Regulation* 2(2):59-65, June 2000.

Patrick, L., and Blodgett, A. "Selecting Patients for Falls-Prevention Protocols: An Evidence-based Approach on a Geriatric Rehabilitation Unit," *Journal of Gerontological Nursing* 27(10):19-25, October 2002.

"Postsurgical Patient Falls Out of Bed: Did RIL Apply? Case on Point: *Giegoldt v. Condell Medical Center,* 2002 WL 538017 N.E.2d-IL," *Nursing Law's Regan Report* 42(11):4, April 2002.

Salladay, S.A. "Patient Falls. Walk with Me," *Nursing2002* 32(3):66, March 2002.

Stevens, M., et al. "Preventing Falls in Older People: Outcome Evaluation of a Randomized Controlled Trial," *Journal of the American Geriatrics Society* 49(11):1448-455, November 2001.

Sullivan-Marx, E.M. "Achieving Restraint-Free Care of Acutely Confused Older Adults," *Journal of Gerontological Nursing* 27(4):56-61, April 2001.

Thomas, S.P. "Restraints Must Be a Last Resort," *Issues in Mental Health Nursing* 21(7):651-52, October-November 2002.

FAILURE TO PERFORM REASONABLE PATIENT CARE

WHETHER YOU'RE a registered nurse or licensed practical nurse (LPN), you're always legally accountable for your nursing actions. In any practice setting, your care must meet baseline legal standards. Your care should also:
- reflect the scope of your state's *nurse practice act*
- measure up to established *standards of care*
- consistently protect your patient.

When performing procedures and providing other basic nursing care, act in accordance with standards of care and the policies and procedures of your facility to stay out of court.

Case studies

The following court cases illustrate how failure to uphold standards of care can leave you vulnerable to lawsuits, no matter where you practice nursing.

CASE 1

In an anonymous case (parties not named based on a confidential settlement) in the Superior Court of the state of Washington (2001), an 8-year-old boy fell while climbing a tree in his back yard. He sustained what appeared to be a minor puncture wound on the back of his thigh. His father noted that blood appeared to be pulsating from the wound and took him to a busy emergency department (ED), which was allegedly filled to overflowing with patients.

After the boy waited 3 hours, his wound was sutured and he was sent home. The next day, he developed a slight fever and the affected leg was swollen. The next morning — day 2 after the incident — his father called the pediatrician, who advised him to take the boy back to the ED.

The father and son went back to the same ED, but were then referred to another hospital. At that facility, the wound was surgically explored and a 3-cm piece of wood was removed. However, the boy had already developed necrotizing fasciitis, or "flesh-eating" disease.

Despite antibiotics, hyperbaric oxygen, and repeated surgeries, large portions of the boy's body were affected by the tissue-destroying disease. He eventually required amputation of the right leg at the hip. As a result of the systemic infection, he became partially blind and brain damaged. His parents filed a lawsuit alleging that the first ED, physician, and hospital staff were negligent in failing to explore the wound, to assure that all wood particles were flushed from the wound prior to suturing, and to obtain an adequate history.

The pertinent nursing issues in this case were failure to take an adequate history that might have alerted the staff to check the wound for wood fragments, failure to assist with exploration of the wound for debris, and failure to suggest computed tomography (CT) or ultrasound studies to assess for deeply embedded wood fragments. The fact that the ED was busy that day was no excuse for providing substandard care. All patients are entitled to adequate care, which in this case would have included a thorough history of the injury and examination of the wound and other appropriate interventions.

During mediation, the boy's attorney showed a presentation consisting of similarly sized wood fragments from the same tree, illustrating that the foreign body left in the wound would have been clearly visible on a CT scan or ultrasound. In addition, the attorney presented a videotape of the boy after the injury, in which he struggled to count from 1 to 5. The case was settled for $7.1 million.

CASE 2

In *Lester v. Southwest General Hospital* (2001), a patient over age 60 was suffering from pulmonary disease, had experienced complications, and was in the intensive care unit. She was on a respirator when somehow her tubing became disconnected. The hospital staff responded to the disconnection alarm, but the patient had already suffered brain damage and died just days after this incident.

The patient's family alleged that it had taken approximately 4 minutes for the nursing staff to respond to the disconnection alarm. The case was settled out of court for $200,000.

Legal issues

These cases demonstrate the tragic outcomes that can result when standards of nursing care aren't met.

STANDARDS OF CARE

Standards of care set minimum criteria for your proficiency on the job, enabling you and others to judge the quality of care you and your nursing colleagues provide. States may or may not refer to standards in their nurse practice acts. Unless included in a nurse practice act, professional standards aren't laws — they're guidelines for sound nursing practice.

Some nurses regard standards of nursing care as impracticable ideals that have little bearing on the reality of working life. This is a dangerous misconception. You're expected to meet standards of nursing care for every nursing task you perform. For example, if you're a medical-surgical nurse, minimal standards of care require that you develop a nursing care plan for your patient based on the nursing process, including nursing diagnoses, goals, and interventions for implementing the care plan. Standards also call for documentation in the patient's record, of your completion and evaluation of the plan. When you document patient care, you're really writing a record of how well you've met the standards. Courts often interpret an absence of documentation as an absence of patient care.

Evolution of nursing standards

Before 1950, nurses had only Florence Nightingale's early treatments, plus reports of court cases, to use as standards. As nursing gradually became recognized as an independent profession, nursing organizations stressed the importance of having recognized standards for all nurses. Then, in 1950, the American Nurses Association (ANA) published the "Code of Ethics for Nursing," a general mandate stating that nurses should offer nursing care without prejudice and in a confidential and safe manner. Although not specific, this code marked the beginning of written nursing standards.

In 1973, the ANA Congress for Nursing Practice established the first generic standards for the profession — standards that could be applied to all nurses in all settings. (See *ANA standards of care,* pages 126 to 130.) By 1974, each of the ANA divisions of nursing practice

(such as community health, geriatrics, maternal-child, mental health, and medical-surgical) had established distinct standards for its specialty. The ANA Congress called these ***specialty standards.*** State nursing associations also helped develop specialty standards.

Other organizations have contributed to the development of nursing standards. The Joint Commission on Accreditation of Healthcare Organizations (JCAHO), a private, nongovernmental agency that establishes guidelines for the operation of hospitals and other health care facilities, has also developed nursing standards to be used in hospital audit systems. In some states, JCAHO standards have been incorporated into law, resulting in broadly applicable standards of patient care. In addition, state nursing associations and the specialty nursing organizations actively work with hospital nursing administrators for adoption of standards.

Federal regulations for staffing Medicare and Medicaid services have influenced the development of standards, especially nursing home standards. By suggesting ethical approaches to nursing practice, ethics codes written by the ANA and the International Council of Nurses influence how nursing care standards are developed.

Local or national standards

The courts also have used local standards — reflecting a community's accepted, common nursing practices — to judge the quality of nursing care, although this practice has been eroded in recognition of national standards applied by ac-

(Text continues on page 130.)

ANA standards of care

The American Nurses Association (ANA) developed these standards of clinical nursing practice to provide guidelines for establishing and determining quality nursing care. These standards may be used by the courts, hospitals, nurses, and patients.

The standards of clinical nursing practice are divided into the standards of care, which identify the care provided to recipients of nursing services, and the standards of professional performance, which explain the level of behavior expected in professional role activities. Each standard is followed by measurement criteria that give key indicators of competent practice for that standard.

Standards of care

STANDARD I: ASSESSMENT

The nurse collects patient health data.

Measurement criteria

1. Data collection involves the patient, partners, and health care providers when appropriate.
2. The priority of data collection activities is determined by the patient's immediate condition or needs.
3. Pertinent data are collected using appropriate assessment techniques and instruments.
4. Relevant data are documented in a retrievable form.

5. The data collection process is systematic and ongoing.

STANDARD II: DIAGNOSIS

The nurse analyzes the assessment data in determining diagnosis.

Measurement criteria

1. Diagnoses are derived from the assessment data.
2. Diagnoses are validated with the patient, partners, and health care providers, when possible.
3. Diagnoses are documented in a manner that facilitates the determination of expected outcomes and care plan.

STANDARD III: OUTCOME IDENTIFICATION

The nurse identifies expected outcomes individual to the patient.

Measurement criteria

1. Outcomes are derived from the diagnoses.
2. Outcomes are mutually formulated with the patient and health care providers, when possible.
3. Outcomes are culturally appropriate and realistic in relation to the patient's present and potential capabilities.
4. Outcomes are attainable in relation to resources available to the patient.
5. Outcomes include a time estimate for attainment.
6. Outcomes provide direction for continuity of care.

ANA standards of care *(continued)*

7. Outcomes are documented as measurable goals.

STANDARD IV:
PLANNING

The nurse develops a care plan that prescribes interventions to attain expected outcomes.

Measurement criteria

1. The plan is individualized to the patient's condition or needs.
2. The plan is developed with the patient, partners, and health care providers.
3. The plan reflects current nursing practice.
4. The plan provides for continuity of care.
5. Priorities for care are established.
6. The plan is documented.

STANDARD V:
IMPLEMENTATION

The nurse implements the interventions identified in the care plan.

Measurement criteria

1. Interventions are consistent with the established care plan.
2. Interventions are implemented in a safe, timely, and appropriate manner.
3. Interventions are documented.

STANDARD VI:
EVALUATION

The nurse evaluates the patient's progress toward attainment of outcomes.

Measurement criteria

1. Evaluation is systematic, ongoing, and criteria-based.
2. The patient, partners, and health care providers are involved in the evaluation process when appropriate.
3. Ongoing assessment data are used to revise diagnoses, outcomes, and the care plan as needed.
4. Revisions in diagnoses, outcomes, and the care plan are documented.
5. The effectiveness of interventions is evaluated in relation to the outcomes.
6. The patient's responses to interventions are documented.

Standards of professional performance

STANDARD I:
QUALITY OF CARE

The nurse systematically evaluates the quality and effectiveness of nursing practice.

Measurement criteria

1. The nurse participates in quality of care activities as appropriate to the nurse's education and position. Such activities may include:
   – identifying aspects of care important for quality monitoring
   – identifying indicators used to monitor quality and effectiveness of nursing care

(continued)

ANA standards of care *(continued)*

– collecting data to monitor quality and effectiveness of nursing care

– analyzing quality data to identify opportunities for improving care

– formulating recommendations to improve nursing practice or patient outcomes

– implementing activities to enhance the quality of nursing practice

– participating on interdisciplinary teams that evaluate clinical practice or health services

– developing policies, procedures, and practice guidelines to improve quality of care.

2. The nurse uses the results of quality of care activities to initiate changes in practice.

3. The nurse uses the results of quality of care activities to initiate changes throughout the health care delivery system as appropriate.

STANDARD II:
PERFORMANCE APPRAISAL

The nurse evaluates her own nursing practice in relation to professional practice standards and relevant statutes and regulations.

Measurement criteria

1. The nurse engages in performance appraisal on a regular basis, identifying areas of strength as well as areas where professional development would be beneficial.

2. The nurse seeks constructive feedback regarding his or her own practice.

3. The nurse takes action to achieve goals identified during performance appraisals.

4. The nurse participates in peer review as appropriate.

5. The nurse's practice reflects knowledge of current professional practice standards, laws, and regulations.

STANDARD III:
EDUCATION

The nurse acquires and maintains current knowledge and competency in nursing practice.

Measurement criteria

1. The nurse participates in ongoing educational activities related to clinical knowledge and professional issues.

2. The nurse seeks experiences that reflect current clinical practice in order to maintain current clinical skills and competency.

3. The nurse seeks knowledge and skills appropriate to the practice setting.

STANDARD IV:
COLLEGIALITY

The nurse interacts with, and contributes to the professional development of, peers, health care providers, and others as colleagues.

Measurement criteria

1. The nurse shares knowledge and skills with colleagues and others.

ANA standards of care *(continued)*

2. The nurse provides peers with constructive feedback regarding their practice.
3. The nurse interacts with colleagues to enhance her own professional practice.
4. The nurse contributes to an environment that is conducive to clinical education of nursing students and other health care students as appropriate.
5. The nurse contributes to a supportive and healthy work environment.

STANDARD V:
ETHICS

The nurse's decisions and actions on behalf of patients are determined in an ethical manner.

Measurement criteria

1. The nurse's practice is guided by the Code for Nurses.
2. The nurse maintains patient confidentiality.
3. The nurse acts as a patient advocate and assists patients in developing skills so they can advocate for themselves.
4. The nurse delivers care in a nonjudgmental and nondiscriminatory manner that is sensitive to patient diversity.
5. The nurse delivers care in a manner that preserves and protects patient autonomy, dignity, and rights.
6. The nurse seeks available resources to help formulate ethical decisions.

STANDARD VI:
COLLABORATION

The nurse collaborates with the patient, partners, and health care providers in providing patient care.

Measurement criteria

1. The nurse communicates with the patient, partners, and health care providers regarding patient care and nursing's role in the provision of care.
2. The nurse collaborates with the patient, family, and health care providers in the formulation of overall goals and the care plan, and in decisions related to care and delivery of services.
3. The nurse consults with health care providers for patient care as needed.
4. The nurse makes referrals, including provisions for continuity of care as needed.

STANDARD VII:
RESEARCH

The nurse uses research findings in practice.

Measurement criteria

1. The nurse uses interventions substantiated by research as appropriate to the individual's position, education, and practice.
2. The nurse participates in research activities as appropriate to her position and education. Such activities may include:
   – identifying clinical problems suitable for nursing research

(continued)

ANA standards of care *(continued)*

– participating in data collection
– participating in a unit, organization, or community research committee or program
– sharing research findings with others
– conducting research
– critiquing research for application to practice
– using research findings in the development of policies, procedures, and guidelines for patient care.

**STANDARD VIII:
RESOURCE UTILIZATION**

The nurse considers factors related to safety, effectiveness, and cost in planning and delivering patient care.

Measurement criteria

The nurse evaluates factors related to safety, effectiveness, and cost when two or more practice options would result in the same expected patient outcome.

creditation agencies. Today's nurses are more often held to a national standard.

Local standards are established in two ways: by individual health care facilities, through their policies and procedures, and by local or state expert witnesses who testify in court cases that involve nurses. Every facility establishes standards to fit its own community's needs. An expert witness interprets local standards by testifying about how nursing is commonly practiced in the community.

LEGAL SIGNIFICANCE OF STANDARDS

Even though they aren't law, nursing standards have important legal significance. The allegations that a nurse failed to meet appropriate standards of care, and that breach of these standards caused the harm to the patient, is the basic premise of every nursing malpractice lawsuit.

During a malpractice trial, the court will measure the defendant nurse's actions against the answer it obtains to the following question: What would a reasonably prudent nurse, with like training and experience, do under these circumstances?

To answer this question, the plaintiff patient, through his attorney, has the burden to prove that certain standards of care exist and that the defendant nurse failed to meet those standards in her treatment of him. He also must prove the appropriateness of those standards, show how the nurse failed to meet them, and show how that failure caused him injury.

When the standard of care is at issue, the plaintiff patient must present expert witness testimony to support his claims. The defendant nurse and her attorney also will produce expert witness testimony to support her claim that her actions didn't fall below accepted standards of care and that she acted in a reasonable and prudent manner.

The court may consider written standards when considering the standards of care involved in a nursing malpractice lawsuit. The court seeks information about all the national and state standards applicable to the defendant nurse's actions. The court may take into consideration professional organization standards and clinical practice guidelines. The court also may seek applicable information about the policies of the defendant nurse's employer.

Because of two trends — uniform nursing educational requirements and standardized medical treatment regimens — national standards are gaining increasing favor with the courts. These trends have made the ANA's standards more influential than local standards of other organizations.

As the role of nurses is expanding across the country, so is the standard of care. Nurses who perform the same medical services are subject to the same standard of care and liability as physicians.

FACILITY POLICIES

Every hospital and other health care facility has **policies** — a set of general principles by which it manages its affairs. You're obligated to know those policies and to follow the established procedures that flow from them. But never do this blindly. As a nurse, you're also obligated to maintain your professional standards, and these standards may sometimes conflict with your employer's policies and procedures. At times, you may be forced to make decisions and take actions

that risk violating those policies and procedures. As a nurse, you must do what's best for the patient. If it's unsafe to follow policy, then don't — but be sure to document the reasons you didn't and notify your supervisor.

At times like these, you need help balancing your duty to your patient with your responsibility to your employer. Your best help is a nursing department policy manual that states relevant, clear guidelines based on up-to-date standards of care that are generally accepted by the profession. A typical problem with policies is that they aren't practical, are too restrictive, or involve standards too difficult to meet. In addition, there may be so many policies that nurses aren't familiar with all of them.

A policy manual that states relevant, clear guidelines based on up-to-date standards of care is the mark of a successful nursing department — one whose first concern is delivering high-quality patient care.

Qualities of a good nursing department manual

Although manuals will differ, most good ones:
● explain how general policies apply to the nursing department
● outline the nursing department's roles and responsibilities, internally and in relation to other departments
● identify the expected limits of nursing action and practice
● offer guidelines for handling emergency situations
● contain procedures that show compliance with state and federal laws such as **patient antidumping laws**

- provide **standing orders** for nurses in special areas, such as the intensive care unit and cardiac care unit
- explain the steps to be taken before — and after — arriving at nursing care decisions.

These steps provide the basis for the facility's nursing care standards. The manual itself might be used as evidence in malpractice cases.

However, policies are frequently:
- too specific
- too restrictive
- too idealistic
- irrelevant
- so voluminous that nurses don't know them all.

Any good nursing department manual should be subject to regular revision, so today, most health care facilities are rapidly revising and expanding their basic policies and procedures. Some procedure and policy changes result from efforts to streamline and standardize patient care. Others result from efforts to comply with new state, jurisdictional, territorial, and federal regulations or to implement recommendations of JCAHO.

Deviating from standards, policies, or procedures

The following case illustrates how providing top-notch care can be undermined by failure to provide basic nursing care. In this case against a university hospital (settled confidentially), nurses in the neonatal intensive care unit (NICU) took care of a significantly premature baby. After overcoming life-threatening respiratory and cardiac problems requiring weeks of care in the NICU, the infant was finally stable and progressing.

Unfortunately, his nurses failed to observe the infant's I.V. insertion site according to the facility's established policy and procedure. The infant had been wrapped snugly and covered with blankets; the condition of the I.V. site was overlooked as the infant had progressed. Hours later, a nurse finally checked the site. By this time, the I.V. fluid had infiltrated the surrounding tissue, and the infant's fingertips on the hand in which the I.V. was inserted were black. It was too late to reverse the damage to the fingertips, necessitating that all four fingertips plus the tip of the thumb be allowed to auto-amputate, or fall off. (See *Anticipating patients' needs*.)

●●▶ **LESSONS IN PRACTICE** Become very familiar with facility policy and procedure governing routine care that you provide on a daily basis. I.V. lines and other access lines have become commonplace pieces of equipment in today's facilities, and even in the home setting. Most facilities have specific time periods for which I.V. or other access lines should be checked, and that's the standard you'll be expected to follow.

Basic nursing care could have prevented the injuries in each case cited previously. Undoubtedly, the facilities involved had a protocol on monitoring I.V. sites and lines, as well as other catheters and lines. Undoubtedly, in each case that protocol wasn't followed.

After a case is filed, attorneys on both sides are allowed to go through a **discovery** process. During this process, the patient's attorney will ask for all relevant health care facility policies and procedures that were in effect at the time of the in-

RELATED CASES

Anticipating patients' needs

In a confidential case, a man in his 50s survived extensive neurosurgery that successfully treated a brain aneurysm. He was taken from the recovery room to a neurosurgical nursing ward. He had a percutaneous sheath system placed for anesthesia, and this equipment remained in place postoperatively. His room was very small, and his bed was located so close to the bathroom that he could reach out and touch the bathroom door.

By postoperative day 2, the patient's urinary catheter had been removed, and he was told to notify the nursing staff if he needed to use the bathroom. He hadn't had a bowel movement since the surgery.

The patient put on his call light for assistance, and when a nurse didn't respond, he got out of bed unassisted to use the bathroom.

When the nurses finally responded, they found him in the bathroom lying in a pool of blood — the percutaneous sheath had become dislodged. The nurses then failed to

position the patient properly and to notify the appropriate personnel immediately of the incident, and the patient died soon after.

There was controversy regarding whether the device had a luer-lock on it, which might have prevented the catheter from dislodging if it had been properly secured. The nurses argued that the device did have a luer-lock and that the lock was checked; however, research indicated that if the device had, in fact, had a luer-lock in place, the incident wouldn't have occurred. The dispute was settled in favor of the patient's family.

The nursing staff should have recognized the lack of appropriate equipment, and they should have responded in a timely manner to the patient's call light. If they had anticipated the patient's need to use the bathroom and provided assistance, he might not have attempted to get out of bed by himself, thereby dislodging the percutaneous sheath and causing a fatal loss of blood.

cident in question. It makes the patient's attorney's job very easy to prove negligence to a jury when he can present a specific facility policy or procedure as evidence and point out precisely where the care given deviated from it. With this approach, the patient's attorney's burden of proof is lessened as he doesn't have to independently prove what the standard of care was from journals or other sources — al-

though this could be added for emphasis.

STANDARDS FOR AGENCY NURSES

In the case of *Guerra v. Diamond Central Nurses, Inc., Diamond Central Personnel Services, Inc., and Feeley Medical Services* (2001), Diamond Central Nurses were to provide home care to a patient with

Parkinson's disease. This care included serving meals. Due to the Parkinson's disease, the patient had problems swallowing, necessitating careful preparation of her meals. In March of 1998, Diamond was short-staffed and subcontracted with Feeley Medical Services to provide nursing care to the patient. She was served a food that wasn't appropriate for her, and she choked to death.

The estate sued, arguing negligent hiring, negligent supervision, and improper care. A jury found against Diamond Central in the amount of $802,421.09. Even though they had utilized an agency to provide care to their patient, they remained ultimately responsible and liable for the nursing care.

Working as an agency nurse

Temporary nursing service agencies represent an innovative approach to the delivery of nursing services — one response to the constant demand for practical, efficient, and cost-effective nursing care. Many nurses decide to work for a temporary nursing service to achieve greater work schedule flexibility and the right to choose their own hours. In addition, most agencies pay higher salaries than hospitals.

When you work for an agency, you have an employee-employer relationship with that agency. The agency charges the client a fee for your services, from which it pays your salary. It also may provide such benefits as social security and other tax deductions, workers' compensation, sick pay, and professional liability insurance. Traditional nursing registries don't enter into employee-employer relationships with private-duty nurses when they provide client referrals.

Few clear-cut policies

A nurse's professional responsibilities as an agency worker are commonly vague. No set of uniform policies and procedures has yet been formally identified or administratively defined. For example, if a registered nurse and an LPN are assigned to care for the same patient in his home but on different shifts, what responsibility does the registered nurse have for the LPN's work? Does the registered nurse have the responsibility for supervising home health aides? Also, should communication between the registered nurse and the patient's physician be direct, or channeled through an agency supervisor?

Large agencies, especially those with nationwide placement, may have specific policies to deal with situations like these. But smaller, more regional agencies may not. Without clear-cut guidelines, you may have to rely heavily on your professional nursing judgment. But remember, the courts apply the same legal principles governing staff nurse malpractice cases to agency nurse malpractice cases.

Determining liability

A nurse is liable for her own wrongful conduct. But if an agency nurse is judged to have been working within the legally permissible scope of her employment, then the agency may be required to pay any damages awarded to the plaintiff. The court may use the doctrine of ***respondeat superior*** to interpret the nurse's legal status, making the employer responsible for the negligent acts of his nurse employees. If the court finds that the nurse exceeded the scope of her employment, however, she may be solely responsible for any damages.

As an agency employee, you may be assigned to work in a patient's home, to care for a single patient in a hospital or other health care facility, or to temporarily supplement a facility's staff. Different practice circumstances can influence how a court determines liability. Any malpractice lawsuit that involves an agency nurse will probably name as defendants the nurse, the temporary-nursing service agency and, if applicable, the hospital or other health care facility in which the alleged malpractice happened. When you work as an agency nurse in a patient's home, your agency-employee status usually is clear-cut. The same is true when you care for a single patient in a hospital or other health care facility.

The courts have more difficulty assigning legal liability in cases that involve agency nurses working as supplemental hospital or institutional staff. In this situation, you're still an agency employee, but you're also in the "special service" of another "employer" — the hospital or facility. In such cases, courts may apply the **borrowed servant** (or ostensible agent) doctrine, holding that the regular employer (the agency) isn't liable for injury negligently caused by the nurse-employee (the "servant") while in the special service of another employer (the hospital, agency, or facility). When a court interprets a case this way, the legal liability shifts from the agency to the hospi-

tal or facility. However, under the doctrine of **dual agency,** the nurse may be held to be the agent of both the agency and the hospital, making both potentially liable.

Professional guidelines

To help protect yourself against a lawsuit, be sure you fully understand what's expected of you when you accept an agency job. (See *ANA guidelines for temporary nurses,* page 136.) Be prepared to adjust to different policies and procedures by reviewing policy manuals and gaining a clear understanding of what they contain. When you work in a patient's home, for example, your agency's policies and procedures govern your actions. Be sure you understand them thoroughly and follow them carefully. How competently you follow procedure may affect such matters as whether a claim for workers' compensation is allowed or whether your agency will be included as a defendant with you in a malpractice suit. Don't perform any non-nursing functions when you work in a patient's home or arbitrarily change his nursing regimen policies and procedures from what your agency has specified. If you do and the patient or his family decides to sue, you may find yourself solely liable.

Working with an agency nurse

If you're a hospital staff nurse and an agency nurse is assigned to your unit, your responsibilities as a coworker are no different than when working with others on the health care team. If you see her performing a procedure in a way that may harm her patient, you have the

---

ANA guidelines for temporary nurses

The American Nurses Association (ANA) has issued guidelines outlining the responsibilities of temporary-nursing agencies and agency nurses. These guidelines state that an agency has a duty to select, orient, evaluate, and assign nurses and to provide them with professional development.

According to these guidelines, agency nurses should:

- keep their licenses current
- select reputable employers
- maintain their nursing skills
- observe the standards of professional nursing practice
- document their nursing practice
- adhere to the policies and procedures of their agencies and clients.

The last point is particularly important if an agency assigns you to work in a hospital or other health care facility. As always, you must be sure you understand the hospital's or facility's policies and procedures for the nursing tasks you're expected to perform. Get to know the head nurse or unit supervisor, and seek clarification from her whenever you're in doubt.

The hospital or facility, in turn, is obligated to supply equipment you need for patient care and to keep its promises and equipment in safe condition.

---

same responsibility to stop the procedure that you have when working with your regular health care team colleagues. If you see an agency nurse performing a procedure incorrectly but without potential harm to the patient, report your observation to your nursing supervisor.

YOUR DUTY TO REPORT PATIENT INCIDENTS

As the case studies discussed previously illustrate, deviations from standards of care, policies, and procedures can result in harm to the patient then become incidents. An *incident* is an event that's inconsistent with the health care facility's ordinary routine, regardless of whether injury occurred. In most

health care facilities, any injury to a patient requires an *incident report.* Whether you're a registered nurse, an LPN, a nursing assistant, a staff nurse, or a nurse-manager, you have a duty to report any incident of which you have first-hand knowledge. Not only can failure to report an incident lead to your being fired, but it can also expose you to personal liability for malpractice — especially if your failure to report the incident causes injury to a patient.

If you're the staff member who knows the most about the incident at the time of its discovery, you should complete the incident report. When you do so, include only the facts: what you saw when you came upon the incident, or what you heard that led you to believe an incident had taken place. If your information is second-hand, place it within quotation marks and identify the source. After completing the incident report, sign and date it. You should complete it during the same shift in which the incident occurred or was discovered.

An incident report should include only the following information:

• the names of the persons involved and the names of any witnesses

• factual information about what happened and the consequences to the person involved (supply enough information so the health care facility's administration can decide whether the matter needs further investigation)

• any other relevant facts (such as your immediate actions in response to the incident, for example, notifying the patient's physician).

Never include the following types of statements in an incident report:

• opinions (such as a reporter's opinion of who's at fault or the patient's prognosis)

• conclusions or assumptions (such as what caused the incident)

• suggestions of who was responsible for causing the incident

• suggestions to prevent the incident from happening again.

Including this type of information in an incident report could seriously hinder the defense in any lawsuit arising from the incident. Remember, the incident report's purpose is to notify the administration that an incident has occurred. In effect, it says, "Administration: Note that this incident happened, and decide whether you want to investigate it further." Such items as detailed statements from witnesses and descriptions of remedial action are normally part of an investigative follow-up; don't include them in the incident report itself.

Potential pitfalls

Be especially careful that your health care facility's reporting system doesn't lead to improper incident reporting. For example, some facilities require nursing supervisors to correlate reports from witnesses and then file a single report. Also, some incident report forms invite inappropriate conclusions and assumptions by asking, "How can this incident be prevented in the future?" If your facility's reporting system or forms contain such potential pitfalls, alert the administration to them.

Reporting an incident

An incident report is an administrative report, and therefore doesn't become part of the patient's *medical record.* In fact, the record shouldn't even mention that an incident report has been filed because this serves only to deflect the medical record's focus. The record should include only factual clinical observations relating to the incident. (Again, avoid using value judgments.)

Entering your observations in the nurses' notes section of the patient's record doesn't take the place of completing an incident report. Nor does completing an incident report take the place of proper documentation in the patient's chart.

An incident report, once it's filed, may be reviewed by the nursing supervisor, the physician called to examine the patient, appropriate department heads and administrators,

Filing an incident report

This chart provides a comprehensive overview of incident report routing in most facilities.

```
┌─────────────────────────────────────────────────────────────┐
│                   Patient incident occurs.                   │
└─────────────────────────────────────────────────────────────┘
                              ▼
┌─────────────────────────────────────────────────────────────┐
│    Record significant medical and nursing facts in patient's chart.    │
└─────────────────────────────────────────────────────────────┘
                              ▼
┌─────────────────────────────────────────────────────────────┐
│      Write incident report during the shift on which the incident      │
│                    took place or is discovered.                    │
└─────────────────────────────────────────────────────────────┘
                              ▼
┌─────────────────────────────────────────────────────────────┐
│              Give incident report to supervisor.              │
└─────────────────────────────────────────────────────────────┘
                              ▼
┌─────────────────────────────────────────────────────────────┐
│  Unit supervisor forwards report to appropriate administrator within 24 hours.  │
└─────────────────────────────────────────────────────────────┘
                              ▼
┌─────────────────────────────────────────────────────────────┐
│                  Administrator reviews report.                  │
└─────────────────────────────────────────────────────────────┘
                              ▼
┌─────────────────────────────────────────────────────────────┐
│     Administrator forwards pertinent information from the report     │
│        to the appropriate department for follow-up action.        │
└─────────────────────────────────────────────────────────────┘
                              ▼
┌─────────────────────────────────────────────────────────────┐
│      Incident reports are collected and summarized to detect patterns      │
│               and trends and highlight trouble spots.               │
└─────────────────────────────────────────────────────────────┘
                              ▼
┌─────────────────────────────────────────────────────────────┐
│     Administrator reviews patterns and trends, using this information     │
│  in continuous quality improvement projects for a single nursing unit  │
│                  or a multidisciplinary committee.                  │
└─────────────────────────────────────────────────────────────┘
            ▼                               ▼
┌──────────────────────────┐    ┌──────────────────────────┐
│  Refer information to existing │    │    Use information as the basis    │
│  quality improvement teams.  │    │       for establishing new       │
│                          │    │    quality improvement projects.    │
└──────────────────────────┘    └──────────────────────────┘
```

the facility's attorney, and the facility's insurance company and its attorneys. (See *Filing an incident report.*) The report may be filed under the involved patient's name or by the type of injury, depending on the facility's policy and the insurance company's regulations. Reports are rarely placed in the reporting nurse's employment file.

If you're asked to talk with the facility's insurance adjuster or attorney about an incident, be cooperative, honest, and factual. Fully disclosing what you know early on will help the facility decide how to handle any legal consequences of an incident. And it preserves your testimony in case you're ever called to testify in court.

Using incident reports as courtroom evidence

Controversy exists over whether a patient's attorney may "discover" (request and receive a copy of) an incident report and introduce it into evidence in a malpractice lawsuit. The laws on this issue vary from state to state. To avoid discovery, the facility may send copies of the incident report to its attorney, or the facility's attorney may write a letter stating that the report is being made for his use and benefit only. This practice may serve to make the document an attorney's work product, which isn't discoverable. The facility may make the incident report an integral part of the quality assurance process and label it as such.

Concern about incident report discovery should be minimal if an incident report contains only properly reportable material. When an incident report contains secondhand information, opinions, conclusions, accusations, or suggestions for preventing such incidents in the future does discovery of the incident report become an important issue for attorneys and the courts.

Avoiding litigation

Any time that you provide care that falls short of current legal and nursing standards, you make yourself a target for a malpractice suit.

In most situations, you can prevent this from happening to you by following the guidelines here in your daily practice.

STAY CURRENT

Here are some effective ways to stay up to date on nursing practices: read nursing journals, attend clinical programs, attend inservice programs, and seek advice from nurse specialists. If your facility doesn't offer needed inservice programs, ask for them.

Remember, ignorance of new techniques is no excuse for substandard care. If you're ever sued for malpractice, your patient care will be judged by current nursing standards, regardless of whether your employer has offered you the necessary training.

KNOW YOUR POLICY MANUAL

Review the policies at least yearly. If you think policies should be added, amended, or omitted, ask for them. If you're ever involved in a malpractice lawsuit, a well-prepared manual and your knowledge of nursing policies could be important to your defense.

USE WHAT YOU KNOW

Use your nursing knowledge to make nursing diagnoses and give clinical opinions. You have a legal duty to your patient not only to make a nursing diagnosis, but also to take appropriate action to meet his nursing needs. Doing so helps protect your patient from harm and you from malpractice charges.

USE THE ENTIRE NURSING PROCESS

Taking shortcuts risks your patient's well-being and your own. If you're charged with malpractice, and the court finds that you took a dangerous patient care shortcut, the court may hold you liable for causing harm to your patient.

DOCUMENT THOROUGHLY

Document every step of the nursing process for every patient. Chart your observations as soon as possible (while facts are fresh in your mind), express yourself clearly, and always write legibly. If you're ever involved in a lawsuit, a complete patient care record could be your best defense.

S*elected references*

Blegen, M.A., et al. "Nurse Experience and Education: Effect on Quality of Care," *Journal of Nursing Administration* 31(1):33-39, January 2001.

Foley, M.E., et al. "Identifying and Using Tools for Reducing Risks to Patients and Health Care Workers: A Nursing Perspective," *Joint Commission Journal on Quality Improvement* 27(9):494-99, September 2001.

Hansten, R.I., and Washburn, M.J. "Facilitating Critical Thinking," *Journal for Nurses in Staff Development* 16(1):23-30, January-February 2000.

Lee, N.G. "Proving Nursing Negligence," *AJN* 100(11):55-56, November 2000.

Retzke, R.E. "Emotional temperatures. Even Following Care Procedures May Not Prevent Lawsuits," *Contemporary Longterm Care* 24(11):13-16, November 2001.

Showers, J.L. "What You Need to Know About Negligence Lawsuits," *Nursing2000* 30(2):45-48, February 2000.

"Stop! ...In The Name of Quality Care," *Revolution* 1(1):6-8, January-February 2000.

BREACH OF CONFIDENTIALITY

"I SOLEMNLY PLEDGE myself before God and in the presence of this assembly...to practice my profession faithfully;...I will do all in my power to maintain and elevate the standard of my profession and will hold in confidence all personal matters committed to my keeping...in the practice of my calling...." This Nightingale Pledge, written in 1893, illustrates the importance Florence Nightingale attached to the concept of *confidentiality*.

It has been said that confidentiality is a key component of trust between patients and health care providers. Some studies have indicated that a lack of *privacy* may deter some patients from obtaining preventive care and treatment. A 1999 report entitled "Promoting Health: Protecting Privacy," published by the California Health Care Foundation and Consumers Union, states that "many people fear their personal health information will be used against them: to deny insurance, employment, and housing, or to expose them to unwanted judgments and scrutiny."

It's difficult for a value to be assigned to privacy protection, but once it's breached, the potential for injury to the patient is incalculable and may be far-reaching. Furthermore, patient delays in seeking treatment out of fear of disclosure of personal medical information account for poorer treatment outcomes and increased health care costs to the individual, to health care providers, and to the insurance industry.

Case studies

The following court cases illustrate the potential for harm to patient — and nurse — when a nurse breaches confidentiality.

CASE 1

In *Nolan vs. Jefferson Parish Hospital* (2001), a licensed practical nurse (LPN) who had been employed in the stepdown cardiology unit for nine years brought a wrongful termination and defamation action against her hospital, individual su-

141

pervisors, and coworkers. She sought reinstatement of her job, lost wages, an injunction to remove certain reprimands from her record, and damages.

While appearing earlier before the Board of Review for the Office of Employee Security in order to have a written warning removed from her employment record, the LPN had attached certain patient records to establish her claim that she had been given a verbal order by a pharmacist to change patients' medications. The hospital terminated her for violating its patient confidentiality policy. However, the Board of Review found that while she was discharged for violation of company policy, she didn't technically recopy the patient's medical record and didn't ignore instructions given to her in the meeting she had had with the facility. Further, she didn't understand that, by presenting the information to the Personnel Department, she had breached the patient confidentiality policy. The Board determined that she didn't deliberately violate company policy, and that the termination wasn't for misconduct connected with her employment. She was found to be entitled to the benefits she had requested.

This LPN may have been fortunate that this case was found in her favor, because not all Boards of Review will look back to see whether the breach of confidentiality was deliberate or merely an oversight. Some find that any breach, deliberate or otherwise, is justification for termination. This case also illustrates that confidentiality breaches may occur when records are recopied by a nurse, or when she sub-

mits documents to another department — even the personnel department — to support any claims made against her. Extreme caution must be exercised in dealing with patient confidentiality issues because most facilities have policies that state a nurse may be terminated for violating a patient's right to confidentiality or privacy.

CASE 2

In the Texas case of *Anderson v. Texas Health System* (2000), the plaintiff, Ms. Anderson, was a nurse employed by a temporary staffing agency that contracted with a local hospital to provide nurses. On September 5, 1997, the hospital received a complaint from a patient who had been hospitalized there the month before, claiming that Anderson had discussed the details of her hospitalization with someone not authorized to receive the information. The hospital's Director of Nursing, James Bryant, contacted the temporary staffing agency to terminate Anderson due to her alleged breach of patient confidentiality. He also reported her to the state board of nursing for the breach.

Thirteen days later, Anderson requested a hearing regarding the patient complaint. On December 3, 1997, the peer review committee granted the request, and Anderson and her attorney presented their defense. However, there's no indication of the committee ever having ruled on the issue, and there's no dispute that Anderson hasn't worked at the hospital since September 5, 1997.

Her lawsuit against the hospital, its owner, and Bryant claimed violations of several Texas statutes on two counts: first, because the peer review committee failed to issue a formal ruling on the allegation made against her and, second, because she was prohibited from working in the hospital. Her claims were dismissed because she didn't cite any malicious acts taken during the peer review proceeding, or any due process rights, which were violated under state law, regarding her subcontractor relationship with the hospital.

As this case shows, even complaints that may be unsubstantiated can result in prohibition from providing patient care in certain facilities. Some facilities are so concerned with patient confidentiality that they may not take a chance that a nurse who has been accused of breaching patient confidentiality will do it again.

Legal issues

Protection of a professional confidence is one of the most important — and most basic — of any of the obligations owed to the end consumer in any professional relationship, be that relationship nurse-patient, physician-patient, attorney-client, priest-penitent, accountant-client, or any other. Any violation of that basic obligation damages or destroys the professional relationship. Health care accreditation organizations have developed standards pertaining to the privacy of personal and medical information. (See *Protecting patients' right to privacy,* page 144.)

PRIVILEGE DOCTRINE
The state courts have been strong in protecting a patient's right to confidentiality of his medical information. Even in court, your patient is protected by the ***privilege doctrine,*** which states that individuals who have a protected relationship, such as that between a physician and patient, can't be forced to reveal communications between them unless the person who benefits from the protection agrees to it. In other words, the patient must agree before confidential information can be revealed in court. The purpose of the privilege doctrine is to encourage the patient to reveal confidential information that may be essential to his treatment. However, when a patient sues, his privilege is waived. (See *Exceptions to privilege,* page 145.)

Nurse-patient relationships
Only a few states (including New York, Arkansas, Oregon, and Vermont) recognize the nurse-patient relationship as protected, but some courts have said the privilege exists when a nurse is following a physician's orders. Whether the privilege granted by the courts applies to LPNs as well is uncertain.

Extent of privilege
State laws also determine the extent of privilege in protected relationships. In *Hammonds v. Aetna Casualty and Surety Co.* (1965), the court reinforced the privilege doctrine by declaring that protecting a patient's privacy is a physician's legal duty. It further ruled that a patient could sue any unauthorized person who disclosed confidential medical information. Similarly, a patient can

Protecting patients' right to privacy

The right to privacy has received a great deal of attention at the state level. Ten states — Alaska, Arizona, California, Florida, Hawaii, Illinois, Louisiana, Montana, South Carolina, and Washington — have written a privacy provision into their constitutions. Nearly all states recognize the right to privacy through ***statutory law*** or ***common law***.

The Joint Commission on Accreditation of Healthcare Organizations (JCAHO) protects a patient's right to privacy regarding videotaping or filming. The JCAHO standard *Clarification on Patient Rights and Informed Consent When Videotaping or Filming* (effective July 28, 2000, and most recently updated February 23, 2001)

states that health care organizations or their designated agents may film or videotape patient care activities in the emergency department only with the patient's consent, and that the health care organization must maintain control of the videotape, not release it to anyone or use it for any purpose, until appropriate informed consent is obtained. If consent isn't given, then the patient is either removed from the film or the tape is destroyed. The hospital or emergency center has an obligation to inform the community it serves that videotaping may be occurring, and signage provided to advise the public of such.

---

sue for invasion of privacy if any unauthorized personnel, such as student nurses, observe him without his permission. The only health care facility personnel who have a right to observe a patient are those involved in his diagnosis, treatment, and related care.

THE PRIVACY ACT

A major piece of legislation involving privacy issues is the Privacy Act of 1974, which became effective on September 27, 1975. The Act laid the groundwork for privacy standards. It established a "code of fair information practices" which attempted to regulate the collection, maintenance, use, and dissemina-

tion of personal information by Federal government agencies. However, due to imprecise language and somewhat outdated regulatory guidelines, the Act was rendered difficult to decipher and apply. After more than 20 years of administrative and judicial analysis, many issues still remain unclear.

The Act focused on four basic policy objectives:
● To restrict disclosure of personal records maintained by agencies.
● To grant individuals increased rights of access to agency records maintained on them.
● To grant individuals the right to seek amendment or supplementation of their records, if those

records aren't accurate, relevant, timely, or complete.

• To establish a code of "fair information practices" requiring agencies to comply with statutory norms for collection, maintenance, and dissemination of records.

Generally, the Privacy Act applies only to Federal agencies rather than to state or local agencies or private entities. An exception, however, is the Social Security number usage restrictions of Section 7 of the Privacy Act, which don't apply to private entities but do apply to local and state governments as well as Federal agencies.

The Department of Justice (DOJ) is charged with investigation and enforcement of this Act. As noted in the DOJ overview cited above, privacy rights are recognized as personal to the individual and can't be assumed by others. Of course, the parent or legal guardian of any minor or the legal guardian of a person legally considered incompetent may act on behalf of that individual when asserting rights under the Privacy Act.

H.I.P.A.A. AND THE PRIVACY RULE

In 1996, Congress passed the Health Insurance Portability and Accountability Act (HIPAA), calling for the Department of Health and Human Services (HHS) to adopt national standards for electronic transactions, claims attachments and formats, and health data privacy and security. The act was also intended to allow patients access to their own medical information and

> ## Exceptions to privilege
>
> In some states, a patient automatically waives his right to physician-patient privilege when he files a personal injury or **workers' compensation** lawsuit.
>
> A hospital or physician can't invoke the privilege doctrine if the motive is self-protection. In *People v. Doe* (1978), a New York nursing home was being investigated for allegedly mistreating its patients. The court ruled that the nursing home's attempt to invoke patient privilege was unjust, since the issue at hand was the patient's welfare.

protect them from unnecessary disclosure of this information.

On November 3, 1999, in compliance with the Act, HHS published a notice of proposed rule making entitled "Standards for Privacy of Individually Identifiable Health Information." The public was encouraged to comment on the proposed confidentiality provisions prior to their adoption. The concerns addressed included protecting personal health information given the availability of computer-based patient record systems, electronic medical information transmission systems, information sharing situations, research, and employment or forensic situations that might involve sharing or exchange of protected personal medical informa-

Breach of confidentiality?

In the case of the *Commonwealth v. Brandwein* (2002), the defendant robbed a bank in 1998. He escaped from capture and sought treatment the following day from a nurse in an emergency clinic.

During his visit with the nurse, he stated that he had done "something very stupid" and that he didn't want to "go to jail." He then handed her an envelope that he wanted given to his daughter, stating that he had overdosed on medication. He also showed the nurse burned areas on his chest, which he stated happened when he had robbed a bank and the money "exploded."

Fearing that the patient might be suicidal, the nurse arranged for an ambulance. The patient then disclosed to the nurse that he had a gun, which he turned over to her when asked to do so. The patient again stated that he didn't want to go to jail, and asked his nurse not to tell anyone.

Even though the nurse hadn't contacted the police, a police officer arrived to offer assistance, unaware of any crime. The nurse immediately pointed out the patient as the person who had overdosed. She also told the police officer that the patient had brought a gun to the clinic and that it was locked in her office. The patient was taken to a local hospital.

The officer remained at the clinic and again spoke with the nurse. The nurse turned the gun and its bullets over and provided the officer with more details about the patient's visit, stating that he'd been in a distraught and suicidal state, had a gun with him, had turned it over on request, and had stated to the nurse that he had robbed a bank and the stolen money had burned him. Police officers were sent to the hospital and, upon the patient's discharge, arrested the patient on firearms charges.

The patient was interviewed at the police station, where he confessed to the bank robbery. However, he argued that his confession should have been suppressed because of the nurse's wrongful disclosures in violation of her obligation to keep patient information confidential.

Because the nurse didn't make her disclosure during a court proceeding, she wasn't protected by an immunity provision in Massachusetts statutes. The court detailed the ethical duty the nurse had to "safeguard the client's right to privacy by judiciously protecting information of a confidential nature…" The duty isn't absolute, however, when innocent parties are in direct jeopardy. The nurse acknowledged that the principles of her profession included a requirement that patient communications not be disclosed "unless she felt that the client was a danger to himself or others." Her disclosures were determined to be a violation of professional ethics, because by the time the officer had arrived at the clinic, the patient had already

---

Breach of confidentiality? *(continued)*

turned the gun over to the nurse, and he was no longer a danger to himself or others.

The court determined that the nurse acted correctly in turning the gun over to the police; she wasn't required to maintain "secret possession" of a possibly illegal firearm merely because a patient handed it to her. The court further stated that her disclosures of the patient's pos-

session of the gun and his involvement in a robbery were a violation of her professional obligation to keep patient communications confidential. However, even though the nurse violated the patient's confidentiality rights, the court found no police misconduct when the officer reacted to her voluntary disclosures by proceeding with firearms charges against the defendant.

---

tion. The revised Standards (known as the Privacy Rule) became effective April 14, 2001, although health plans and health care providers covered by the Rule were given until April 2003 to comply with the new requirements.

The Rule created national standards protecting medical records and other personal health information, including oral information, from intentional or unintentional use or disclosure. Covered entities must reasonably safeguard protected health information by implementing appropriate administrative, technical, and physical safeguards to protect the privacy of the information. Under the Rule, government-operated health plans and health care providers must meet substantially the same requirements as private providers for protecting the privacy of individual identifiable health information.

In addition, all Federal agencies must also meet the requirements of the Privacy Act of 1974, which restricts the information about individual citizens, including any personal health information that can be shared with other agencies and with the public. For example, the Rule specifically prohibits disclosure of certain information, including deoxyribonucleic acid (DNA) information, absent a warrant or evidence of some other legal requirement.

The Privacy Rule created under HIPAA also requires health care providers to obtain permission from persons who have been victims of domestic violence or abuse before disclosing their information to law enforcement. (See *Breach of confidentiality?*)

Here are key provisions of the Privacy Rule:

• Patients have more control over their health information.

• The Rule establishes appropriate safeguards to protect the privacy of health information.

• Violators are held accountable, with civil and criminal penalties that can be imposed if they violate patients' privacy rights.

The disclosure debate

For years, health care experts have debated the merits of letting a patient see his medical records. Proponents argue that knowing the information helps the patient to better understand his condition and care and makes him a more cooperative patient.

Opponents, usually physicians and hospitals, argue that the technical jargon and abbreviations found in medical records may confuse or even frighten a patient. In addition, opponents claim that opening medical records to a patient will increase the risks of malpractice lawsuits. No evidence exists to support this assertion.

The "right to access" issue has spawned an important legal debate. The first issue the courts had to answer involved ownership. The second issue the courts had to resolve involved access.

Determining ownership

The hospital owns the hospital medical records, and the physician owns his office records, according to court decisions. Most courts have decided that a patient sees a physician for diagnosis and treatment, not to obtain records for his personal use.

Right to access

While granting ownership of medical records to physicians and hospitals, the courts have supported patients' rights to obtain records they need for a case review. For this reason, any patient in any state can file a lawsuit to **subpoena** his medical records.

However, some court decisions and some states' laws have given patients the right to direct access. In fact, many states guarantee a patient's right to his medical information. In *Cannell v. Medical and Surgical Clinic S.C.* (1974), the court ruled that a physician had a duty to disclose medical information to his patient. The court also ruled, however, that physicians and hospitals needn't turn over the actual files to the patient. Instead, they need only show the complete medical record — or a copy — to the patient.

The court based the patient's limited right to access on two important concepts:

- A patient has a right to know the details about his medical treatment under common law.
- A patient has a right to the information in his records because he pays for the treatment.

Setting up roadblocks

Despite the laws and court decisions, hospitals don't always make it easy for a patient to gain access to his records. Some hospitals discourage a patient from seeing his medical records by putting up bureaucratic barriers. But while requiring the patient to have an attorney make the request can stifle a patient's attempt to gain access to his records, it may also encourage him to consult a malpractice lawyer. Other hospitals charge high copying fees to discourage patient record requests. Some states, such as Pennsylvania, have laws that require reasonable copying fees.

- The Rule strikes a balance when public responsibility requires disclosure of some forms of data such as to protect public health. An example is the reporting of human immunodeficiency virus (HIV) infection and acquired immunodeficiency syndrome (AIDS) cases, which maintains patient confidentiality while tracking these diseases.
- Patients may now find out how their information may be used and what disclosures of their information have been made.
- The Rule limits release of information to the minimum reasonably needed for the specific purpose.
- Patients now have the right to examine and obtain a copy of their own health records and request corrections. (See *The disclosure debate.*)

Prior to HIPAA, a patchwork of Federal and state laws protected personal health information and how it could be distributed. With HIPAA or, more specifically, with the Privacy Rule, we now have Federal safeguards to protect the confidentiality of medical information. To the extent that state laws provide stronger privacy protections, they will continue to apply over and above the new Federal privacy standards.

Under the Privacy Rule, the average health care provider or health plan is required to perform certain activities:

- Provide patients with information about their privacy rights and how their information can be used.
- Adopt clear privacy procedures for its practice, health care facility, or plan.
- Train employees so that they understand the privacy procedures.
- Designate an individual to be responsible for seeing that the privacy procedures are adopted and followed.
- Secure the patient records containing individually identifiable health information so that they aren't readily available to those who have no legitimate need to access such private and confidential information. (See *HIPAA questions and answers,* page 150.)

Penalties for noncompliance with HIPAA guidelines may result in civil monetary penalties on a per-person, per-violation basis, with strong penalties (significant fines and prison terms) for misuse of the medical or health information with knowledge and intent. The penalties may apply to the individual who violated HIPAA, and may also apply to the organization or its officers.

Consent under HIPAA

Under the Privacy Rule, health care providers must obtain patients' consent to use or disclose health information to carry out treatment, payment, or health care operations. An exception is granted in cases of emergency or when there are substantial communication barriers. The provider must exercise professional judgment to determine whether obtaining consent would interfere with the timely delivery of necessary health care. The provider must obtain consent for release, use, or disclosure of the information obtained during the emergency treatment as soon as reasonably practicable after the treatment.

Authorization under HIPAA

The Privacy Rule differentiates between authorization and consent. An authorization is more specific and restrictive than consent; it has

HIPAA questions and answers

Who's governed by HIPAA regulations?

Health care providers, health plans, and medical information clearinghouses, and those who are affiliated with them as business associates, contractors, consultants, or researchers using personably identifiable health information, are covered by regulations of the Health Insurance Portability and Accountability Act (HIPAA) of 1996.

What's the purpose of HIPAA regulations?

The regulations were created to prevent inappropriate disclosure and use of a person's identifiable health information, and to ensure that organizations or individuals who have access to or use this health information protect it and the systems which store, transmit, and process it.

HIPAA also defines the rights of individuals with respect to their own health information. For example, individuals have the right to obtain copies of the information practices of the health care provider or organization. They have the right to access, review, and correct information contained in their own records. They have the right to an accounting of disclosures made to individuals who aren't involved in the provision of care.

Does HIPAA protect all personal medical information?

The short answer is that not all personal medical information is protected. For example, under certain circumstances, it's mandatory that health information be disclosed. All states have laws requiring health care providers to report cases of specific diseases to public health officials. The Privacy Rule allows only those disclosures that are required by law to be made without the patient's consent. It allows disclosures to public health authorities that are authorized by law to collect or receive information for public health purposes. To protect the public health, it's often necessary for public health officials to obtain information about the persons afflicted with a disease in order to determine the cause of the disease and make possible the prevention of further illness.

Examples of information that may be shared with public health authorities concerning protected health are reportable diseases (such as tuberculosis, syphilis, and acquired immunodeficiency syndrome) or injuries, deaths, births, investigations of the occurrence and cause of injury and disease, and monitoring adverse outcomes related to food, drugs, biological products, and dietary supplements.

an expiration date and may also limit the purpose for which the information may be used or dis-

closed. The Privacy Rule requires providers to obtain authorization to use or disclose health information maintained in psychotherapy notes for treatment by persons other than the originator of the notes, for payment, or for certain health care operations purposes. Mental health records are entitled to a heightened level of security and protection.

Notice and consent under HIPAA

The Privacy Rule also stipulates that patients be given notice of privacy practices before consent is obtained. However, the Rule doesn't require the patient to read or understand the notice, nor does it require that the covered entity explain to the patient everything that's in the notice. Merely giving notice is sufficient.

The Rule also provides specific guidelines regarding patient consent. The consent is a general document giving a health care provider permission to use and disclose health information. Health care services may be conditioned on the individual providing this consent, and one consent may cover all uses and disclosures by that provider, without an expiration date. If a patient refuses to consent to the use or disclosure of their health information, the health care provider may refuse to treat the patient. Revocations or limitations of consent must be in writing.

Health plan organizations and health care clearinghouses (such as laboratories that interact with physicians rather than patients) don't have to obtain a patient's consent for treatment. These organizations may use and disclose health information for purposes of treatment without obtaining a patient's consent. Instead, authorizations are required under most such circumstances.

The consent document may be brief and written in general terms. However, it must be written in plain language that informs the individual that information may be used and disclosed. It must state the patient's rights to review the provider's privacy notice, to request restrictions, and to revoke consent, and it must be dated and signed by the individual or his representative.

Minimum necessary disclosures

HIPAA explicitly exempts from the "minimum necessary" standard all disclosures to providers for treatment purposes. Also exempted are all requests by health care providers for information to be used for treatment purposes. As a result, information will flow freely between and among providers involved in treatment. The provisions in the HIPAA regulation that require special justification for disclosing the entire medical record don't apply to treatment-related disclosures because they aren't subject to the minimum necessary standard in the first place. Uses of health care information for treatment purposes, under HIPAA, allows the use of the entire medical record when it's specifically justified as the amount that's reasonably necessary to accomplish the purpose of the use.

HIPAA and the internet

Most online health activities aren't covered by HIPAA. The rules only apply to certain types of Web sites:
● those established by health care providers, such as hospitals or physicians' offices

● those belonging to health insurance carriers, such as Aetna U.S. Healthcare or Kaiser Permanente
● those belonging to health care clearinghouses that process health insurance claims information in a specific format for providers and insurers such as WebMD Office.

Commonplace online health-related activities — for example, sites offering general nutrition or fitness or discussing medical conditions and treatment options — may not be covered by HIPAA. Also excluded from protection are sites selling drugs without a prescription, online mental health counseling sites that accept only credit card payments, and pharmaceutical company Web sites.

COMPUTERIZED MEDICAL RECORDS

The legal implications of computerized medical records are evolving. Most computer records are legitimate substitutes for manual records, but some states still require practitioners to keep written records as well. Various laws protect the privacy of computerized medical records, but there are no guarantees that unauthorized persons won't gain access to computerized records.

The most pressing legal questions concern the threat to patient privacy and confidentiality. With traditional records, information is restricted simply by keeping the record on the unit, whereas computer records can be called up at any terminal in the facility. The primary safeguard is the use of a password that limits access to computerized information. Passwords

may limit all access to a particular record, or allow access only to certain portions of a record. For example, a nurse's code might allow access to a patient's entire record, but a technician's code might restrict access to only information pertinent to his special function.

Health care facilities must show that their computer systems are trustworthy enough to be used in court. For example, they should use software that automatically records the date and time of each entry and each correction as well as the name of the author or anyone who modifies a record. When an error is corrected, the software should preserve both the original and corrected versions and identify each author. (See *Challenging a computer record in court*.)

FAXED RECORDS

Care must also be taken to safeguard patient information sent by fax machine. In particular, policies and procedures should be established to prevent confidential patient information, such as a positive result on an HIV test, from being transmitted by fax machine — especially one that's centrally located and easily seen by many staff members.

PATIENT PRIVACY AND SPECIFIC CONDITIONS

Nurses should be aware of confidentiality issues regarding the handling of sensitive medical information about conditions, such as cancer, HIV infection, and AIDS as well as genetic testing.

RELATED CASES

Challenging a computer record in court

In 1977, a patient in New York charged that a computerized record system was an invasion of his privacy. In *Whalen v. Roe* (1977), the patient challenged the constitutionality of a state law requiring patients buying certain prescription drugs to list their name, address, age, the drug, dosage, and prescribing physician's name for a state database. The state then entered all the information into a computer.

The Supreme Court upheld the law but acknowledged the threat to privacy implicit in the system. The Court reasoned that central storage and easy accessibility of computerized data vastly increase the potential for abuse of the information contained therein.

Cancer

Early detection and early treatment are crucial in the treatment of cancer. However, if a patient is concerned that results of screening procedures may be disclosed, making him vulnerable to discrimination by insurers or employers, he may decide not to have the screening.

In fact, a pilot study documented 206 instances of discrimination as a result of access to genetic information, culminating in loss of employment and insurance coverage or ineligibility for benefits. It also found that one in three women invited to participate in a breast-cancer study using genetic information refused, fearing just such discrimination or loss of privacy.

HIV infection and AIDS

All states require that cases of AIDS be reported to the state or local health department. The majority of states require that cases of HIV infection be reported as well. Almost all states protect its confidentiality under other statutes or provisions, but do allow for disclosure of HIV-related information in certain circumstances. The most commonly cited permissible disclosures are to a health care provider involved in the patient's care, sexual or needle-sharing partners, parties with a subpoena or court order, blood banks or organ donors, epidemiologists and researchers, correctional facilities, school officials, health-maintenance organizations, health care facilities or mental health facilities, and insurance companies. Only a few states allow disclosure of the name of the source patient. Some states make mandatory notification of spouses and partners. (See *Contact notification,* page 154.)

Informed consent may be required by other statutes, common law, regulations, or policies for HIV testing or release of information. In more than half of the states, minors are allowed to consent to HIV testing. In a majority of states, some

EXPERT OPINION

Contact notification

The patient's right to privacy may conflict with your duty to prevent the spread of the disease. The patient may balk when you request that he inform his partner that he's human immunodeficiency virus (HIV)-positive. You must respect the patient's right to confidentiality, but you should also try to help him understand that it's crucial for the other person to know they've been exposed to HIV. Anonymous contact notification programs may provide assistance. For example, with the patient's consent, you can refer the problem to the county health department, which will attempt to locate and inform contacts of their exposure.

Many married patients are reluctant to notify their spouses, especially if the infection can be traced back to an extramarital affair. Legally, you can't compel patients to tell their spouses, but you can explore options that may make it easier to do so. For example, you can ask patients whether they'd prefer that a family physician related the information. A counselor can help reduce the anxiety related to this type of disclosure and to support the patient through the disclosure process.

Laws dealing with contact notification continue to evolve and vary widely from state to state. For example, a Utah law barring individuals with HIV from marrying was challenged in 1993 by two HIV-infected women. They feared that their families would lose financial benefits if their marriages were ruled invalid by the courts.

A compelling reason for informing sex partners is the fact that many states charge HIV-infected individuals with murder when they have unprotected sex with partners whom they didn't inform of their infection. In 1991, a man in Oakland, California, was sentenced to 3 years in prison for this offense. In Jackson, Florida, a 22-year-old man was convicted of attempted second-degree murder for knowingly engaging in intercourse while infected with HIV. He was sentenced to 4 to 5 years in jail and 13 years of probation.

situations may occur where informed consent for HIV testing is waived, most commonly for persons charged or convicted of specific sex offenses, emergency workers who were exposed to a patient's blood, prison or jail inmates, patients who are incapable of consenting but require testing to provide medical treatment, for research or epidemiological purposes, and for blood, tissue, or organ donations.

Almost all states have either criminal or civil penalties for unauthorized disclosure of HIV related information. Some have both criminal and civil penalties.

 LESSONS IN PRACTICE Because each state has passed legislation regarding the confidentiality of

The "biological underclass"

Insurance companies have been among the first to be charged with genetic discrimination. From the company's point of view, it's a sound business decision to increase premiums or deny coverage to anyone with a serious medical condition or at high risk for developing such a condition.

Unfortunately, predictive tests don't always tell the whole story. A single faulty gene may not cause trouble unless other, related genes are also defective, or the gene may never be expressed unless it's set off by an environmental trigger. A patient who's seen as "certain to become disabled" rather than "at risk" for disability could easily join the ranks of the uninsured — with little legal recourse.

Employers represent another source of potential genetic discrimination. In times of increasing health care costs, employers may avoid hiring someone who's likely to incur large medical bills. Industry officials also argue that genetic screening can identify workers who might be especially sensitive to industrial toxins. A more ethical approach would be to clean up the workplace so that the risk is decreased for all workers.

HIV status, nurses must be aware of their state's laws regarding confidentiality and regarding mandatory reporting.

Genetic information

Prior to HIPAA, no Federal legislation existed relating to genetic discrimination in individual insurance coverage or in the workplace. The primary public concern is that insurers will use genetic information to deny, limit, or cancel insurance or that employers will use genetic information against existing workers or for screening of potential employees. (See *The "biological underclass."*) Concern also exists because DNA samples can be held indefinitely and used for purposes other than those for which they were gathered.

In February 2000, President Clinton signed an Executive Order prohibiting Federal departments and agencies from using genetic information in hiring or promotion actions. The Order was supported and endorsed by the American Medical Association, the American College of Medical Genetics, the National Society of Genetic Counselors, and the Genetic Alliance. The mandate provided strong privacy protections for any genetic information used for medical treatment and research.

Under the Order, obtaining or disclosing genetic information about employees or potential employees is prohibited, except when it's necessary to provide medical treatment to employees, ensure workplace health and safety, or provide occupational and health researchers access to data. In every case where genetic information about employees is obtained, it will be subject to all Federal and state privacy protections.

The most likely current source of protection against genetic discrimination in the workplace is provided by laws prohibiting discrimination based on disability, such as the Americans with Disabilities Act, which is enforced by the Equal Employment Opportunity Commission (EEOC), or the Rehabilitation Act of 1973. None of these explicitly address genetic information, but do provide some protections against disability-related genetic discrimination in the workplace. However, the HIPAA Federal law directly addresses the issue of genetic discrimination by:

• prohibiting group health plans from using any health status–related factor including genetic information as a basis for denying or limiting eligibility for coverage or for charging an individual more for insurance coverage.

• limiting exclusions for preexisting conditions in group health plans to 12 months and prohibiting such exclusions if the individual has been covered previously for that same condition for 12 months or more.

• stating explicitly that genetic information in the absence of a current diagnosis of illness shall not be considered a preexisting condition.

• not prohibiting employers from refusing to offer health coverage as part of their benefits packages.

Persons who believe they've been subjected to workplace discrimination based on genetic information should be able to file a charge with the EEOC, Department of Labor, or other investigatory Federal agency.

Avoiding litigation

Your best approach to avoiding lawsuits regarding patient privacy or confidentiality issues is to know your responsibility in protecting privacy, to know what information you may disclose, and to know what information you must disclose.

PROTECTING PATIENT PRIVACY

Despite legal uncertainties regarding your responsibilities under the privilege doctrine, you have a professional and ethical responsibility to protect your patient's privacy, whether you're a registered nurse or an LPN.

This responsibility requires more than keeping secrets. You may have to educate your patients about their privacy rights. Some may be unaware of what the right to privacy means, or even that they have such a right. Explain to the patient that he can refuse to allow pictures to be taken of his disorder and its treatment, for example. Tell him that he can choose to have information about his condition withheld from others, including family members. Make every effort to ensure that the patient's wishes are carried out.

WHEN TO DISCLOSE CONFIDENTIAL INFORMATION

Under certain circumstances, you may lawfully disclose confidential information about your patient. For example, the courts allow disclosure when the welfare of a person or a group of people is at stake. Consider the patient who's diagnosed with epilepsy and asks you not to tell his family. Depending on the circumstances, you may decide that this isn't in the patient's and his family's best interest, particularly in terms of safety. In that situation, inform the patient's physician; he may then decide to inform the family to protect the patient's well-being. In most states, the physician is required to inform the Department of Motor Vehicles of uncontrolled epilepsy.

You're also protected by law if you disclose confidential information about a patient that's necessary for his continued care or if your patient consents to the disclosure. However, be careful not to exceed the specified limit of a patient's consent.

PROTECTING THE PUBLIC

The courts have granted immunity to health care professionals who, in good faith, have disclosed confidential information to prevent public harm. A controversial California case established a physician's right to disclose information that would protect any person whom a patient threatened to harm. In *Tarasoff v. Regents of the University of California* (1976), a woman was murdered by a mentally ill patient who had told his psychotherapist that he intended to kill her. The victim's parents sued the physician for failing to warn their daughter. The Supreme Court found the physician liable because he didn't warn the intended

victim. The Court ruled similarly in *McIntosh v. Milano* (1979), and many states have now adopted this position.

When you must disclose confidential information

In some situations, the law requires you to disclose confidential information.

CASES OF ABUSE

All 50 states and the District of Columbia have *disclosure laws* for cases of *child abuse,* elder abuse, and spouse or partner abuse. Except for Maine and Montana, all states also grant immunity from legal action for a *good faith* report on suspected abuse. In fact, there may be a criminal penalty for failure to disclose such information. Courts also may order you to disclose confidential information in cases of child custody and child neglect.

CRIMINAL CASES

Some laws create an exemption to the privilege doctrine in criminal cases so that the courts can have access to all essential information. In states where neither a law nor an exemption to the law exists, the court may find an exemption to the doctrine in criminal cases.

GOVERNMENT REQUESTS

Certain government agencies can order you to reveal confidential information, including Federal agencies, such as the Internal Revenue Service, the Environmental Protection Agency, the Department of Labor, and HHS. State agencies that may order you to reveal confidential information include revenue or tax bureaus and public health departments. For example, most state public health departments require reports of all communicable diseases, births and deaths, and gunshot wounds.

PUBLIC'S RIGHT TO KNOW

The newsworthiness of an event or person doesn't make disclosure acceptable. In such circumstances, the public's need for information doesn't outweigh a person's right to keep his medical condition private. For example, newspapers routinely publish the findings of the President's annual physical examination in response to the public's demand for information, but only after the President has authorized the disclosure.

Other events for which the public's right to know may outweigh the patient's right to privacy include breakthroughs in medical technology (the first successful hand transplant) and product tampering cases, for example. In 1999, the national media gave wide exposure to an incident in New York state in which nine people died from mosquito bites that transmitted a flavivirus that cause St. Louis encephalitis.

However, even when the public has a right to know about a confidential matter, the courts won't allow public disclosure to undermine a person's dignity.

FURTHER PROTECTION

Once you're familiar with patient privacy issues, don't forget to follow the basics: never discuss patient information with a person not entitled to that information or in a public place where a third party might overhear your conversation. This includes your family members. Reassuring the patient that you'll keep information confidential will help put you both at ease.

More than 100 years ago, Florence Nightingale understood the importance of protecting the confidences of her patients' personal matters. She also understood that the standard of the profession was one that she could elevate, by both her personal commitment and pledge. The issues of confidentiality and privacy are still with us. Only now, as health care providers who form the "front line" for collecting and protecting personal health information, we have discovered so many more ways that it can be breached! As we look to the future and navigate uncharted courses when deciding what personal health information to collect, use, and share, the concept hasn't changed all that much since 1893. It's still very much in our hands.

Privacy? Confidentiality? It's a matter of earned trust, which can determine whether or not our patients will even seek out health care; and if they do, whether or not they provide their physicians and nurses with full and complete information to allow the system to work best for them.

S*elected references*

Allender, M. "HIPAA Compliance in the OR," *AORN Journal* 75(1):121-25, January 2002.

Bergren, M.D. "HIPAA Hoopla: Privacy and Security of Identifiable Health Information," *Journal of*

School Nursing 17(6):336-41, December 2001.

Cain, P. "Respecting and Breaking Confidences: Conceptual, Ethical, and Educational Issues," *Nurse Education Today* 19(3):175-81, April 1999.

Gallagher, T. "Patient Dignity Equals Privacy," *Nursing Times* 97(48):21, November-December 2001.

Gordon, E.L. "Release of Behavioral Health, Developmental Disabilities, HIV, and Substance Abuse Information: Guidelines for Legal Compliance," *Health Care Law Monthly* 3-16, December 2000.

Haggerty, L.A. and Hawkins, J. "Informed Consent and the Limits of Confidentiality," *Western Journal of Nursing Research* 22(4):508-14, June 2000.

"HHS Announces Final Regulation Establishing First-Ever National Standards to Protect Patients' Personal Medical Records," *Health Care Law Monthly,* p. 17-19, December 2000.

Hutton, A. "The Private Adolescent: Privacy Needs of Adolescents in Hospitals," *Journal of Pediatric Nursing* 17(1):67-72, February 2002.

Kaiser, J. "Patient Privacy. Researchers Say Rules Are Too Restrictive," *Science* 294(5549):2070-71, December 2001.

Kalina, C.M. et al. "How Does the HIPAA Privacy Standard Affect Case Management?" *AAOHN Journal* 49(11):508-11, November 2001.

Maltz, A. "Keeping Pace with New Patient Privacy Rules," *RN* 64(9):71-72, 74, 82, September 2001.

Shuren, A.W. and Livsey, K. "Complying with the Health Insurance Portability and Accountability Act. Privacy Standards," *AAOHN Journal* 49(11):501-507, November 2001.

Chapter Nine ●●●●●●●●●●●●●●●●●●●●●●●●●

CRIMINAL ACTIONS

BEING SUED for ***malpractice*** is a distressing experience, but being charged with a crime for making a mistake, following the attending physician's orders, or complying with the patient's wishes can be devastating. In most cases, to be considered a crime, an act must be performed with the intention to cause pain, injury, or distress to another person.

One potential problem for nurses, pertaining to pain management, arises when the line blurs between an act that's intended to cause pain and one that's intended to relieve pain, but is nevertheless viewed as a crime. This broad definition of crime means nurses and other health care providers walk a fine line — if, for example, you overmedicate a patient you might be at risk for being charged with unnecessary use of restraint or even murder; yet if you undermedicate a patient, you might be at risk for being charged with neglect or abuse.

Nurses who are charged criminally commonly end up facing civil malpractice as well; a plaintiff's attorney could argue that any behav-

ior leading to a criminal charge (even if ultimately found not guilty) deviates from the standard of care and amounts to malpractice.

Case studies

The following court cases illustrate how medication administration can result in criminal actions against nurses.

CASE 1

Sharon LaDuke, a registered nurse in New York, was investigated for possible criminal behavior in her management of a terminally ill woman's care (*Sharon LaDuke v. Hepburn Medical Center* [1997]). In December 1994, a 76-year-old woman with end-stage lung disease and pneumonia was admitted to the intensive care unit (ICU) because she was in acute respiratory failure. Her family requested that the patient be weaned from life support. However, her I.V. infusion was never discontinued.

On January 11, 1995, the patient appeared restless and uncomfortable; her physician ordered that fentanyl, a potent opioid analgesic, be continued by I.V. The physician also ordered that the patient receive injections of fentanyl every 30 minutes, as needed, if she became agitated or restless. The nurses' notes indicated that LaDuke gave the patient an injection of fentanyl and administered another dose of fentanyl 15 minutes afterward, instead of 30 minutes afterward as the physician ordered; 5 minutes later, the patient died.

LaDuke's actions were investigated despite the fact that the family had requested her to provide better pain management and subsequently supported her actions. The investigation revealed that because nurse LaDuke had administered the final dose by increasing the I.V. drip rate, rather than using a syringe, it violated the medical center's policy. Although the district attorney concluded that insufficient evidence of homicide existed, LaDuke's employer terminated her on the grounds that she had euthanized the patient.

CASE 2

A patient admitted for long-term care in a nursing home received a whirlpool bath from a certified nursing assistant as part of her routine care. The two nursing assistants responsible for the patient were working under the supervision of a licensed practical nurse. While preparing the patient's bath, the nursing assistant tested the water with a double-gloved hand and, assuming it was the correct temperature, placed the patient in the bath. After the patient had been placed in the whirlpool, the second assistant left the room. Shortly thereafter, the remaining nursing assistant realized that some supplies were missing and stepped out of the room to obtain the items she needed, leaving the patient alone for several minutes.

The first assistant returned and continued with the bath. The patient didn't complain of pain or have obvious signs of distress. The second assistant returned to take the patient back to her room, and the supervising nurse noted that the patient's foot was bleeding. Upon further examination, the nurse realized that the patient's legs and lower body had received scalding second-degree burns.

The supervising nurse said she would report the incident to the appropriate authorities, but failed to do so. The patient developed a severe infection and died a few weeks later; the medical examiner ruled that the patient died as a result of an infection directly attributed to the burns she sustained. The nurse and one of the nursing assistants were charged with negligent homicide. They each received a 2-year suspended sentence and a 5-year *probation period* and voluntarily surrendered their licenses.

Legal issues

As the cases discussed here clearly illustrate, it's easy for a well-meaning nurse to step into the legal minefield of criminal liability.

CRIMINAL LIABILITY

Abuse is physical, sexual, or emotional mistreatment that harms, or is likely to harm, the recipient. Recent statutes have expanded the definition of abuse to include any unjustified physical contact, including but not limited to:

● excessive force in the course of a prescribed treatment or therapy
● unnecessary physical contact when providing care, comfort, or assistance to the patient
● retaliation against the patient.

Physical abuse is the use of force that results in bodily injury, physical pain, or physical impairment. It may involve acts of violence, such as striking, pushing, shoving, shaking, slapping, kicking, pinching, and burning. It may also include the inappropriate use of medication, restraints, force-feeding, and physical punishment of any kind.

Sexual abuse involves unwanted touching or any type of sexual contact, including coerced nudity, assault, and battery. Sexual misconduct is a very gray area that doesn't always indicate an act that's willful or deliberate. In fact, malpractice insurance will cover charges of sexual misconduct for acts that aren't willful and deliberate and don't fall outside the scope of employment.

Emotional or psychological abuse involves the infliction of pain or distress through verbal or nonverbal acts. It may include verbal assaults, insults, threats, intimidation, humiliation, and harassment. Emotional and psychological abuse may involve the use of abusive language, silence, or isolation.

Criminal assault is defined as a threat or attempt to inflict offensive physical contact or bodily harm on a person (such as by lifting a fist in a threatening manner) that puts the person in immediate danger or apprehension of such contact or harm. When the threat of an assault is carried through, the act of criminal battery occurs. Battery is defined as an offensive touching or use of force on a person without the person's consent. However, keep in mind that the language of specific criminal laws varies from state to state.

By 1993, all 50 states had enacted criminal elder abuse statutes punishing unintentional behavior, such as "wanton" or "reckless" action, mistreatment, criminal negligence, or criminal neglect, in addition to punishing intentional acts.

MISTREATMENT AND NEGLECT

Mistreatment includes the use of medication, isolation technique, or restraint that harms, or is likely to harm, the patient. It includes, but isn't limited to:

● exceeding a patient's prescribed medication dosage
● using medication, restraints, or isolation as a means of retaliation
● keeping a patient confined to a closet, locked room, or other enclosed area
● preventing or restricting a patient's communication with others
● using restraints without appropriate orders
● forcing a patient to take medication against his wishes
● forcing a patient to submit to a procedure or therapy despite his objection. (See *Acting despite a patient's wishes.*)

Neglect is the refusal or failure to fulfill a health care provider's or health care facility's obligations to a patient, failure to provide treatment or services necessary to maintain the health or safety of a patient. It may also include failure of a person who has financial responsibility to provide care. Neglect typically means the refusal or failure to provide life necessities, such as food, water, clothing, shelter, personal hygiene, medicine, comfort, personal safety, and other essentials included in an implied or agreed-upon responsibility to a patient.

Neglect includes, but isn't limited to:
● failing to provide medical, dental, nursing, or other treatments or services
● failing to carry out care plans or specific treatments
● failing to provide dietary requirements
● failing to provide for hygienic needs
● failing to provide safety measures
● failing to provide assistance with activities of daily living (ADLs), such as bathing and dressing.

On January 22, 2001, the governmental agencies known as the Centers for Medicare & Medicaid Services issued new protective regulations regarding restraints and seclusion, to which all facilities accepting Medicare or Medicaid payments must adhere. The regulations guarantee patients freedom from restraints or involuntary seclusion utilized for coercion, discipline, retaliation, or convenience. The regulations also guarantee the patient's right to participate in his own treatment decisions, including the use of *advance directives.*

Acting despite a patient's wishes

Medication, isolation techniques, or restraints may be administered against a patient's wishes, but only in limited circumstances:
● when a patient has refused treatment and the court issues an order authorizing the medication, isolation technique, or restraint
● when the patient engages in behavior that presents imminent injury to himself (as in attempted suicide or repetitive injurious behavior) or another person (when a patient is committing violent acts against the staff or other patients)
● when the treatment is the least restrictive available means to prevent harm and provide reasonable care.

Federal regulations also provide guidelines for the way facilities function. To receive Medicare and Medicaid reimbursement, health care facilities and nursing homes must comply with Federal requirements for long-term care facilities. Under these regulations, a nursing home must:
● have sufficient nursing *staff*
● conduct an initial comprehensive and accurate assessment of each resident's functional capacity
● develop a comprehensive care plan for each resident

- prevent the deterioration of a resident's ability to bathe, dress, groom, transfer and ambulate, use a toilet, eat, and communicate
- provide the necessary services to maintain good nutrition, grooming, and personal oral hygiene if a resident can't carry out ADLs
- ensure that each resident receives proper treatment and assistive devices to maintain vision and hearing abilities
- ensure that each resident does not develop pressure ulcers and, if a resident has pressure ulcers, provide the necessary treatment and services to promote healing, prevent infection, and prevent new sores from developing
- provide appropriate treatment and services to an incontinent resident to restore as much normal bladder functioning as possible
- ensure that the resident receives adequate supervision and assistive devices to prevent accidents
- maintain acceptable parameters of nutritional status
- provide each resident with sufficient fluid intake to maintain proper hydration and health
- ensure that each resident is free from significant medication errors
- promote each resident's quality of life
- maintain the dignity and respect of each resident
- ensure that the resident has the right to choose activities, schedules, and health care
- provide pharmaceutical services to meet the needs of each resident
- be administered in a manner that enables the facility to use its resources effectively and efficiently

- maintain accurate, complete, and easily accessible clinical records on each resident.

●●▶ **LESSONS IN PRACTICE** Mistreatment and neglect can be avoided by adhering to state and Federal regulations and standards.

PALLIATIVE CARE AND END-OF-LIFE ISSUES

Before 1990, criminal law was very murky regarding the prosecution of end-of-life issues. Terms, such as *mercy-killing,* **euthanasia,** and **right-to-die laws** were used interchangeably, and states made their own laws on a case-by-case basis. However, in 1990, the legal landscape pertaining to end-of-life care shifted when the U.S. Supreme Court ruled, in the case of *Nancy Cruzan v. Director, Missouri Department of Health* (1990), that patients have a constitutional interest in refusing unwanted medical care, including life-sustaining therapy, such as nutrition and hydration.

Since 1990, criminal prosecutions arising from care of the dying and attempts to manage pain in the terminally ill have fallen into three broad categories: withdrawal of life-sustaining treatment and the accompanying use of pain medication (without the consent of the patient or family), the administration of morphine or other analgesics and sedatives, and terminal care that includes the use of a potentially fatal agent, such as potassium chloride, insulin, or chloroform.

The use of controlled substances or opioids to treat a patient's pain need not be, and usually isn't, an intentional criminal act. To charge a health care provider with a crime, prosecutors must find evidence of that person's intent to kill or a reckless disregard for a patient's well-being.

Double-effect doctrine

These distinctions raise several important issues, not the least of which is the controversial doctrine of the "double-effect." While the doctrine has clear criteria, which must be met for it to be applied, it's arguable that it's misinterpreted in some situations.

The doctrine of double effect states that a harmful effect of treatment, even if that effect results in death, is permissible if death isn't intended and occurs as a side effect of a beneficial action.

In order for this doctrine to apply, the following criteria must exist:

● The intended effect must be a good one.
● The harmful effect must be foreseen but not intended.
● The harmful effect must not be a way of producing the good effect.
● The good effect must, on balance, outweigh the harmful effect.

The use of morphine in the dying patient is a classic illustration of this principle in action. The good effect of the morphine is the relief of suffering; the harmful effect is the possible hastening of death. The first condition of the principle of double effect is met because when the nurse administers morphine to the patient, the nurse doesn't bring about the relief of suffering by means of weakening the patient's condition. Therefore, the harmful effect isn't the means to the desired effect, so the second condition is also satisfied. The in-

tent of the nurse is to relieve the patient's suffering, not to kill the patient. The adverse effect, possibly hastening the patient's death, comes from dangers inherent in the use of the drug. Death isn't intended, but is a necessary risk. Third, the good and the evil effects result simultaneously. The risk of hastening the patient's death occurs at the same time as the benefit of relieving the patient's pain.

The relief of suffering in the dying patient is vitally important. The caregiver's primary duty is to relieve the patient's pain and suffering when curative efforts have ceased. This duty provides sufficient reason for using the morphine in whatever dosage is necessary to accomplish that goal. Therefore, the principle of double effect entirely justifies the use of enough morphine and other analgesic drugs to relieve pain in terminally ill patients, even at the risk of shortening their lives. (See *Murder or mercy?,* page 166.)

Underlying motivation

Ethicists distinguish morally permissible care that results in death from inappropriate killing by applying this rule. This fact helps to explain why a health care provider is permitted to administer high doses of painkillers to relieve a terminally ill patient's severe pain, even in amounts that would cause a patient to die sooner. The more severe and intractable a patient's pain, the greater the justification for risking premature death. The swiftness with which the dosage of opioids is increased must be proportional to a patient's pain and suffering.

RELATED CASES

Murder or mercy?

In a highly publicized, Massachusetts trial (*Commonwealth v. Anne Capute* [1982]), a hospital licensed practical nurse, was charged with murder. The prosecution alleged that Nurse Capute intended to kill a patient when she administered 195 mg of morphine that had been ordered by a physician for pain during one 8-hour period. The prosecution argued that the amount of morphine given to the patient was what caused her death, and that the patient wouldn't have died if it hadn't been for the administration of the morphine.

Nurse Capute's attorney argued that the patient had a terminal disease that caused her death. Facing a possible life sentence if convicted, Capute told the jury that she administered the morphine to help the patient, and that the jury and the attorneys could not understand the patient's pain and suffering because they hadn't been there to witness it.

Because the jury didn't believe that the prosecution proved that the medication had caused the patient's death, Capute was acquitted of murder.

relievers, even when dying patients are suffering. According to some, this reluctance stems from ethical and legal fears about hastening death and from moral or psychological rejection of the alleged difference between the intent to cause death and the foreseen possibility of causing death.

Research indicates that, in providing end-of-life care, clinicians commonly have more than one motive when using sedatives and analgesics in ICUs. Sometimes hastening death is a motivation, but not the most important one, for some physicians and nurses. At least one author has suggested that this amounts to the caregivers' rejecting the differences between actions intended to hasten death, as opposed to actions foreseen to do so. However, the courts maintain a strong distinction between those deaths that are the result of the "double effect" of treating interminable pain and those deaths that are brought on by injections of potassium chloride. Potassium chloride has no palliative function and doesn't treat pain; the rule of "double effect" doesn't apply.

Assisted suicide

What does this mean in terms of assisted suicide? In 1994, the voters of the state of Oregon passed the Death with Dignity Act, the nation's first statute permitting physicians to prescribe lethal medications to allow terminally ill patients to kill themselves, although this act is now under appeal at the Federal level. Other states have considered legislation legalizing physician-assisted suicide but, as yet, no statutes have been passed.

Despite this, some physicians and nurses have been reluctant to use sufficient doses of opioid pain-

Uncontrolled pain remains an important motivation behind many patients' desire for suicide. One survey demonstrated that a significant majority of terminally ill patients and recently bereaved caregivers support euthanasia and physician-assisted suicide for patients with unremitting pain. Yet the same study indicates that as many as 95% of these patients can get adequate pain relief if the right medications are administered in the right quantities. Part of the problem is simply a lack of education.

In addition to expertise in pain management, the National Association of Home Care's affiliate, the Hospice Association of America, has developed a model bill of rights for all individuals receiving hospice care, based on the patient rights currently enforced by law.

●▶▶ **LESSONS IN PRACTICE** Working with organizations, such as the National Association of Home Care and the Hospice Association of America, and familiarizing yourself with the guidelines and techniques used by these organizations is one of the best ways to defend yourself from accusations of improper behavior. (See *Legal considerations in hospice care.*)

SEXUAL MISCONDUCT

All nurses have a professional responsibility in their nurse-patient relationships to inspire confidence in their patients, act in their best interests, and respect their dignity. This professional responsibility means that nurses should promote independence and should refrain from seeking personal gain at their patients' expense and from inappro-

RELATED CASES

Legal considerations in hospice care

If you work in a hospice, be aware of your special legal responsibilities.

Standing orders
A hospital staff nurse can follow standing orders for pain medication. However, when working in a hospice, never rely on standing orders as authorization to administer pain medication. Always obtain specific orders signed by the patient's physician.

Advice on making a will
In a hospice, never give your patient advice concerning his will. If he asks for advice, tell him you can't help him. Suggest that he discuss the matter with his attorney or family members.

Living wills
Unlike the hospital nurse, whose duty with respect to living wills varies from state to state, the nurse who works in a hospice must respect the patient's living will. Don't violate it unless a court order instructs you to do so.

priate involvement in their personal relationships.

One of the best ways to achieve and maintain this integrity is through the understanding and establishment of professional boundaries. Professional boundaries in

RELATED CASES

Risking sexual misconduct

The following case illustrates the risks in becoming physically or emotionally involved with a patient.

Nurse Terri, a home health care nurse, was caring for Michael, a paraplegic Gulf War veteran, over the course of 6 months. Early in the professional relationship, Michael began making sexual advances toward Nurse Terri, which she gently rebuffed. As months went by, Michael persisted in his advances, and Nurse Terri began a sexual relationship with him. She requested that another nurse take over his care and started seeing him socially.

After about 6 weeks, Nurse Terri realized this wasn't a relationship she wished to continue, and broke up with Michael. He then filed a complaint in which he alleged that Nurse Terri sexually assaulted him, and she was charged with second-degree sexual assault. Pursuant to a plea agreement, Nurse Terri agreed to 1 year of probation and a 1-year suspension of her license.

nursing are limits protecting the space between the power of the professional and the vulnerability of the patient. The power imbalance present in a professional relationship places the patient in a position of vulnerability and of potential exposure to exploitation or abuse if trust isn't respected. The burden is on the nurse to maintain a therapeutic relationship. Whether initiated by the patient or the nurse, it's the nurse's responsibility to identify the crossing of a boundary and deal with issues professionally and therapeutically. (See *Risking sexual misconduct*.)

Boundary violations can occur when the needs of the nurse are confused with those of the patient. Each situation is unique, but the presence of one or more of the following boundary warning signs tells the nurse to stop and take another look at a particular relationship with a patient. By paying attention to these boundary warning signs, many issues can be resolved before a boundary is crossed or the care of the patient is adversely affected.

Some of the warning signs indicating that professional boundaries should be attended to are:
● frequently thinking of the patient when away from work
● frequently planning other patients' care around the subject patient's needs
● spending personal time with the patient
● sharing personal information or work concerns with the patient
● communicating in a flirtatious manner, perhaps with sexual innuendo, off-color jokes, or offensive language
● noticing more physical touching than is appropriate or sexual content in interactions with the patient

- favoring one patient's care at the expense of another's
- keeping secrets with the patient
- swapping patient assignments with other staff
- communicating in a guarded and defensive manner when questioned regarding interactions or relationships with the patient
- changing dress style for work when working with the patient
- receiving gifts or continuing contact or communication with the patient after discharge
- denying the fact that the patient is, in fact, a patient
- acting or feeling possessive about the patient
- giving special attention or treatment to a patient that differs from that given to others
- denying that you have crossed the boundary from a therapeutic to a nontherapeutic relationship.

So what do you do if you become aware of feelings of sexual attraction to a patient? Discuss such feelings with a supervisor or trusted colleague. Arrange to transfer the care of that patient to another nurse. In addition to recognizing that such feelings are neither wrong nor abnormal, you should seek help to understand and resolve them.

This doesn't mean that a nurse can never date or marry a former patient. The key word here is *former.* Some of the important factors that need to considered when thinking about entering into such a relationship would be:

- What is the length of time between the nurse-patient relationship and the dating?
- Is there still a power imbalance?

- What kind of therapy did the patient receive? There's a difference between assisting a patient with a short-term problem, such as a broken leg, and providing long-term care for a chronic condition.
- Is there a risk to the patient? In the case of Nurse Terri, she failed to consider her patient's psychological and emotional vulnerability and the long-term implications; the consequences cost her dearly.

Even in instances where no criminal accusations or charges are made, the nurse may face a civil claim of malpractice from a patient's claim that boundary violations deviate from the standard of care. Careful consideration and thoughtfulness are paramount; too many careers have been seriously damaged or destroyed because of poor judgment.

Avoiding litigation

Most nurses and nursing assistants are excellent caregivers who are experienced with doing physically difficult and emotionally draining jobs, but one of the most challenging aspects of nursing is dealing with verbal and physical aggression from patients and residents.

MANAGING STRESS

Abuse, mistreatment, or neglect may usually be prevented by understanding and changing the situation. Acknowledging that your emotions and feelings are valid is one of the first steps to controlling stressful situations that may arise out of working with challenging patients. There are a number of other ways to control stress and anger, after you've acknowledged your feelings. First, take a few deep breaths and reassess the situation. Approach an aggressive patient calmly. Call for help at the first sign of trouble. Remain calm, never argue with a patient, and never force a patient to do anything against his will.

START WITH PREVENTION

Prevention is the best plan in ensuring staff and patient safety. To untrained observers, the instinctual reaction would be to avoid, ignore, or flee from acts of aggression. Proper training, which identifies types and levels of aggressive behavior, helps to confront and control aggression problems immediately. Direct patient-care nursing staff and support staff who are present on the unit should receive frequent training that includes learning how to communicate problems among themselves in language that's simple, consistent, and easily understood. Training decreases fear and hostility and educates staff members on how to maintain a professional, therapeutic environment.

Identifying potential problems early is key to preventing explosive situations and maintaining order. Regular staff meetings, with postincident review and evaluation, can help educate everyone about what could have been handled differently and what was done right. Discussions should include behavior modification and management techniques that could have been used. Similarly, litigation arising from negligence can be avoided by learning patients' rights, adhering to standards of nursing care, and documentation. Standards of nursing care can be found in recommendations of professional organizations, facility policies and job descriptions, textbooks and periodicals, federal regulations, and state nurse practice acts. Some groups that set standards for public and private health care facilities as well as home health care nursing include the American Nurses Association; the National Institutes of Health Clinical Center; the American Public Health Association, public health nursing section; the National League for Nursing; and the National League for Nursing Accrediting Commission. The standards for health care facilities are set forth by the Joint Commission on Accreditation of Healthcare Organizations and Community Health Accreditation Program.

The Federal government became deeply involved in the oversight of nursing home care with the passage of the Nursing Home Reform Amendments of the Omnibus Budget Reconciliation Act (OBRA) of 1987. The nursing home amendments of OBRA (1987) provide specific guidance about what caregivers must document. Every long-term care facility is required to document a comprehensive assessment and care plan for each resident to ensure that the resident's abilities don't diminish, if avoidable. Facilities must maintain the highest practical physical, mental, and psychological status for each resident.

Congress also set forth specific patient rights regarding abuse and the use of restraints:

- The right to be free from physical or mental abuse, corporal punishment, involuntary seclusion, or disciplinary use of restraints.
- The right to be free from restraints used for the convenience of the staff rather than the well-being of the resident.
- The right to have restraints used only under orders written by a physician or nurse to treat a resident's medical symptoms and ensure his safety and the safety of others.
- The right to be given psychopharmacologic medication only as ordered by a physician as a part of a written care plan for a specific medical symptom, with annual review for appropriateness by an independent, external expert.

THE IMPORTANCE OF GOOD DOCUMENTATION

Good documentation can protect you from allegations of abuse, sexual misconduct, mistreatment, and neglect and can be the basis for defending you against such allegations. Documentation, in addition to including information regarding the patient's clinical status, should also show communication of information between the staff and the patient's family members regarding advanced directives and surrogate decision-makers.

Documentation is particularly important with regard to pain management in palliative and end-of-life care, to prevent accusations or allegations such as those against nurses Anne Capute and Sharon LaDuke. There are two predominantly useful tools for nurses dealing with palliative care and hospice

patients: the first is the World Health Organization analgesic ladder, a simple, well-validated, and effective method for optimum treatment of cancer pain.

The second tool is the recognition of pain as "The Fifth Vital Sign" — the first four vital signs are blood pressure, pulse, respiratory rate, and temperature. This phrase, proposed in 1997, has been adopted by the American Pain Society to increase the awareness of pain and pain management for health care providers. Once a level of pain has been documented, appropriate pain management can begin. Because nurses are primarily responsible for the assessment and management of pain, they should be aware of the legal implications for undertreating pain. To protect yourself, document defensively by including:

- location, frequency, type, and severity of pain
- drug, dose, and route of the patient's current medications
- information gathered from the patient used to determine the type of treatment that would provide optimal pain relief
- actions taken to reduce the patient's pain and his response to them.

LESSONS IN PRACTICE Proper documentation of all patient care, treatment, and interventions is your best protection against invalid accusations, allegations, or criminal liabilities.

Nurses affect countless lives by providing a comforting, honest, human touch in times of great grief, misery, and distress; nurses immortalize this perception by developing caring relationships with patients and their families, maintaining their clinical and professional competence, knowing their legal responsibilities, and being an advocate for the patient.

Selected references

Burgess, A.W., et al. "Sexual Predators in Nursing Homes," *Journal of Psychosocial Nursing and Mental Health Services* 38(8):26-35, August 2000.

Burgess, K.L. "The Criminalizing of Long-term Care," *Provider* 27(5): 47-48, May 2001.

Carlson, E.M. "Videotaping to Protect Nursing Facility Residents: A Legal Analysis," *Journal of the American Medical Directors Association* 2(1):41-44, January-February 2001.

Crane, M. "Treating Pain: Damned If You Don't," *Medical Economics* 78(22):66-68, November 2001.

"Defending Against Sexual Assault Charges," *Nursing1999* 29(6):71, June 1999.

Dowdell E.B., and Prentky R.A. "Sexual Abuse of Nursing Home Residents," *Journal of Psychosocial Nursing and Mental Health Services* 38(6):10-18, June 2000.

Galloro, V. "Watching Out for Nursing Home Residents: Cameras Could Help Curb Abuse but Others Argue They Invade Privacy," *Modern Healthcare* 31(20):24-26, May 2001.

Greene, J. "The Medical Workplace: No Abuse Zone," *Hospitals and Health Networks* 76(3):26, 28, March 2002.

Hirst, S.P. "Resident Abuse: An Insiders Perspective," *Geriatric Nursing* 21(1):38-42, January 2000.

Marchionda, C.G. "Patient Abuse: When Prevention Strategies Fail," *Provider* 27(8):35-38, August 2001.

McCarthy, M. "Report Finds Abuse in U.S. Nursing Homes Goes Unreported and Unpunished," *Lancet* 359(9309):860, March 2002.

Michael, J.E. "What Home Healthcare Nurses Should Know About Fraud and Abuse," *Home Healthcare Nurse* 17(9):564-72, September 1999.

Neumann, J.L. "Ethical Issues Confronting Oncology Nurses," *Nursing Clinics of North America* 36(4): 827-41, December 2001.

Pasero, C., and McCaffery, M. "The Undertreatment of Pain," *AJN* 101(11):62-65, November 2001.

"'Reckless' Neglect of Elders Violates Elder Abuse Act," *Regan Report on Nursing Law* 39(11):1, April 1999.

Taylor, K.J. "Unmasking Fraud and Abuse. The Pursuit is On Via Internal Compliance Programs," *Contemporary Longterm Care* 24(2):34-36, 38, February 2001.

"Were Nurses Fired for Refusing To Participate in Fraud?" *Nursing Law's Regan Report* 42(9):1, February 2002.

West, J.C. "Hospital May Be Liable for Actions of Nurse Who Molested Child: *E.P. v. McFadden,* So.2d, 2000 WL 303063, No. 298 (Ct. Civ. App. Ala. March 24, 2000)," *Journal of Healthcare Risk Management* 21(2): 46-47, Spring 2001.

ADVOCACY, ETHICS, AND LEGAL DUTIES

I N PRACTICE, nurses find themselves at the center of the confluence of multiple independent and interdependent issues that include professional obligations and personal ***ethics.*** For example, ethical dilemmas may arise when the nurse finds herself in the middle of conflicting duties and responsibilities to the patient, her employer, her peers, and herself. Ethical dilemmas can involve diverse problems, from patient advocacy to whether to report a colleague's inappropriate conduct. You need to find a way to understand and balance these issues and potential conflicts and know your legal responsibilities.

Case studies

The following hypothetical cases illustrate the nurse's duty in ethical situations.

CASE 1

Marjie May, a registered nurse, has worked at the Reproductive Sci-

ences Center (RSC) of the University Research Hospital in a large city for 6 years. The RSC has a reputation for using cutting-edge technology and has received many public and privately funded grants for developing innovative procedures and techniques to help couples with infertility problems. The RSC has sperm and egg banks that provide semen and ova for the artificial inseminations and in vitro fertilization (IVF) procedures conducted at the center. As a circulating nurse at RSC, Nurse May assists in routine IVF procedures.

One day, Nurse May's closest friend, a technician in the IVF laboratory where the eggs are fertilized, tells her that Dr. Floral, head of RSC and the person most responsible for its funding, has been experimenting with somatic cell nuclear transfer technique and that he's planning to use cloned embryos for one of the IVF procedures that Nurse May is to assist with the next morning. The woman to be implanted with the cloned embryo thinks that she's getting an IVF embryo from one of her own eggs harvested ear-

173

lier and fertilized by the sperm of an unknown donor.

Ms. May believes that not telling the truth to the woman is a violation of the principles of veracity and informed consent. Before the center closes for the day, Ms. May expresses her concerns about the ethics of the procedure to the nurse-manager. The nurse-manager states that because the woman didn't know the semen donor, not knowing that it was a cloned embryo was basically the same thing.

The nurse-manager also reminds Nurse May that Dr. Floral is the main authority at the center and that questioning him and going against his wishes by telling the woman the full facts might result in Nurse May's termination. Moreover, revealing the cloning techniques used at RSC might jeopardize the center's funding and close it permanently because the government has banned human cloning. The nurse-manager reasons, "If the center shuts down, we won't be able to help any of those sad couples who come here with infertility problems. Do you want that to happen?"

Nurse May has difficult ethical and legal decisions to make in this case. Would she be acting as an advocate knowing that the patient's right to informed consent was denied? Would she be held liable knowing that a true informed consent was not obtained? What about her concerns regarding her facility?

CASE 2

Linda Beatty is a nurse on a medical-surgical unit; she's friendly with one of her fellow nurses on the unit, Joy DeBeers. In March,

Nurse Beatty observed Nurse DeBeers slurring her words and falling asleep at work. Nurse DeBeers' behavior continued for a few weeks, and Ms. Beatty began to notice that Nurse DeBeers' postoperative patients are having more complaints of pain than other postoperative patients. She suspects that Nurse DeBeers is stealing the patients' narcotics.

In early April, Nurse Beatty confronts Nurse DeBeers with her suspicion, and DeBeers emphatically denies stealing and using narcotics. Nurse DeBeers is so upset with the accusation that she threatens Nurse Beatty with a defamation suit if she continues to pursue her concerns and act on her suspicions.

In mid-April, Nurse Beatty advises her nursing supervisor of her suspicions and contacts the State Board of Nursing.

Legal issues

There's no single, all-encompassing set of guidelines to help nurses navigate these issues. Rather, you're expected to be aware of the resources in your area — such as your state's nurse practice act, practice standards, ethical codes, hospital ethics committees, and ethical theories. You should be able to distinguish nursing ethics and the *law* so that choices, decisions, and implementations (both actions and inactions) can be accomplished for and on behalf of the patient. (See *Nursing ethics and the law.*)

Nursing ethics and the law

When you make decisions, your choices and actions should consider — and, ideally, fulfill — three criteria:

- They should be the best practice clinically.
- They should be legally within the scope of policies, procedures, and acts.
- They should be morally the right thing to do.

However, ethics, law, and best practice don't always coincide. Certain actions may be considered by some people to be morally or legally ambiguous. Each type of situation shown below can present potential moral dilemmas for nurses.

ETHICAL	**UNETHICAL**

Legal

Type 1: Actions of this type are the ideal — ethical and legal, they aren't always free from complications and inconveniences. *Example:* While prepping and medicating a patient for surgery, a nurse realizes that the patient doesn't want the operation, but has given consent only because her husband insisted. Because this isn't a valid consent, the nurse contacts the patient's physician, even though this action will alter surgical schedules and planned outcomes.

Type 2: Actions of this type might be considered unethical, but are legal. *Example:* A nurse caring for a 12-year-old cancer patient learns that he has accepted the fact that he's dying and wants to stop chemotherapy. His parents have consented to try a new, aggressive course of chemotherapy. The nurse goes ahead and administers the chemotherapy as ordered by the physician.

Illegal

Type 3: Actions of this type might be considered ethical by some, but are nevertheless illegal. *Example:* A nurse is caring for an elderly patient with dementia and cancer. The patient's husband asks for information about "terminal sedation" — what type and how much medication could be used to bring about a peaceful death. The nurse gives him this information, and arranges for the patient to be discharged home in her husband's care.

Type 4: Actions of this type are illegal and unethical. *Example:* A physician informs a nurse that he routinely prescribes antidepressants for every new resident admitted to a nursing home. If residents ask about the medication, he instructs the nurse to say, "This is just a pill your physician ordered," because telling them more might upset them. The nurse follows the physician's orders because he's politically powerful and she doesn't want to cross him.

DEFINITIONS

Familiarity with the language of ethics ensures uniformity and consistency when you're communicating. The following is a list of frequently used terms and definitions in ethics.

● *Ethics* is the area of philosophic study that examines values, actions, and choices to determine right and wrong.

● *Normative ethics* presents standards of right or good action for the guidance and evaluation of conduct.

● *Descriptive ethics* is a factual investigation of moral behavior and beliefs.

● *Laws* are binding rules of conduct authored and enforced by formal authorities, such as legislatures, courts, and governmental agencies.

● *Rights* are entitlements that one deserves according to just claims, legal guarantees, or moral principles. For every right, there's a correlative duty or obligation.

● *Morals* are fundamental standards of right and wrong that an individual learns and internalizes. An individual's moral orientation is generally based on religious and personal beliefs.

● *Values* are ideals or concepts that give meaning to the individual's life and are commonly derived from societal norms, religion, and family orientation.

● ***Moral dilemmas*** arise when two or more clear ethical principles apply, but support mutually inconsistent courses of action.

● *Moral distress* occurs when an individual knows and wants to take the right ethical action, but can't do so because of real or perceived system constraints or pressures.

ETHICAL PRINCIPLES

Principles are generally less abstract and easier to understand and apply than theories. Principles serve to specify obligations, define rights, protect interests, and establish models of conduct. There are five significant ethical principles that can assist nurses in ethical decision making and issue resolution. (See *Ethical principles in conflict: A case study.*)

● *Justice* is the principle that individuals have the right to be treated equally. An example of this principle's application is fair and just allocation of health care resources. This would include human resources (as in nursing staff), procedures, and capital (financial) resources.

● ***Beneficence*** is the principle that individuals are obligated to do what's good as opposed to what's harmful. Another way of understanding beneficence is to understand it in terms of producing a benefit. Dilemmas typically occur when health care providers, patients, and family members disagree about what course of action is "in the patient's best interest." Beneficence is usually understood as a ***duty*** that's inherent in the role of nurses, physicians, or other health care professionals — but the extent to which beneficence is a duty for health care professionals isn't a black-and-white concept. The recognized duty may be questioned in cases when a physician is the researcher and the patient is the subject, as in case 1. In these types of cases, there's a possibility for conflict because the researcher's purpose is to acquire knowledge, which may be at odds with the principle of helping the patient.

Ethical principles in conflict: A case study

Nurses commonly identify ethical principles, such as beneficence, nonmaleficence, autonomy, justice, and fidelity, and strive to honor them in making ethical decisions and choosing courses of action. This way of making ethical decisions is called principlism. It's effective only as long as ethical principles aren't in conflict. In the reality of a nurse's daily responsibilities, ethical principles can — and typically do — conflict with each other.

ETHICAL PRINCIPLES	ETHICAL ISSUE
The principle of beneficence	A 45-year-old patient is brought by ambulance to the emergency department. He's anxious, pale, diaphoretic, and complains of severe substernal pain. An assessment, electrocardiogram, and other initial tests are inconclusive to rule out myocardial infarction. The patient receives medication for pain and is admitted to the chest pain clinic for further observation. After 30 minutes, the patient tells his nurse he's pain-free.
The principle of autonomy	This patient insists that because he's now feeling fine again, he's leaving the hospital because he absolutely has to be at an important business meeting. He says he has already called a taxi.
Beneficence and autonomy conflict	The nurse tells the physician, who orders her to convince the patient to stay in the hospital for his safety and well-being. How should the nurse interpret and carry out the physician's order while respecting her patient's autonomy? Does "convince" mean "coerce"? Even if the patient is willing to sign out against medical advice, is letting him leave the right thing to do?

● **Nonmaleficence** is the principle of the avoidance of harm. These issues often involve a nurse's responsibility to "blow the whistle" if she sees others compromising the patient's safety. The principle of nonmaleficence is the second duty imposed on nurses, physicians, and other health care workers. This principle can be violated in many ways; for example, a nurse who abuses a chemical substance (either narcotics or alcohol) while she's on duty intentionally compromises the patient's safety. The principle can also be violated when there's no malice or intention to do harm; for example, a nurse's careless or negligent actions can result in a medication error that harms the patient. If the error results in an unavoidable patient injury, the nurse violated the principle of nonmaleficence. This principle doesn't demand perfection; it's recognized that the results of treatment are often uncertain and that human beings, who are fallible, make and act on decisions that may be unwise. Professional organizations expect members to uphold standards of conduct or performance that, at minimum, require members to possess the knowledge and skills relevant to the proper discharge of their duties. The legal profession defines these as standards of due care; failure to meet these standards is cause for legal maleficence.

● *Autonomy* is the principle that individuals have the right to self-determination, freedom, and independence. For example, when a patient executes a living will, he's exercising his right to autonomy. A nurse applies and respects the principle of autonomy when she has the patient direct and take responsibility for his own care.

● *Fidelity* is the principle that individuals are obligated to be faithful to their commitments. Dilemmas of fidelity may include the extent and limits of a nurse's role and duties to a patient that might conflict with other duties, such as to the hospital or physician. Fidelity also involves *confidentiality* — respecting privileged information — a patient's right to privacy must be balanced against society's right to be informed of potential threats to public health. Last, fidelity involves a commitment to *veracity* — telling the truth by fully informing a patient of his medical condition.

Ethical conflicts

Today, the ethical commitment nurses bring to their work affects patients and their families, colleagues, and the health care delivery system as a whole. As nurses gain power and influence, they're becoming a more visible force in resolving the ethical dilemmas that confront modern health care. Three ethical responsibilities of the professional nurse include patient advocacy, blowing the whistle on misconduct by colleagues, and responding to the problem of substance abuse among coworkers.

PATIENT ADVOCACY

Most health care providers interpret patient advocacy as informing, advising, or counseling the patient to facilitate his autonomy as well as his recovery. The patient advocacy movement began in the early 1970s, with the nurse's role described vaguely as an assertion of ethico-legal responsibility.

During the 1980s, some questioned whether nurses had a right to advocate on a patient's behalf and many nurses experienced a backlash from acting as patient advocates. Despite concerns that patient advocacy might be used as a tool to advance a nurse's self-interest, the practice was legitimized as part of the nursing role when it was included in college nursing curricula.

In the 1990s, ethical decision-making and autonomy for nurses became a major theme, linked specifically with advocacy. Nursing literature and curricula defined patient advocacy as a nursing role that provided a great deal of credibility and visibility for nurses.

Nurses now understand that their professional role is multidimensional and includes being a patient advocate, even when there's significant risk, peril, or pressure for the nurse. Patient advocacy is seen as a mandate in nursing ethical codes. In fact, in most states, the nurse can be subject to administrative discipline from her state board of nursing, if there's a meritorious claim against her for placing the patient in harm's way.

Acting as a patient advocate

Acting as a *patient advocate* is undoubtedly one of your most important moral obligations. When a patient must make a decision regarding his care, it's your responsibility to help him in ways that enhance his values, priorities, freedom, dignity, and *quality of life.* As an advocate, you must never impose your own agenda or values on a patient. By listening carefully to the patient and asking thoughtful questions, you may be able to help the patient and his family make a decision.

A patient advocate should also seek to protect a patient's rights from infringement. (See *Interpreting patients' rights,* page 180.) The patient's right to informed consent was the issue Nurse May needed to deal with in case 1. Nurse May could, in fact, have been held liable if it was discovered that she allowed the procedure to go forward despite the fact she knew the patient hadn't been informed. Other patient rights that nurses are required to advocate include the right to privacy, and to refuse treatment.

Guidelines for advocating patient's rights

The best way for you to act as an advocate for the patient is to become familiar with your employer's stated policy on the patient's rights. If no such stated policy exists, consider the National League for Nursing (NLN) position statement on the role of nursing in the patient's rights. You may want to make a copy of the patient's bill of rights and talk to your nurse-manager about implementing it at your facility.

The NLN encourages you to view the patient as a partner in the health care process. In planning his care, recognize his right to participate in decisions. Help him set realistic goals for his health care, and teach him the various approaches he can use to achieve them.

LESSONS IN PRACTICE Throughout the decision-making process, contine to assess the patient's understanding of his illness. When he needs and wants more information, first determine whether you or the physician should provide it. Then, let the patient participate in the development of his care plan, which must address the patient's unique needs as well as his rights.

WHISTLE-BLOWING

Whistle-blowing refers to an employee's disclosure of illegal, immoral, or illegitimate practices under an employer's control. The American Nurses Association's (ANA) Code for Nurses outlines the

Interpreting patients' rights

The theory of patients' rights is clear, but the practice is full of conflict. In defending a patient's rights, you might risk exceeding the bounds of nursing practice.

Consider the case of *Tuma v. Board of Nursing* (1979). A patient with myelogenous leukemia was admitted to an Idaho hospital for chemotherapy. Although she had agreed to this treatment, she was openly distressed about it. Instead of asking her physician about alternative treatment, she asked Jolene Tuma, RN, MSN, a nursing instructor at the College of Southern Idaho, who supervised nursing students at the hospital.

Ms. Tuma told the patient, in detail, about alternative treatments. She discussed Laetrile therapy and various natural food and herbal remedies, comparing their adverse effects with those of chemotherapy. She also gave the patient the name of a therapist who practiced alternative treatments and offered to arrange an appointment.

Ms. Tuma didn't encourage the patient to alter her treatment plan or indicate that alternative treatments were better than the prescribed therapy or would cure her.

At the patient's request, Ms. Tuma also discussed the alternative treatments with the patient's son and daughter-in-law. They told the patient's physician and, as a result, he interrupted the chemotherapy until he could discuss the situation with the patient. The next day the patient again agreed to undergo chemotherapy. Two weeks later, she went into a coma and died.

The patient's physician demanded that the hospital remove Ms. Tuma from her teaching position at the college. At the hospital's request, the board of nursing conducted an investigation and hearing. The board interpreted Ms. Tuma's behavior as unprofessional. They agreed that she had interfered with the physician-patient relationship and suspended her nursing license for 6 months.

Ms. Tuma appealed, lost the appeal, and appealed again. This time, 3 years after the incident, the Idaho State Supreme Court declared her not guilty of unprofessional conduct. The Court ruled that the Idaho Nurse Practice Act neither clearly defined unprofessional conduct nor provided guidelines for avoiding it.

Unanswered questions

In failing to define the nurse's specific role in upholding a patient's right to information, the decision left several troubling questions unanswered.

For example, Ms. Tuma's patient asked her, not the physician, for information about alternative therapies. The physician testified that he wasn't knowledgeable about these therapies. If a physician can't or won't answer such questions, does the patient have the right to get answers from a nurse? Until the courts or legislatures address such questions, you won't find easy answers.

nurse's obligation to report acts of **negligence** and **incompetence** by other health care providers. It states that "the nurse acts to safeguard the patient and public when health care and safety are affected by incompetent, unethical, or illegal practice by any person."

ANA guidelines on reporting incompetent, unethical, or illegal practices identify helpful parameters for judging problematic conduct. Incompetent nursing practice is measured by nursing standards, unethical practice is evaluated in light of the Code for Nurses, and illegal practice is identified in terms of violations of the law. As a patient advocate, you must be willing to take appropriate action — in short, to blow the whistle.

When to blow the whistle

A health care professional who makes a mistake usually wants to ensure that it won't happen again. Correcting an error usually involves admitting the mistake, expressing honest regret, and completing an incident report. At times, though, you may encounter a health care professional who makes repeated mistakes, attempts to cover them up or minimize them, and engages in suspect or misleading behaviors. To uphold the ethical standards of your profession, you need to blow the whistle.

Implications of whistle-blowing

Many nurses equate whistle-blowing with heroic self-sacrifice: a moral victory in the midst of a professional defeat. In fact, some nurses have had their reputations tarnished, lost their jobs, or been named in libel suits after reporting professional misconduct. Fortunately, such bitter retaliation isn't the norm. Keep in mind, however, that the higher the professional standing of the individual who commits misconduct, the greater the risk you face when you need to blow the whistle. (See *Whistle-blowing: A systematic approach,* page 182.)

Reporting nurse misconduct

Usually, channels exist at health care facilities through which you can report the misconduct of another nurse or nursing assistant without fear of reprisal. Often, a nurse-manager and the personnel office assume joint responsibility for investigating allegations of misconduct. For you, the only drawback is animosity from the affected staff member — and possibly from her acquaintances or sympathizers. The benefits, however, include correcting an injustice, preventing future harm, and strengthening your sense of moral integrity.

Reporting medical or management misconduct

If you report the misconduct of a physician, nursing supervisor, nurse-manager, or member of the facility's administration, expect stiffer resistance and, possibly, more severe retaliation, especially if management has cooperated in concealing the misconduct. Be prepared for a lengthy and hard-fought battle. That's because the accused professional may attempt to discredit you — or have you terminated — rather than face the allegations honestly.

Consider the case of Barry Adams, a nurse in Boston, who was

Whistle-blowing: A systematic approach

Like other nursing actions, whistle-blowing can be carried out successfully if it's planned, systematic, and purposeful.

Gathering facts

Begin by gathering all the facts, and then put in writing the misconduct you want to report. Be sure to include the incident's date and time, the person or people involved, and the source of your information. Record just the facts. Above all, avoid accusations and personal opinions.

Stating the problem

Clearly state the problem and identify causative factors. Was incompetence or negligence involved? Were supplies adequate? Did equipment malfunction? Was facility policy at fault?

When answering these questions, try to eliminate your personal biases. If possible, review the problem with a trusted colleague.

Determining your objective

State your objective in confronting the problem. For example, you may want to eliminate threats to patient safety; eliminate illegal, immoral, or illegitimate practices; uphold professional ethical standards; or affect changes in facility policy.

Confronting the problem

Confront the person who committed the misconduct in a constructive, nonthreatening way. Express your concerns and ask for an explanation of the incident. Seek reassurance that the problem will be addressed.

Making your decision

After a reasonable duration, determine whether the problem has been corrected. If it hasn't, identify the pros and cons of whistle-blowing. The pros include correction of a harmful or potentially harmful situation, retained moral integrity, and an enhanced sense of moral accountability. The cons include alienation, stress and, possibly, loss of reputation, professional standing, and job. After you weigh the pros and cons, talk over the issue of whistle-blowing with your attorney.

Next, realistically appraise your situation. Will you be able to cope if you blow the whistle? Are you secure professionally and financially? Do you have the support of your family, colleagues, or administration? How much help can you count on?

Make your decision based on your analysis of the severity of the incident, the consequences of whistle-blowing, and your resources. If you elect to blow the whistle, carefully devise a strategy that follows facility channels.

If you fail to get satisfaction through facility channels, consider consulting professional organizations, regulatory agencies and, as a last resort, the press. Be sure to document each step you take.

terminated after reporting allegedly unsafe working conditions to the administration of the now-closed Youville Health Care Center in Cambridge. The National Labor Relations Board validated his complaints of retaliation, and then he issued a complaint with the Massachusetts Board of Nursing (Docket No. RN-99-183) against one of the center's executives, Ann Poster, alleging unprofessional and unethical conduct in connection with allegedly unsafe patient conditions at the center. In September 1999, the Massachusetts Board of Nursing dismissed these allegations.

Working through channels

Whistle-blowing can be pursued by one of two ways: by proceeding through the facility's chain of command or by going public (which includes going to outside regulatory agencies). You should make every effort to correct the situation internally before going public. If you work successfully through the chain of command, you should be able to accomplish your goals with a minimum of exposure. Ethically, you owe management an opportunity to change the situation before going public. For your own legal protection, you should maintain a record of your efforts to work through channels before considering more drastic measures.

If you fail to get satisfaction from the facility's chain of command, contact the appropriate regulatory agencies. Contact the media only as a last resort.

Providing adequate documentation

Document your disclosure carefully. Write a clear, objective summary of the relevant facts. Explain why the information is significant and what needs to be done. Avoid focusing on personalities because personal accusations detract from the disclosure and may invite a lawsuit for *libel* or *slander.* Have other professionals verify the information, if possible, to lend objectivity to the information and, possibly, shield you from retaliation.

Surviving the setbacks

No matter how carefully you approach whistle-blowing and how much backup you have, be prepared for possible retaliation. Management may find it more convenient to attack the whistle-blower than to address the problem. Colleagues may start giving you the cold shoulder, and you might even experience overt harassment. Rumors that you're dishonest or incompetent may spread through the facility.

To protect yourself and to maintain pressure on management, meticulously document everything, including continued incidents of incompetence or negligence. Consider photocopying all incident reports you file. Be especially vigilant in your practice, and document your nursing actions carefully. Your employer may try to distract attention from the disclosure by portraying you as a troublemaker; to counter this tactic, maintain friendly, diplomatic relations with as many colleagues as possible.

If you anticipate that whistle-blowing will cause severe personal hardship, consider mapping out a self-protection strategy. Retain an attorney who will provide you with competent legal advice throughout your ordeal. Seek out friends and colleagues who have the moral integrity to stand behind you.

SUBSTANCE ABUSE

An estimated 7% of the 1.9 million nurses in the United States are addicted to alcohol or drugs. In one state study, researchers found that more than 90% of disciplinary hearings for nurses in the state were related to alcohol and drug abuse. These statistics aren't surprising in light of the high stress levels in nursing today. Nurses can experience frustration and feelings of powerlessness when trying to act as patient advocates. Frequent floating to unfamiliar units, unrealistic workloads, and long or double shifts may bring on fatigue and loneliness. Many nurses today must shoulder tremendous family and financial obligations while trying to meet professional demands. And, of course, nurses aren't immune to the harsh social realities of modern life. Combined with the availability of controlled substances, such stressors commonly lead a nurse to substance abuse.

In the past, nurses who were caught abusing drugs or alcohol were punished. The prevailing ethic held that a nurse who abused drugs violated the public trust and the standards of her profession and deserved to be subject to strong disciplinary action. Nursing administrators were expected to report suspected substance abusers to their state nursing board. The board would then investigate the allega-

tion and, if it found the nurse guilty, impose punishment that commonly included revocation of her license.

In practice, however, many administrators didn't report substance abuse, but chose instead to terminate the nurse. In addition, colleagues of a suspected substance abuser commonly didn't report their suspicions because they knew the nurse's job would be in jeopardy. Aware of the harsh treatment that awaited them, nurses who abused drugs or alcohol switched jobs frequently rather than endure the repercussions that would follow an admission of abuse.

Helping the abuser

From an ethical viewpoint, the punitive approach to substance abuse left much to be desired. Administrators who fired a substance abuser abnegated their ethical responsibility to help nurses in need and to prevent qualified nurses from abandoning the profession. Colleagues who didn't report substance abuse ignored the best interests of the addicted nurse and her patients. The substance abuser usually switched jobs rather than ask for help. She had little motivation to change, knowing that she was unlikely to receive understanding or rehabilitation.

Fortunately, society is learning to view substance abuse as a treatable disorder, and the emphasis is on rehabilitating chemically dependent nurses rather than punishing them. Within the nursing profession, there's greater understanding of the importance of peer support for the nurse who's struggling with addiction. Nurse practice acts commonly include provisions that encourage or mandate chemically dependent nurses to complete a treatment program.

Many facilities now have policies for dealing with substance abuse among employees, from initial reporting through rehabilitation and returning to work. In addition, treatment programs have become commonplace, and associations for recovering nurses are available to provide needed support.

Recognizing substance abuse

Be aware that allegations of substance abuse are serious and potentially damaging. To make an accurate assessment, you need to be familiar with the signs of substance abuse.

Signs of drug or alcohol abuse may include:
- rapid mood swings, usually from irritability or depression to elation
- frequent absences, lateness, and use of private quarters such as bathrooms
- frequent volunteering to administer medications
- excessive errors or problems with controlled substances, such as reports of broken vials or spilled drugs
- illogical or sloppy documentation
- inability to meet deadlines or minimum job requirements
- avoidance of new and challenging assignments
- increased errors in treatment, particularly in dosage computation
- poor personal hygiene and appearance
- inability to concentrate or remember details
- alcohol odor on the breath
- slurred speech, unsteady gait, flushed face, or red eyes

- discrepancies in narcotics supplies detected at the end of the nurse's shift
- narcotics signed out to patients only on the nurse's shift
- patient complaints of no relief from narcotics supposedly administered when the nurse is on duty
- preference for working alone or on the night shift, when supervision is minimal
- social withdrawal
- memory loss
- alcohol-induced complications, including jaundice, bruises (from falls), and delirium.

Reporting substance abuse

Nurse Beatty, in case 2, had a clear duty to her patients and to her employer to report her suspicion and to provide support for that suspicion. Most state practice acts for all health care disciplines require reporting of certain observed or suspected situations, such as coworker impairment, elder abuse, child abuse, abuse of mentally ill patients, and sexual abuse. Practice acts that require this type of reporting provide penalties, including criminal and disciplinary actions, for a professional who knows, observes, or suspects these situations, but doesn't report them.

If you detect signs of substance abuse, your first step is to document them. Include the time, date, and place of the incident; a description of what happened; and names of witnesses. Be sure to omit personal opinions and judgments. Instead, for example, say, "At about 9 p.m. on November 15, 2001, Mrs. Fox in room 501 told me that my injections of morphine were much better than those the other nurse gives. I asked what she meant. She told me that June Barrett's injections never seemed to take away her pain, but that mine always did. Two nights later, at 10:15 p.m., I went to use the restroom. When I opened the door, I saw June Barrett injecting a solution into her thigh using a hospital syringe. She told me to get out. I did. We didn't talk about it afterward."

Never confront or accuse the suspected nurse on your own. After you've documented the incident, discuss it with your nurse-manager. She'll need to gather additional information by examining patient charts, medication records (especially for narcotics), and reports from patients and other nurses. After the nurse-manager completes this review, she'll try to determine if the evidence corroborates your report.

● ▶▶ **LESSONS IN PRACTICE** Document and report your suspicions. You have a legal and ethical obligation to report suspected impairment on the job. Your license is at stake if you don't.

Confronting the substance abuser

If the nurse-manager concludes that substance abuse is likely, she'll need to confront the nurse with the facts and explain the options. In most facilities, these options include treatment and perhaps eventual reinstatement in her position. If you're asked to be present for this confrontation, keep in mind that you best fulfill your moral obligation to the substance abuser by being honest, compassionate, and nonjudgmental and by expressing your willingness to help. Expect that she'll feel threatened and may

attempt to deny her condition, even if the facts are fully substantiated.

In most substance abuse cases, if the nurse is willing to enter a treatment program and successfully completes it, no disciplinary action will be taken against her. If the nurse refuses to enter treatment, she may be reported to the state board of nursing, suspended, or terminated.

The road back

In most instances, the recovering nurse can return to work. She may be placed under a special contract that stipulates conditions for continued employment. These conditions may include:
● attending weekly meetings with a counselor
● participating in a 12-step program and meetings with other recovering nurses
● submitting to random blood and urine screenings
● remaining drug-free.

The chemically dependent nurse's colleagues must use their professional training to try to understand her condition. Coworkers play a crucial role in the recovering nurse's ultimate success or failure. When recovering from addiction, a person's needs include:
● finding ways to improve self-esteem, including assertiveness training
● developing a stronger support system
● developing stress management and coping techniques
● learning to come to terms with past traumatic experiences such as physical or sexual abuse.

Welcoming a recovering nurse back to the work setting and offering support during the critical transition period is as important as detecting and reporting signs of abuse. From an ethical point of view, working with a colleague who's a substance abuser can be frustrating and uncomfortable, but helping a nurse recognize her problem and begin the process of recovery is an act of significant moral courage and humanity.

A*voiding litigation*

Your duty as a patient advocate should be a top priority in your daily practice. From checking physician orders for appropriateness to supporting a patient's right to refuse treatment, you should continuously advocate that the patient must always remain the primary focus in decisions about health care access, quality, and cost.

In instances of whistle-blowing and impaired provider status, keep in mind that you may be held liable for information you were aware of but failed to report. You have duties to the patients and the facility in which you practice as well as to the profession and practice of nursing. In impaired provider cases, the nurse practice acts in all states address the responsibility of all nurses to report observed substance abuse. In fact, if a nurse observes (or has reason to believe or suspect) another nurse abusing drugs on the job or stealing a patient's drugs and doesn't report this, she's subject to disciplinary proceedings.

Today's nurses are involved in a complex health care landscape. The practice of clinical nursing is only one aspect that the nurse has to master. Nurses should take proactive steps to understand their role as a patient advocate and to understand their legal duties and obligations. A comprehensive understanding of these concepts will aid in decision-making and in managing actual and potential risks.

S*elected references*

Adams, J. "Professional Ethics. A Case Study of Infusion Nurse Consultants," *Journal of Intravenous Nursing* 23(6):371-77, November-December 2000.

Coverston, C., and Rogers, S. "Winding Roads and Faded Signs: Ethical Decision Making in a Postmodern World," *Journal of Perinatal and Neonatal Nursing* 14(2):1-11, September 2000.

Frais, A. "Whistleblowing Heroes — Boon or Burden?" *Bulletin of Medical Ethics* (170):13-19, August 2001.

Galloro, V. "Shelter for Whistleblowers. Appeals Court Reinstates False Claims Act Lawsuit," *Modern Healthcare* 32(4):18, January 2002.

Hewitt, J. "A Critical Review of the Arguments Debating the Role of the Nurse Advocate," *Journal of Advanced Nursing* 37(5):439-45, March 2002.

Milton, C.L. "Ethical Codes and Principles: The Link to Nursing Theory," *Nursing Science Quarterly* 12(4):290-91, October 1999.

Mitchell, G.J., and Bournes, D.A. "Nurse as Patient Advocate? In Search of Straight Thinking," *Nursing Science Quarterly* 13(3):204-209, July 2000.

Turkoski, B.B. "Home Care and Hospice Ethics: Using the Code for Nurses as a Guide," *Home Healthcare Nurse* 18(5):308-16, May 2000.

LEGAL RISKS OF UNDERSTAFFING

NURSING SHORTAGES as well as ongoing staffing problems, including *floating*, mandatory overtime, and other employment-related issues, make nurses increasingly vulnerable to lawsuits, job termination, or other disciplinary actions. Today, more than ever, you need to understand your rights as a nurse-employee. You need to know how to assert your rights and make your employer aware of your expectations.

Case studies

The cases discussed in this chapter will show you pitfalls to avoid, particularly in relation to staffing and other employment issues.

CASE 1

The decision in the landmark case of *Darling v. Charleston Community Memorial Hospital* (1965) was based partly on the issue of understaffing. A young man broke his leg while playing football and was taken to Charleston's emergency department, where the on-call physician set and cast his leg. The patient began to complain of pain almost immediately. Later, his toes grew swollen and dark, then cold and insensitive, and a stench pervaded his room. Nurses checked the leg only a few times per day and failed to report its worsening condition. When the cast was removed 3 days later, the necrotic condition of the leg was apparent. After making several surgical attempts to save the leg, the surgeon amputated below the knee.

After an out-of-court settlement with the physician who had applied the cast, the court found the hospital liable for failing to have enough specially trained nurses available at all times to recognize the patient's serious condition and to alert the medical staff. (See *Important court rulings*.)

CASE 2

In the case of *Merritt v. Karcioglu* (1996), a 92-year-old woman was admitted to a cardiac care unit for the treatment of heart failure and pulmonary edema. She was being given Lasix and frequently wanted to go to the bathroom. Despite the fact that she had been told repeatedly not to get out of bed unassisted, the patient continued to get out of bed without asking for help.

The nurses and the patient's physician were aware of the fact that she wasn't fully oriented because she thought she was at home despite being reminded repeatedly that she was in the hospital's intensive care unit (ICU). Even though the nurses carefully documented the fact that the patient repeatedly tried to get out of bed without assistance and all attempts to change this behavior were unsuccessful, the physician decided not to order restraints for the patient.

Three hours after the physician had been in to assess the patient, she got out of bed; once again, she thought she was at home and wanted to go to her kitchen to fix dessert for her family. In her effort to get out of bed, the patient fell and sustained a fractured right hip, which required open reduction and internal fixation.

The patient recovered from her fractured hip and was discharged to her home only to return to the hospital 6 months later, at which time she died from complications related to heart failure. After the patient died, her family decided to sue the hospital because she had fallen and sustained a hip fracture. This case went to trial and was then appealed to the Louisiana Court of Appeal. The court found that the physician's decision not to order restraints wasn't negligent and that the nurses weren't negligent in not requesting that the patient be restrained.

> **RELATED CASES**
>
>
> ## Important court rulings
>
> Since the *Darling* case, several similar cases have been tried — for example, *Cline v. Lun* (1973), *Sanchez v. Bay General Hospital* (1981), and *Harrell v. Louis Smith Memorial Hospital* (1990). Almost every case involved a nurse who failed to continuously monitor her patient's condition — especially his vital signs — and to report significant changes to the attending physician. In each case, the courts have emphasized:
>
> - the need for sufficient numbers of nurses to continuously monitor a patient's condition
> - the need for nurses who are specially trained to recognize signs and symptoms that require a physician's immediate intervention.

However, the court found that the hospital had been negligent and that its negligence led to the patient's fall and subsequent injury. The court's decision was influenced by the fact that the nurse assigned to the 92-year-old woman was also expected to respond to any code that was called in the ICU. The nurse had been assigned to care for the patient on a one-to-one basis because the woman needed close monitoring to maintain her physical well-being. However, at the time that the patient got out of bed, the nurse assigned to her was following hospital guidelines — assisting in a code situation that caused her to leave the patient unattended. The court stated that the hospital guidelines were inappropriate and that they were indicative of a poor staffing pattern. The court further stated that a nurse can be in only one place at a time and that the hospital requirement that the nurse assist in a code situation allowed harm to come to her assigned patient.

Staffing issues

Staffing issues abound across the country in almost every nursing care setting. They may reflect the current shortage of nurses; many agencies and facilities simply aren't able to find nurses to fill open positions. The nursing shortage has worsened a number of staffing problems, including but not limited to inappropriate nurse-patient ratios, voluntary and mandatory overtime, inappropriate floating, and lack of appropriate breaks during working hours.

Every health care facility has a responsibility to provide enough adequately trained nurses to care for the patients in its facility. If the facility can't employ the number of nurses needed to care for its patient population, it should transfer patients to other facilities and refuse to accept new admissions until it has enough staff to care for each patient in a way that will meet all expected standards of care.

The health care facility should assess the needs of current and potential patient populations for nursing care. The assessment should include the acuity level of the patients to help determine the level of nursing skills required for the care of each patient. Each agency or facility must be concerned with establishing and maintaining an acceptable nurse-patient ratio as well as ensuring that the nursing staff is trained to care for patients of various competencies. In addition, when a nursing agency or health care facility is determining its staffing needs, it should allow for well-trained and competent per diem staff to fill in staffing gaps that might occur due to an influx of patients, more patients requiring one-on-one care, staff absences (due to vacations, illnesses, or other causes), and other situations that might necessitate extra nurses or nurses to fill in for absent nurses.

Unfortunately, there's no magic formula for maintaining appropriate staffing, nor are there absolute figures for nurse-patient ratios in every health care setting. In fact, California is the only state with a law requiring specific nurse-patient ratios as a minimum standard. (See *What constitutes "adequate" staffing?*) If you're responsible for staffing your facility — or even a single unit within that facility — you should be familiar with existing standards of care relative to nurse-patient ratios and with existing standards pertaining to general staffing considerations, floating nurses to other patient care areas, mandatory overtime, and the use of per diem and agency nurses to fill staffing needs.

One source of staffing guidelines is a brochure published by the American Nurses Association (ANA). "Principles for Nurse Staffing" was developed by a 10-

What constitutes "adequate" staffing?

Unless you work in a nursing home or skilled nursing facility, determining whether your unit has too few nurses or specially trained nurses may be difficult. The few guidelines that do exist vary from state to state and are limited mainly to specialty care units (such as the intensive care unit). Even the Joint Commission on Accreditation of Healthcare Organizations (JCAHO) offers little help. The JCAHO staffing standard sets no specific nurse-patient ratios; rather, it offers the general recommendation that health care facilities provide "an adequate number of staff whose qualifications are commensurate with defined job responsibilities and applicable licensure, law and regulation, and certification."

California is the only state that requires hospitals to meet minimum nurse-patient ratios in all units, mandates additional staffing based on patient acuity, and prohibits nurses from being assigned to areas for which they lack adequate orientation or clinical training. The bill establishing these requirements was passed in October 1999, and became law in January 2002. Although other states haven't yet passed similar legislation, they may follow suit if California is able to improve staffing patterns with this law.

In the absence of well-defined staffing guidelines, the courts have had no reliable standard for ruling on cases of alleged understaffing. Each case has been decided on an individual basis.

member expert panel, with five additional contributing members. The brochure provides policy statements about staffing, including nine principles of staffing divided into three subsections: patient care unit issues, staff-related issues, and facility-related issues. The brochure can be found on-line at *www.nursingworld.org/readroom/ stffprnc.htm,* and copies can be ordered by calling ANA publications at 1-800-637-0323.

The following example illustrates various staffing issues. A 12-bed ICU needs a minimum of 6 nurses available each shift to adequately care for patients (in general, the appropriate staffing in an ICU is no

more than two patients for every nurse). However, an ICU may have, at any given time, a number of patients who require one-on-one attention. In addition, regular staff members may be absent or on vacation. Therefore, the person responsible for staffing this ICU would require extra, available, competent intensive care nurses for each shift should the need arise. This means the hospital should either have its own pool of per diem nurses who have the training and experience needed to work in an ICU and have been appropriately oriented to the ICU, or it should have established relationships with staffing agencies able to supply the hospital with competent intensive care nurses to fill in the staffing gaps. If the hospital can't maintain safe staffing levels for the number of patients in its care, it must transfer patients to other facilities and refuse new admissions.

Carrying the example a bit farther, if the same 12-bed ICU had 9 patients and 3 empty beds, a physician might want to admit another patient to the unit. If the night shift is staffed with 5 nurses, there's adequate staff to care for the current patients even if one patient needs one-on-one attention. However, if another patient were admitted to the unit or one of the five nurses were to call out sick, the hospital should be prepared with adequately trained, competent nurses to fill in.

The bottom line is that an agency or health care facility should have enough staff to meet current patient care needs and provide coverage for needed staff breaks, and it should have extra staff available on-site or on call should an emergency arise. Failure by an agency or facility to assure an appropriate level of staffing at all times is a breach in the standard of care.

UNDERSTAFFING

Understaffing occurs when the health care facility's administration fails to provide enough professionally trained personnel to meet the needs of the patient population. Most nurses are familiar with the problems that understaffing can cause.

Attorneys for the **plaintiff** frequently argue that understaffing is widespread and results in substandard bedside care, increased mis-takes and omissions, and hasty documentation — all of which increase nurses' (and their employers') liability. For example, if a patient is harmed while hospitalized and can demonstrate that the harm resulted from the hospital's failure to provide sufficient qualified personnel, the hospital may be held liable.

FLOATING

Occasionally, situations arise in which there isn't enough staff on one unit, but more staff than needed on another unit. When this occurs, some facilities want to float staff between patient care units, sending the "extra" nurses to the unit that's short-handed. A facility that floats nurses to short-staffed units should have established policy that clearly states the competencies required of nurses asked to float to a unit other than the one where they usually work. The facility should also have a contingency plan if no such nurses are available. The floating policy should also delineate the method of orientation for nurses who are floated to another unit.

In the case of *Winkelman v. Beloit Memorial Hospital* (1992), Nurse Winkelman sued Beloit Memorial Hospital for wrongful discharge after she was terminated because she refused to float to the medical-surgical and geriatric units. Nurse Winkelman had worked for the hospital for 16 years at the time of the incident that led to her discharge; during her entire employment, she had worked in the neonatal nursery. She had never been asked to float to another unit despite the fact that the hospital had a policy that nurses would be floated as needed.

RELATED CASES

Termination for refusal to float

In the case of *David W. Francis v. Memorial General Hospital* (1986), David Francis, a critical care nurse, refused to float to an orthopedic unit, where he had been assigned to function as the charge nurse. His refusal to float earned him a 2-day suspension

When Nurse Francis returned to work after his 2-day suspension, he stated that he would refuse to float again if and when he was asked to float to a unit where he didn't feel qualified to function. The hospital gave Nurse Francis the option of being oriented to all of the nursing units in the hospital to help him feel prepared to float. Nurse Francis refused this offer, and Memorial General terminated his employment.

When the court decided this case, it considered the fact that Nurse Francis had refused the option of being oriented to other units and didn't attempt to find out whether he could feel comfortable in other areas of nursing. Nurse Francis' principles regarding the issue of floating were very important to him, and he allowed these principles to preempt a compromise with the hospital on floating. Therefore, the court ruled that the termination of Nurse Francis by Memorial General Hospital was justified.

When Ms. Winkelman was asked to float from the neonatal nursery to an adult unit, she stated that she didn't feel qualified to care for adult patients and that if she agreed to float, she would be putting her patients, her nursing license, and the hospital in jeopardy. According to Nurse Winkelman, her nursing supervisor responded to her refusal to float by offering her three options: she could float as requested, find a replacement nurse to float for her, or take an unexcused absence and go home. Nurse Winkelman chose to go home rather than float.

At the time of trial, Nurse Winkelman's supervising nurse testified that she hadn't offered the option to go home, further stating that Nurse Winkelman had, in essence, abandoned her job responsibilities and had thereby resigned her position. Ms. Winkelman tried to get reinstated at Beloit, but was refused on the grounds that she had voluntarily resigned.

The court found that Ms. Winkelman had been terminated because she refused to float and awarded her $40,000 in lost wages. The court stated that Ms. Winkelman's refusal to float was reasonable in that, in the court's opinion, "the sick should be given care by those who in fact are qualified to do so," and that the mere fact that one is licensed to practice as a nurse doesn't make one qualified to practice in all areas of nursing. (See *Termination for refusal to float*.)

If a nurse is asked to accept an assignment that isn't appropriate or to float to a patient care area in

Floating: Understanding your legal responsibility

For many nurses, an order to float to an unfamiliar unit triggers worry and frustration. It may cause worry about using skills that have grown rusty or frustration at being pulled away from familiar or enjoyable work.

A necessary evil

Unfortunately, floating is necessary. Hospitals must use it to help solve their understaffing problems, and the courts sanction it as being in the public's best interest.

Exceptions

You can't refuse to float simply because you fear that the skills you need for the assignment have diminished or because you're concerned about legal risks in the assigned unit. If you do, you may be vulnerable to disciplinary action or termination by your employer. You'll need to go along with an order to float unless:

- you have a union contract that guarantees you'll always work in your specialty
- you can prove you haven't been taught to do the assigned task.

Tell your supervisor if you haven't been taught a task she has assigned you. Usually, she'll accommodate you by providing you with immediate training or changing your assignment. However, if she insists that you perform a task that you don't know how to do, refuse the assignment. If the hospital reprimands or fires you, you may be able to appeal the action taken against you in a court of law.

---

which she feels uncomfortable — either because she's unfamiliar with the unit's specialty or because the number of patients she's been asked to manage is greater than that dictated by the standard of care guidelines — she has three options (if she has no labor agreement):

- The nurse can accept the assignment. However, this may leave her open to civil liability if a patient suffers an injury that stems from an act of commission or omission by the nurse or by another employee for whom she's responsible. Furthermore, the nurse's license may be jeopardized if she knowingly accepts a role beyond her level of competence.

- She can accept the assignment, but subsequently file an appeal to try to avoid this type of problem in the future. This approach won't help if a problem occurs during the course of the assignment; however, it's always appropriate to document problems that occur as a result of an improper assignment. Such documentation may include writing a letter or memo to the staffing supervisor. The nurse should also be sure to fill out an incident report if adverse events occur as a result of the assignment.

● She can reject the assignment. This may leave the nurse vulnerable to disciplinary action — even to being terminated.

Deciding whether to accept an assignment for which you don't feel qualified or that you feel may compromise the standard of care your patients deserve is complicated. If you choose to accept the assignment, you may be putting your license at risk by performing tasks for which you aren't trained — but if you refuse it, you may jeopardize your job. Civil suits and licensure problems can result from situations in which a nurse's refusal of an assignment wasn't justified and may actually have been a breach of contract.

Some facilities suggest that a nurse who's untrained to work in a unit different from her regular unit act as a nursing assistant instead, but this should never be done. A nurse is held to the standard of care expected of a nurse, regardless of whether she has been told to float and fill in as a nursing assistant. (See *Floating: Understanding your legal responsibility.*)

BREACH OF CONTRACT

Unjustified failure to perform a contractual duty is a **breach of contract.** The breach may be considered partial; that is, only one element of the contract was breached, or substantial, in which the entire agreement was broken. If only part of the agreement was breached, the remaining contract may still be in effect. Both parties may want to continue the relationship, with some clarification. Substantial breaches, however, are never lawful, and legal damages may result. Breaches can be avoided if both parties carefully consider the terms and conditions of the contract and understand what they're promising each other.

Employee breach of contract

When you agree to perform (or not to perform) a duty or action by signing an employment contract, and you don't perform as promised, you may be in breach of the contract and subject to litigation forcing you to perform as promised. You may even be required to reimburse your employer for the cost of hiring someone to do the job and to pay his court costs and legal fees.

Of course, the terms and conditions of a contract can be changed or modified by verbal or written agreement. For example, your facility may need you to work at a different location, and may request a renegotiation or verbal modification of the original contract. If the option is available, it's better to change a contract than to breach it. Good communication may prevent a perceived breach, and renegotiation is cheaper than litigation.

Employer breach of contract

Sometimes an employer breaches a contract — for example, by failing to give you the vacation time agreed to. If you discover a breach, follow procedures outlined in your employee handbook.

Misunderstandings can usually be resolved by talking with the proper people in the chain of command (always in a professional and unemotional manner). If documents are involved, they're important proof. If you have a union con-

Charge nurse's liability

A nurse put in charge of a unit, even temporarily, may find herself personally liable in understaffing situations, including:

- She knows understaffing exists but fails to notify the hospital administration about it.
- She fails to assign her staff properly, and then also fails to supervise their actions continuously.
- She tries to perform a nursing task for which she lacks the necessary training and skills.

Viable defenses

A charge nurse isn't automatically liable for mistakes made by a nurse on her staff. Most courts won't hold the charge nurse liable unless she knew, or should have known, that the nurse who made the mistake:

- had previously made similar mistakes
- wasn't competent to perform the task
- had acted on the charge nurse's erroneous orders.

Remember, the plaintiff-patient has to prove two things: that the charge nurse failed to follow customary practices, thereby contributing to the mistake, and that the mistake actually caused the patient's injuries.

---

tract, tell your representative as soon as you're aware of the breach.

If you exhaust all channels of appeal, you may need to discuss the problem with an attorney with contract expertise, using a written log of your attempts to rectify the situation, including statements made, with dates and times.

MANDATORY OVERTIME

Another issue that frequently arises as a direct result of staffing problems is the practice of requiring mandatory overtime. Most nurses work overtime voluntarily when emergencies (such as a nurse calling in sick or unexpected admissions) necessitate additional nurses. However, when mandatory overtime becomes the rule rather than an exception to the rule, many

nurses protest that it's wrong to demand that they work overtime. For some facilities, mandatory overtime is a chronic, inappropriate response to poor staffing policies. Instead of anticipating and working to fill the needed coverage gaps, such facilities demand mandatory overtime in the form of staying past the end of a scheduled shift or overusing an on-call system.

Some nurses who have refused to work overtime because they needed to pick up children at day care or be elsewhere have been told that they would be terminated if they didn't stay and work or that choosing to leave amounted to abandoning patients. All nurses should have the right to refuse to work beyond their shift when the extension of the work day results from an avoidable understaffing problem.

A matter of safety

The use of mandatory overtime may also raise safety issues when a nurse who has already worked 12 hours is too tired to continue working safely. In addition, nurses forced to work mandatory overtime may be unhappy with the situation; their unhappiness and potential distraction may also increase the potential for errors, causing injuries to patients.

In response to the outcry regarding mandatory overtime and unsafe staffing, a bipartisan bill was introduced in the U.S. House of Representatives and the U.S. Senate on November 14, 2001, to limit mandatory overtime for nurses. It's believed that limitations on mandatory overtime will bring about a significant reduction in medical errors and an improvement in the quality of patient care. This bill, the Safe Nursing and Patient Care Act (H.R.3238/S. 1686), was still in committee as of mid-February 2002.

TEMPORARY EMPLOYEES

Another significant problem that can be caused by poor staffing is that facilities often have to hire agency nurses or traveling nurses to fill the gaps. Hiring temporary nurses presents its own unique set of challenges. Every time an agency or traveling nurse comes to a facility, the supervising nurse should provide orientation and assess the nurse's competencies before making patient care assignments. Failure on the part of the supervising nurse, who's usually the charge nurse on duty, to appropriately assess the competencies of the nurses that she supervises can

open the door to a breakdown in the standard of care, especially if the temporary nurse lacks the requisite competencies and thereby causes harm to a patient. (See *Charge nurse's liability*.)

Facility liability

Courts have assigned primary liability to health care facilities in lawsuits in which nursing understaffing is the key issue. A health care facility can be found liable for patient injuries if it accepts more patients than it or its nursing staff can accommodate. The health care facility controls the purse strings and, in the court's view, is the only party that can resolve the problem.

DEFENDING UNDERSTAFFING

Health care facilities accused of failing to maintain adequate nursing staffs have offered various defenses. Some have argued that they acted reasonably because their nurse-patient ratio was comparable to other area hospitals. This argument fails if applicable rules and regulations contradict it.

Other facilities have defended understaffing by arguing that no extra nurses were available. However, the courts have hesitated to accept this defense, especially when facilities have knowingly permitted an unsafe condition to continue for a long period. Still other facilities have excused understaffing by pleading lack of funds, but the courts have repeatedly rejected this defense.

The emergency defense

Facility liability for understaffing isn't automatic. If the facility couldn't have provided adequate staff by reasonable means — for example, because a nurse suddenly called in sick and no substitute could be found — the facility may escape liability. This is known as the **sudden emergency exception** when used as a defense during trial; that is, the emergency couldn't have been anticipated.

Except for the sudden emergency exception defense, a facility has only two alternatives for avoiding liability for understaffing: either hire sufficient personnel to staff an area adequately or else close the area or restrict the number of beds until adequate staff can be found.

Avoiding litigation

The best way to avoid litigation resulting from staffing issues is to make sure the facility's staffing needs have been accurately assessed and that all reasonable steps have been taken to fulfill those staffing needs. If the staffing needs can't be fulfilled, the facility should take immediate action to reduce the patient care load to a level that can be handled by available staff. Assuring an appropriate nurse-patient ratio will greatly enhance the safety of the patients and the quality of care at the facility.

COPING WITH A SUDDEN OVERLOAD

Like other nurses, you're probably all too familiar with understaffing. You begin your shift and suddenly

you find yourself assigned more patients than you can reasonably care for. What can you do to protect yourself?

First, make every effort to protest the overload and get it reduced. Begin by asking your supervisor or director of nursing services to supply relief. If they can't or won't, notify the facility's administration. If no one there will help either, write a memorandum detailing exactly what you did and said and the answers you received. Don't walk off the job (you could be held liable for abandonment); instead, do the best you can, prioritize your care, and utilize other members of the health care team only as allowed. (See *When coworkers put you at risk*.) After your shift is over, prepare a written report of the facts and file it with the director of nursing.

LESSONS IN PRACTICE Filing a written report doesn't guarantee that you'll be protected from liability if a patient is injured during your shift. You may still be found liable, especially if you could have foreseen and prevented the patient's injury; however, a written report will impress a jury as a sincere attempt to protect your patients. The report could also provide you with a defense if the alleged malpractice involves something you should have done but didn't because of understaffing.

CHRONIC UNDERSTAFFING

Chronic understaffing, if it occurs on your unit, presents you with a dilemma. On one hand, your conscience tells you to try your best to

EXPERT OPINION

When coworkers put you at risk

To help you steer clear of legal dangers when working with a health care team, here are some questions and answers to clarify your liability.

Can I be held liable for mistakes made by a student nurse under my supervision?

Yes, if you have primary responsibility for instructing the student and correcting her mistakes.

If a student performs tasks that only a licensed nurse should perform — with my knowledge, but without my supervision — am I guilty of breach of duty?

Yes, because as a staff nurse, you should know that a student nurse can perform nursing tasks only under the direct supervision of a nurse licensed to perform those tasks. Also, the patient is entitled to a licensed nurse level of care.

What should I do if I see another health care team member perform a clinical procedure incorrectly?

If the incorrect procedure can harm the patient, you have a legal duty to stop the procedure — tactfully, when possible — and immediately report your action to your nursing supervisor. If the incorrect procedure isn't potentially harmful to the patient, use your judgment about whether to stop the procedure. If you don't stop the procedure, report your observation to your supervisor.

Can I face legal action if I ask a hospital volunteer to help me give a patient care and she does something wrong?

Yes. Don't ask a volunteer to participate in a task she isn't trained and professionally qualified to perform.

---

help every patient. On the other hand, you feel compelled to protect yourself from liability.

Collective action

The best protection, as you might expect, is prevention — action taken. Try to work with your facility to develop creative, practical solutions to remedy the understaffing situation. If you and your colleagues act responsibly and collectively to try to bring about change, the law will protect you in several important ways. A case in point is *Misericordia Hospital Medical Center v. National Labor Relations Board* (1980), which

involved a charge nurse who was terminated from her job because her employer found her activities "disloyal."

She belonged to a group of hospital employees called the Ad Hoc Patient Care Committee. The committee was formed after JCAHO, which intended to survey the hospital, had invited interested parties — including hospital staff — to attend a public meeting and submit information on whether accreditation standards were being met. One *complaint* lodged by the nurse and her committee was insufficient coverage on many shifts — a situation the hospital had failed to remedy.

Even though JCAHO examiners approved the hospital, the nurse was terminated shortly afterward. When the National Labor Relations Board (NLRB) ordered the hospital to reinstate the nurse, the hospital appealed. The appeals court upheld the NLRB order, citing a U.S. Supreme Court ruling that employees don't lose protection "when they seek to improve terms and conditions of employment or otherwise improve their lot as employees through channels outside the immediate employee-employer relationship."

EMPLOYEE OR MANAGEMENT?

Although this decision offers nurses some protection in conflicts with employers, especially those in which working conditions directly affect patient care, anyone who's involved in hiring, terminating, scheduling, disciplining, or evaluating employees is considered management and may not be included in the collective bargaining unit if a nurses' union exists in that health care facility. Therefore, a nurse may or may not be covered, depending on the court's interpretation of whether she's management.

An individual nurse or a group of nurses who believe the facility's staffing needs require reassessment and change should first decide how best to proceed. This may entail meetings within the facility to discuss staffing issues in an attempt to come up with a resolution of the problem. Failure by the facility to appropriately address staffing is-

sues, or by an individual nurse or group of nurses to recognize and act to rectify staffing problems, may put the facility and the nurses in jeopardy if adverse events occur while staffing isn't at appropriate levels.

If a nurse can't get her facility to rectify staffing problems, she may need to resign from the facility and work in another health care setting. Continuing to work at a facility that doesn't have appropriate staffing may put a nurse's license at risk, in addition to subjecting her to the potential of a successful lawsuit by a patient who sustained harm as a result of inadequate care. A state board of nursing could easily take the position that a nurse wasn't using good nursing judgment if she continued to work in a setting where she knew there wasn't adequate staffing.

ANOTHER SUCCESS STORY

The nurses at Shore Medical Center put these principles to work to make changes at their facility. They had been concerned for many months about the short staffing of many of their patient care units and about consistent use of mandatory overtime. The nurses' asserted that the short staffing was unsafe and that it significantly affected the quality of care they were able to render to patients. They reinforced their position by supplying actual case examples of adverse events that had occurred with patients, some of which had resulted in injury to patients as a result of understaffing and forcing nurses to work mandatory overtime when they may have been too fatigued to safely work. The nurses repeatedly addressed these issues with nursing management, and finally followed the chain of command to the top level of administrative staff at the facility. The administration responded that they felt current staffing levels were generally sufficient and were, in fact, consistent with the staffing levels at other facilities.

The nurses were discouraged by this response, but determined to effect a change in the staffing. They felt that they had exhausted all avenues of recourse available to them at the facility and decided to lodge a complaint with JCAHO. JCAHO had been at the medical center 1 year earlier and had accredited the medical center without noting a staffing problem.

JCAHO RULES

JCAHO responded to the complaint lodged by the nurses by making an unannounced visit to the hospital. During the course of this unannounced visit, JCAHO representatives interviewed numerous nurses and spent time on many of the patient care units. At the end of the visit, JCAHO concluded that the staffing patterns at the hospital were unsafe and that they must be changed immediately. The facility was given 3 months to rectify the problems that had been identified. With their accreditation at high risk, the hospital was compelled to increase the nurse-patient ratio on all units and to curtail their mandatory overtime practice.

HIGHLIGHTING PATIENT CARE

Make sure you follow the appropriate channels of communication when reporting a potentially dangerous understaffing situation, as the nurses did in the preceding example. Simply report the problem, the number of hours you've been forced to work, and other relevant facts. Then, if you still can't get help and if your complaint involves an alleged ***unfair labor practice*** (and you're a union member), consider contacting the NLRB. Otherwise, consider other agencies that may be able to provide you with assistance, such as state licensing agencies or consumer health care watchdog groups.

Short staffing may significantly affect patient care, and nurses are justifiably concerned about their risk of liability in a short-staffing situation. If you're able to establish that you exercised reasonable professional judgment, established priorities, and communicated problems to nursing and facility management despite short staffing, you can increase your chances of successfully defending a claim based on short staffing.

S*elected references*

Calarco, M.M. "Given the Nursing Shortage, is Mandatory Overtime a Necessary Evil?" *Nursing Leadership Forum* 6(2):33-36, Winter 2001.

Cape, C.S. "The Nursing Shortage is Everyone's Problem," *Healthcare Financial Management* 55(2):14, February 2001.

Capitulo, K.L., et al. "Professional Responsibility Versus Mandatory Overtime," *Journal of Nursing Ad-*

ministration 31(6):290-92, June 2001.

Horem, S., and Reno, K. "Perils of Mandatory OT (Overtime)," *Hospitals and Health Networks* 75(4):28, April 2001.

Kany, K. "The Wild Blue Yonder. Should Nurses be Floating to Unfamiliar Units?" *AJN* 100(8):79, August 2000.

Lee, D. "Overtime — Mandatory or Voluntary?" *British Journal of Perioperative Nursing* 12(2):63, February 2002.

Mee, C.L. "Mandatory Madness... Mandatory Overtime," *Nursing2001* 31(9):6, September 2001.

Principles for Nurse Staffing. American Nurses Association, 1999. *www.nursingworld.org/readroom/ stffprnc.htm.*

Romig, C.L. "The Nursing Shortage Demands Action Now — State and Federal Legislation Passed," *AORN Journal* 74(5):733-38, November 2001.

Romig, C.L. "Developing a Nurse-to-Patient Ratio Policy," *AORN Journal* 72(5):912-16, November 2000.

Seago, J.A. "The California Experiment: Alternatives for Minimum Nurse-to-Patient Ratios," *Journal of Nursing Administration* 32(1):48-58, January 2002.

U.S. Department of Health and Human Services, Health Resources and Services Administration. "Nurse Staffing and Patient Outcomes in Hospitals," Needleman, J., et al. Prepared under contract number 230-99-0021, 2001. *www.bhpr.hrsa.gov/nursing/staffstudy.htm.*

Vernarec, E. "Just Say No to Mandatory Overtime?" *RN* 63(12):69-70, 74, December 2000.

Chapter Twelve

SURVIVING A LAWSUIT

IMAGINE YOU'RE AT the nurses' station, catching up on paperwork, when a stranger approaches and asks for you. He thrusts some legal papers into your hands and starts to walk away. Baffled, you ask, "What's this all about?" He replies, "You've just been served with papers; you're being sued."

As you look over the papers, you recognize the name of a former patient listed as the *plaintiff,* and you see your name listed as the defendant. You learn that you've been accused of "errors and omissions." A nagging worry for most nurses has just become reality: You've been sued for nursing malpractice.

Failing to respond to the complaint could result in a default judgment against you. You need to act immediately. Your next step depends on whether you have professional liability insurance. (See *Responding to a malpractice summons,* pages 204 and 205.)

Contacting appropriate personnel

If you're covered by your employer's insurance, immediately contact the legal services administrator at your health care facility. She'll tell you how to proceed.

If you have your own professional liability insurance, consult your policy and read the section that tells you what to do when you're sued. Every policy details whom you should notify and how much time you have to do it. Call this person immediately and tell him you've been sued. Document the date, time, his name, and his instructions. Then hand-deliver the lawsuit papers to him, if possible, and get a signed, dated receipt. If you can't deliver the papers by hand, send them by certified mail, return receipt requested, so you're assured of a signed receipt. Don't forget to make a photocopy of the lawsuit papers for yourself first.

If you don't contact the appropriate representative within the speci-

Responding to a malpractice summons

If you receive a summons notifying you that you're being sued, your early response can have a significant effect on the outcome of the suit.

Immediately cease communication with the plaintiff, his family, and his attorney. If you have nursing malpractice insurance — and you should — ask your agent to see that your claim is handled by an attentive, experienced claims adjuster and a qualified attorney.

Maintain your own file on the case. Ask for copies of all relevant documents and reports from the claims adjuster, your attorney, and the patient's attorney. Check the status of your case regularly.

Selecting a defense attorney

If the patient names your facility in the lawsuit, the facility's insurance company may supply an attorney to defend you as its employee. Also, your insurance carrier may cover and assist you if only the facility is named in the suit. If you're sued alone, your insurance carrier may appoint an attorney to represent you. If you're uninsured, you must find your own attorney. If the facility's attorney is representing its interest in the lawsuit, you should have a separate attorney to represent your interest. Two codefendants shouldn't have the same attorney.

If the dollar amount for which you're being sued exceeds your insurance coverage, consider hiring a private attorney. He'll be working exclusively for you, not for your insurance carrier. He'll notify your primary defense attorney (the attorney provided by your insurance carrier) and your insurer that, should the judgment exceed your coverage, the carrier may be held liable.

Shop around

To find a qualified attorney:
- consult with your facility's legal services department
- consult with your state nurses' association or other appropriate professional organization
- ask friends or relatives with legal experience, whose judgments you can trust
- call your local bar association, listed in the telephone book.

When you meet with a prospective attorney you've found (or one the insurance company has provided), ask him about his experience with malpractice cases. If he has too little experience or if too many of his cases were decided for the plaintiff, you have the right to seek another attorney (or to ask your insurance carrier to provide a different one).

Working with your attorney

Establish a good working relationship with your attorney. It's your job to educate him about the medical information he needs to defend you. Be prepared to spend many hours reviewing documents, licensing requirements, facility procedures, journals, and texts as well as your professional qualifications and the details of the case. Do the following:

Responding to a malpractice summons *(continued)*

- Give your attorney and insurance company representative all the information you can about the case, including anything you remember that isn't in the record.
- Give your attorney your specialty's nursing practice standards.
- Discuss with him how you feel about settling out of court.
- Develop a list of experts qualified to testify on the standards of care in your specialty and present it to

your attorney. These names might come from your attorney, or from a legal nurse consultant or professional organization. Don't recommend friends; the jury may believe them to be less objective.

- Review all available records, including those obtained by your attorney that are normally inaccessible to you such as the records of the patient's private physician.

fied time, the insurance company can refuse to cover you. To protect yourself, act quickly, document your actions, and remember to get a receipt.

Your employer will almost certainly be named as a codefendant in the lawsuit. Even if that isn't the case, notify your employer that you're being sued. Your insurance company may try to involve your employer as a defendant.

In addition, contact the National Nurses Claims Data Bank established by the American Nurse's Association. Provide a full report of the incident in question, including the date, time, and persons involved. This contact will give you access to national data that may support your case, and your data will in turn help other nurses who are involved in lawsuits. Your name and address will be kept confidential.

Insurance considerations

When you notify your insurance company that you've been sued, it will first consider whether it must cover you at all. The insurer does this by checking for policy violations you may have committed. For example, your insurance company will investigate whether you gave late notice of the lawsuit, gave false information on your insurance application, or failed to pay a premium on time. If the company is sure you've committed such a violation, it will use this violation as a policy defense, and it can refuse to cover you.

If the company thinks you've committed such a violation, but isn't sure it has evidence to support a policy defense, it will probably send you a letter by certified mail informing you that the company may not have to defend you, but that it will do so while reserving the right to deny coverage later, withdraw from the case, or take other actions. Meanwhile, the company will seek a declaration of its rights from the court. If the court decides the company does not have to defend you, the company will withdraw from the case.

Usually, however, an insurance company takes this action only after careful consideration because denying coverage may provide you with grounds for suing the company. If you receive such a letter, hire your own attorney to defend you in the lawsuit and to advise you in your dealings with the insurance company. If your case against the insurance company is sound, your attorney may suggest that you sue the insurer.

If your insurance company doesn't assert a policy defense, its representative will select an attorney or a law firm specializing in medical malpractice as your attorney of record. This attorney is legally bound to do all that's necessary to defend you.

FINDING AN ATTORNEY

If you don't have insurance, either on your own or through your employer, you'll have to find your own attorney. Don't even consider trying to defend yourself. You need an attorney who's experienced in medical malpractice because the case will be complex and the opposition will be composed of experienced attorneys.

Make appointments with a few attorneys who seem qualified to defend you. In most cases, you won't be charged for this initial consultation. When you meet with each

one, ask how long he thinks the lawsuit will take and how much money he'll charge you. Also, try to get a feel for the attorney's understanding of the issues in your case. Then choose one as your attorney of record, and give him a copy of the lawsuit papers. Do this as soon as possible.

Preparing your defense

Your attorney will file the appropriate legal documents in response to the papers you were served. He'll ask you for help in preparing your defense. He should give you a chance to present your position in detail. Remember, all discussions between you and your attorney are *privileged communication,* meaning that your attorney can't disclose this information without your permission.

Your attorney will also obtain complete copies of the pertinent medical records and other documents he or you feel are important in your defense.

THE DISCOVERY PROCESS

Your attorney will use *discovery* methods to uncover every pertinent detail about the case against you. Discovery methods are legal procedures for obtaining information, and may include:

● *interrogatories* — questions written to the other party that require answers under oath

● *depositions* — oral cross-examination of the other party, under oath and before a court reporter

- *defense independent medical examination* — a medical examination of the injured party by a physician selected by your attorney or insurance company.

The plaintiff patient's attorney will also use discovery tools, so you may have to answer interrogatories and appear for a deposition as well. Your attorney will carefully prepare you for these procedures. Neither the interrogatory nor the deposition should be taken lightly. Don't speculate in answering questions. Work closely with your attorney in preparing your written answers to the interrogatory.

However, this doesn't mean that you must say or do whatever he asks. If you feel your attorney is asking you to say or do things that aren't in your best interest, tell him so. You have the right to change attorneys at any time. If you believe an attorney selected by your insurance company is more interested in protecting the company than in protecting you, discuss the problem with a company representative. Then if you still feel that he isn't defending you properly, hire your own attorney. You may have grounds
for subsequently suing the insurance company and the company-appointed attorney.

Preparing for court

Plan on spending a lot of time preparing your case with your attorney before you appear in the courtroom.

DON'T TALK ABOUT THE CASE

You're precluded from speaking directly with the person suing you because he's represented by an attorney. Don't try to placate the person suing you by calling him and discussing the case. Your chances of talking him into dropping his lawsuit are slim, and every word you say to him can be used against you in court. In fact, to prevent information leaks that could compromise your case, don't discuss the lawsuit with anyone except your attorney. To protect your professional reputation, don't mention to your colleagues that you've been sued.

STUDY THE MEDICAL RECORD

Your attorney will ask you to study relevant medical records as soon as possible. Examine the complete medical chart, including nurses' notes, laboratory reports, and physicians' orders.

If you feel the need to take notes on key entries or omissions concerning the records, make sure you do it on a separate sheet of paper. Then give the notes to your attorney so that he can add them to his case file. Your own notes can be used as evidence against you should they be acquired by the plaintiff, but your attorney's case file is protected from discovery rules, so your notes will be safe in his file.

Don't make changes to the medical records as you review them. Remember, you aren't the only person with a copy of the records, so altering them will hurt your case by undermining your credibility.

Settling out of court

Only 10% of malpractice suits filed actually go to court. Of those that go to court, only 10% end with a final judgment. The rest are settled out of court.

Making a compromise

Settling your case out of court isn't an admission of wrongdoing. The law regards settlement as a compromise between two parties to end a lawsuit and to avoid further expense. You may choose to pay a settlement rather than incur the possibly greater expense — financial and emotional — of defending your innocence at trial.

Determining your settlement rights

If you're covered by professional liability insurance, the terms of your policy will determine whether you and your attorney or the insurance company can control the settlement. Most policies don't permit the nurse to settle a case without the insurance company's consent. However, many policies, especially those provided by employers, permit the insurance company to settle without the consent of the nurse involved.

Review your policy to determine your settlement rights. If the policy isn't clear, call the insurance company representative and ask for clarification.

Evaluating a possible settlement

Offer your attorney and your insurance company's representative all the information you can about the case, so the company can evaluate your liabilities as well as a possible settlement with the plaintiff. As an attending nurse, you may be in the best position to provide crucial observations concerning the patient's state of mind — in many cases, the basis of a successful settlement.

PROTECT YOUR PROPERTY

Although many states have ***homestead laws*** that protect a substantial part of the equity in your house as well as other property from a judgment against you, some states don't. Ask your attorney about the laws in your state or province. If you don't have insurance or if damages awarded to the plaintiff exceed your insurance coverage, these particulars can be crucial in deciding how aggressive a defense to mount.

GIVING A DEPOSITION

Before the trial, you'll probably be called to testify at a deposition. This can take place in an attorney's office or in a special room in the courthouse set aside for that purpose. The deposition takes place in a less formal atmosphere than a courtroom, but don't forget that a court reporter will be transcribing every word you and the attorneys say.

In a way, the deposition is a rehearsal for the actual trial. At the trial, the plaintiff's and the defendant's attorneys have the right to use your pretrial testimony to bolster their respective cases. Therefore, your attorney should help you to prepare for your deposition.

EVENTS LEADING TO TRIAL

While your attorney prepares your defense, he'll also explore the desirability of reaching an out-of-court settlement. If he decides an out-of-court settlement is in your best interest, he'll try to achieve it before your trial date. (See *Settling out of court.*)

If your case goes to trial, your attorney will participate in selecting the jury. In this process, attorneys for both sides question prospective jurors, and your attorney will ask your opinion on their suitability. Attorneys may reject a few prospective jurors without reason (a ***peremptory challenge***) and an unlimited number for specific reasons (a ***challenge for cause***). For example, an attorney may reject someone who knows the plaintiff or who has a personal interest in the suit.

To help prepare you to testify, your attorney will ask you to review the complete medical record, your interrogatory answers, and your deposition.

On trial

Be prepared for your trial to last several days or even weeks. After all the witnesses have given their testimony, the jury — not the judge — will decide if you're liable. If the jury finds you liable, it will also as-

sess damages against you. (See *The trial process: Step-by-step,* pages 210 and 211.) In some instances, a jury isn't used; for example, cases tried in Federal court may not have a jury. Also, an arbitration proceeding is sometimes (although rarely) used instead of a jury trial.

TESTIFYING IN COURT

When you're called to testify in a malpractice lawsuit, as a defendant (or as an expert witness in another defendant's trial), you may be expected to respond quickly to a confusing presentation of claims, ***counterclaims***, allegations, and contradictory evidence. You can use many techniques to help reduce stress and enhance the value of your testimony.

Courtroom demeanor

Making a good impression on the jury — when you're on the witness stand and while you're seated beside your attorney — is an essential part of a good defense. This may form the jury's first, and sometimes lasting, impression of your credibility.

Your attorney will help prepare you to testify at the trial. He'll tell you how to dress — conservatively, as if you were going to an important job interview — and how to act. He may recommend, for example, that you sit with both feet on the floor with your hands folded in front of you and pay polite attention to other speakers. Remember that the purpose of these instructions is to help win the case. Remember, too, that failing to cooperate with an attorney provided by an

The trial process: Step-by-step

The chart below summarizes the basic trial process from complaint to execution of judgment. If you're ever involved in a lawsuit, your attorney will explain the specific procedures that your case requires.

Pretrial preparation

1 Complaint
Plaintiff files a complaint stating his charges against the defendant.

2 Summons
Court issues defendant a summons stating plaintiff's charges.

3 Answer or counterclaim
Defendant files an answer and may add a counterclaim to plaintiff's allegations or those of other defendants.

Trial

7 Opening statements
Plaintiff's and defendant's attorneys present facts as they apply to their cases.

8 Plaintiff presents case
Plaintiff's witnesses testify, explaining what they saw, heard, and know. Expert witnesses review documentation and give their opinions about specific aspects of the case.

9 Cross-examination
Defendant's attorney questions plaintiff's witnesses.

13 Defendant closes case
Defendant's attorney may claim plaintiff hasn't presented an issue for the jury to decide.

14 Closing statements
Each attorney summarizes his case for the jury.

15 Jury instruction
Judge instructs the jury in points of law that apply in this particular case.

---

insurance company can be used by the company to deny coverage.

Malpractice lawsuits are notoriously slow-moving. Interruptions occur in the form of recesses, attorneys' lengthy arguments in judges' chambers, and the calling of witnesses out of turn. Be patient no matter what happens. When you're asked to appear, be prompt. You may not score points by your punctuality, but you'll definitely lose a

4 Discovery
Plaintiff's and defendant's attorneys develop their cases by gathering information by means of depositions and interrogatories and by reviewing documents and other evidence.

5 Pretrial hearing
Court hears statements from both parties and tries to narrow the issues.

6 Negotiation by settlement
Both parties meet to try to resolve the case outside the court.

10 Plaintiff closes case
Defendant's attorney may make a motion to dismiss the case, claiming plaintiff's evidence is insufficient.

11 Defendant presents case
Defendant's witnesses testify, explaining what they saw, heard, and know. Expert witnesses review documentation and give their opinions about specific aspects of the case.

12 Cross-examination
Plaintiff's attorney questions defendant's witnesses.

16 Jury deliberation and verdict
Jury reviews facts and votes on verdict. Jury announces verdict before judge and both parties.

17 Appeal (optional)
Attorneys review transcripts. The party against whom the court ruled may appeal if he feels the judge didn't interpret the law properly, instruct the jury properly, or conduct the trial properly.

18 Execution of judgment
Appeals process is completed and the case is settled.

few if you aren't in court when called to testify.

When you testify, the jury doesn't expect you to be letter-perfect or to have instant or total recall. If you don't know the answer, say so. Listen closely to questions, and answer only what the questioner has asked. Always answer the questions simply and in lay terms, and never elaborate or volunteer information. If you're

Courtroom controversy: Nurses as expert witnesses

Testimony by experts is essential for the plaintiff and defendant. In lawsuits against nurses, the court's position holds that a nurse is the appropriate expert witness when dealing with the actions or decisions of a nurse. Before 1980, it was common for physicians to set the standards for nursing care.

No double standard

A standard has been evolving since the late 1970s for expert testimony for lawsuits involving nurses. In the case of *Young v. Board of Hospital Directors, Lee County* (1984), the court concluded that physicians may not determine nursing standards of care. The physician, being unfamiliar with the daily practices of nurses, is unable to set a standard or to testify as to deviation from common nursing practice. The nurse expert witness can explain technology or nursing care in the language jurors can understand. This type of testimony is crucial to dispel common misconceptions or to explain scientific facts as they pertain to nursing care and the care at hand.

Qualifications of an expert

A nurse expert witness testifying for the plaintiff in a negligence case must be able to describe the relevant standard of care, describe how the nurse deviated from the acceptable standard, and explain how failure to meet acceptable nursing standards caused or contributed to the patient's injury. A nurse expert for the defense will testify to the standard and whether the defendant nurse met the standard.

A nurse must meet certain criteria to be considered an expert witness. The first — and only absolute — criterion is current licensure to practice nursing. Experts need not come from your state, although it's better if they do. Also, the expert witness' credentials must match or exceed the defendant's. This includes clinical expertise in the same specialty, certification in the clinical specialty, and recent education relevant to the nursing specialty at issue. Another criterion is a lack of bias; the expert witness should have no professional or personal relationship with anyone involved in the suit.

Expert witness or legal consultant?

A legal consultant differs from an expert witness. A legal consultant may be an expert, but her name and the information and opinions she gives aren't disclosed to the opposition. However, when a nurse agrees to become an expert witness, her name is given to opposing counsel and she may have to testify in court. Also, all comments, notes, or reports she makes may be discovered and reviewed by opposing counsel.

The nurse expert witness faces two dilemmas: the changing standard of care and being maneuvered into stating that only one opinion is correct. She must consider the possibility that the standard of care may

Courtroom controversy: Nurses as expert witnesses *(continued)*

have changed by the time the case goes to trial; thus, it's crucial to know what was acceptable at the time of the incident. When there's more than one acceptable choice, the expert witness must repeatedly emphasize that more than one approach could have been selected and still be appropriate.

Sometimes, a nurse may testify as an expert about a physician's care when he performs a nursing function such as drawing blood.

Case study

In *Prairie v. University of Chicago Hospitals* (1998), an Illinois appellate court held that expert testimony wasn't needed to establish that a nurse acted negligently. A patient underwent a laminectomy; 2 days later a nurse insisted the patient get out of bed despite complaints of severe pain. The patient sued.

The trial court ruled in the nurse's favor because of the plaintiff's failure to present expert testimony on the standard of care. The appellate court overturned the ruling, stating the fact existed that the nurse had acted negligently and that expert testimony wasn't needed to establish the standard because the jury could evaluate the nurse's conduct on the basis of common knowledge.

---

asked to describe a piece of equipment that's unfamiliar to a lay audience, get your attorney's approval to bring it to the courtroom and show it to the jury. Above all, be honest. Avoid the very natural temptation to exaggerate or bend the truth, especially when your testimony must be critical of a colleague or of your facility's policies.

During the trial, your professional reputation will be at stake. Project a positive attitude at all times, suggesting that you feel confident about the trial's outcome. Never disparage the plaintiff inside or outside the courtroom. Characterizing him as a malingerer or fraud, for instance, can only generate bad feelings that may interfere with the settlement. You probably won't be able to speak to him during the trial, but if you do, always be polite and dignified. If he, or his attorney, attempt to goad you into making an angry response, ignore them.

Cross-examination

During **cross-examination,** the opposing attorney will try to discredit your testimony. This may take the form of an attack on your credentials, experience, or education. Don't take the attacks personally or allow them to fluster you. If you're testifying as an expert witness for someone else, follow this same advice. (See *Courtroom controversy: Nurses as expert witnesses.*)

Another ploy the opposing attorney can use to discredit you is the "hedge." He may try to get you to change or qualify an answer you gave previously on **direct examina-**

tion or at the deposition. He may also try to confuse the issue by asking you a similar, but hypothetical, question with a slightly different but significant slant. Just remember: a simple, sincere "I don't know" often reinforces a jury's belief in your honesty and competence. Your best protection against cross-examination anxiety is adequate preparation with your attorney.

Selected references

Duffy, W. "Don't Let a Deposition Ruin Your Disposition," *AORN Journal* 70(1):34-36, 39-40, 42, July 1999.

Grensing-Pophal, L. "Here Comes the Judge," *Nursing2000* 30(6): 80-81, June 2000.

Martin, K., and Cepero, K. "Five Deposition Styles and How to Handle Them," *Nursing Management* 31(2):52, February 2000.

Martin, K., and Cepero, K. "You're Being Deposed? Remain Calm," *Nursing Management* 30(5): 65-66, May 1999.

Sheehy, S.B. "Understanding the Legal Process: Your Best Defense," *Journal of Emergency Nursing* 25(6):492-95, December 1999.

GLOSSARY
COURT CASE CITATION INDEX
GENERAL INDEX

Glossary

A

abuse The physical, sexual, or emotional mistreatment of a person, such as a child, elderly person, or spouse or partner. It may be overt or covert and often results in permanent physical or psychological injury, mental impairment or, sometimes, death. Compare *mistreatment, neglect.*

abuse of process A civil action in which it's alleged that the legal process has been used in an improper manner. For example, an abuse of process action might be brought by a health care practitioner attempting to countersue a patient or by a psychiatric patient attempting to demonstrate wrongful confinement.

actual notice A plaintiff has actual oral or written knowledge of a condition or incident. Compare *constructive notice.*

adjudicated incompetent Declared incompetent by exercise of judicial authority. Note that a patient who has been adjudicated incompetent may still have the mental capacity to make an informed decision about his medical care. Compare *incompetence, mental incompetence.*

administrative review Investigation conducted by the state board of nursing when a nurse is accused of professional misconduct. The board first reviews the complaint and then may hold a formal hearing at which evidence is presented and witnesses examined and cross-examined. Court proceedings — and possibly legal penalties — may result from the board's findings.

admissible evidence Authentic, relevant, reliable information presented during a trial that may be used to reach a decision.

advance directives Documents used as guidelines for life-sustaining medical care of patients with advanced disease or disability who are no longer able to indicate their own wishes.

advance directive system System implemented by health care institutions (including hospitals, nursing homes, and hospices) to ensure that every patient, at admission, is informed of his right to execute a living will or durable power of attorney for health care decisions.

adverse effect (or reaction) A harmful, unintended reaction to a drug administered at normal dosage.

affidavit A written statement sworn to before a notary public or an officer of the court.

affirmative defense A denial of guilt or wrongdoing based on new evidence rather than simple denial of a charge. For example, a nurse who pleads immunity under the Good Samaritan law is making an affirmative defense. The defendant bears the burden of proof in an affirmative defense.

agency A relationship between two parties in which the first party authorizes the second to act as agent on behalf of the first.

agent A party authorized to act on behalf of another and to give the other an account of such actions.

AMA *abbr.* Against medical advice; a patient's decision to leave a health care facility against his physician's advice.

amendment An alteration to an existing law or complaint.

answer The response of a defendant to the claims of a plaintiff. The answer contains a denial of the plaintiff's allegations and may also contain an affirmative defense or a counterclaim. It's the principal pleading on the part of the defense and is prepared in writing, usually by the defense attorney, and submitted to the court.

appeal A request taken to a higher court (called an appellate court) to review a decision of a lower court.

appellate court A court of law that has the power to review the decision of a lower court. An appellate court doesn't make a new determination of the facts of the case; instead, it reviews the way in which the law was applied to the case.

appellee The party in an appeal who won the case in a lower court. The appellee argues that the decision of the lower court shouldn't be modified by the appellate court.

arbitration The settlement of a dispute by an impartial person chosen by the disputing parties.

arbitrator An impartial person appointed to resolve a dispute between parties. The arbitrator listens to the evidence as presented by the parties in an informal hearing and attempts to arrive at a resolution acceptable to both parties.

assault An attempt, or even a threat, by a person to physically injure another person.

attorney of record The attorney whose name appears on the legal records for a specific case as the agent of a specific client.

audit A methodical examination; to examine with intent to verify. Nursing audits examine standards of nursing care.

autonomy The principle of self-determination. The right to make decisions about one's own health care.

B

battery The unauthorized touching of a person by another person. For example, a health care professional who treats a patient beyond what the patient has consented to has committed battery.

beneficence The promotion of good and prevention of harm.

binding arbitration A process of settling disputes in which all parties agree to be bound by the determination of an arbitrator.

borrowed-servant doctrine A legal doctrine that courts may apply in cases in which an employer "lends" his employee's services to another employer who, under this doctrine, becomes solely liable for the employee's wrongful conduct. Also called ostensible agent doctrine. Compare *dual agency doctrine.*

breach of contract Failure to perform all or part of a contracted duty without justification.

breach of duty The neglect or failure to fulfill in a proper manner the duties of an office, job, or position.

C

captain-of-the-ship doctrine A legal doctrine that considers a surgeon responsible for the actions of his assistants when those assistants are under the surgeon's supervision. Similar to the *borrowed-servant doctrine.*

causal connection Of, relating to, or constituting a cause.

causa mortis Latin phrase meaning "in anticipation of approaching death." The state of mind of a person approaching death.

chain of custody Evidentiary rule requiring that each individual having custody of a piece of evidence be identified and that the transfer of evidence from one custodian to another be documented so that all evidence is accounted for. Also called chain of evidence.

challenge An objection by a party (or his lawyer) to the inclusion of a particular prospective juror as a member of the jury that is to hear the party's cause or trial, with the result that the prospective juror is disqualified.

challenge for cause A challenge based upon a particular reason (such as bias) specified by law or procedure as a reason that a party (or his lawyer) may use to disqualify a prospective juror.

child abuse The physical, sexual, or emotional mistreatment of a child. It may be overt or covert and often results in permanent physical or psychological injury, mental impairment or, sometimes, death. Child abuse results from complex factors involving both parents and child, compounded by various stressful environmental circumstances, such as poor socioeconomic conditions, inadequate physical and emotional support within the family, and any major life change or crisis, especially those crises arising from marital strife. Also called battered child syndrome for children under age 3. Compare *child neglect*. See also *abuse*.

child neglect The failure by parents or guardians to provide for the basic needs of a child by physical or emotional deprivation that interferes with normal growth and development or that places the child in jeopardy. Compare *child abuse*.

child welfare Any service sponsored by the community or special organizations that provides physical, social, or psychological care for children in need of it.

circumstantial evidence Testimony based on inference or hearsay rather than actual personal knowledge or observation of the facts in question.

civil defense laws That body of statutory law that's invoked when the jurisdiction is under attack; for example, during a war.

civil penalty Fines or money damages imposed as punishment for a certain activity.

claim A demand for something as rightful due; an assertion of ownership.

claims-made policy A professional liability insurance policy that covers the insured only for a claim of malpractice made while the policy is in effect.

code *1*. A published body of statutes such as a civil code. *2*. A collection of standards and rules of behavior such as a dress code. *3*. A symbolic means of representing information for communication or transfer such as a genetic code. *4*. *Informal*. A discreet signal used to summon a special team to resuscitate a patient without alarming patients or visitors.

codes A system of assigned terms designed by a medical institution for quick and accurate communication during emergencies or for patient identification.

commitment *1*. The placement or confinement of an individual in a specialized hospital or other institutional facility. *2*. The legal procedure of admitting a mentally ill person to an institution for psychiatric treatment. The process varies from state to state but usually involves judicial or court action based on medical evidence certifying that the person is mentally ill. *3*. A pledge or contract to fulfill some obligation or agreement, used especially in some forms of psychotherapy or marriage counseling.

common law Law derived from previous court decisions as opposed to law based on legislative enactment (statutes). Also called case law. In the absence of statutory law regarding a subject, the judge-made rules of common law are the law on that subject.

comparative negligence Determination of liability in which damages may be apportioned among multiple defendants. The extent of liability depends on each defendant's relative contribution to the harm done as determined by the jury. Compare *negligence*.

complaint *1*. In a civil case, a pleading by a plaintiff made under oath to initiate a suit. It's a statement of the formal charge and the cause for action against the defendant. In a criminal case, a serious felony prosecution requires an indictment with evidence presented by a state's attorney. 2. *Informal.* Any ailment, problem, or symptom identified by the patient, member of the patient's family, or other knowledgeable person. The chief complaint is usually the reason the patient has sought health care.

compulsory non-suit A verdict meaning that there isn't sufficient evidence to proceed with a case.

confidentiality A professional responsibility to keep all privileged information private. In some instances confidentiality is mandated by state or federal statutes and case law.

consent form A document, prepared for a patient's signature, that discloses his proposed treatment in general terms.

consequential damages See *special damages.*

constructive-continuing-treatment rule This rule is similar to the termination-of-treatment rule; however, under the constructive-continuing-treatment rule, a patient may file a lawsuit after the last treatment took place. The rationale behind this rule is that the patient's new health care provider(s) might make care decisions based on decisions made by the patient's previous provider. Compare *termination-of-treatment rule.*

constructive notice A defect or dangerous condition is visible and apparent and has existed for a sufficient length of time that the plaintiff should reasonably have discovered it. Compare *actual notice.*

contract defense An answer to an allegation that a breach of contract has occurred. Compare *impossibility defense.*

contract duties Duties defined in a contract such as an employment contract.

contract violations Actions that break

mutually accepted contract provisions such as those of an employment contract.

corporate liability The legal responsibility of a corporation and its officers. A corporation's liability is normally limited to its assets; the shareholders are thus protected against personal liability for the corporation.

counterclaim A claim made by a defendant establishing a cause for action in his favor against the plaintiff. The purpose of a counterclaim is to oppose or detract from the plaintiff's claim or complaint.

countersignature A signature obtained from another health care professional to verify that information is correct and is within the verifier's personal knowledge.

criminal assault A threat or attempt to inflict offensive physical contact or bodily harm on a person (as by lifting a fist in a threatening manner) that puts the person in immediate danger or apprehension of such contact or harm.

cross-examination The questioning of a witness by the attorney for the opposing party.

D

damages The amount of money a court orders a defendant to pay the plaintiff when the case is decided in favor of the plaintiff.

decedent The deceased.

defamation The tort of wrongful injury to another's reputation through either oral or written words. For defamation to have occurred, the allegedly injurious information must be published — that is, revealed to a third party. Compare *libel, slander.*

default judgment A judgment rendered against a defendant because of the defendant's failure to appear in court or to answer the plaintiff's claim within the proper time.

defendant The party that's named in a plaintiff's complaint and against whom the plaintiff's allegations are made. The defendant must respond to the allegations. See also *answer.*

defense independent medical examination In malpractice litigation, a medical examination of the injured party by a doctor selected by the defendant's attorney or insurance company.

delinquency *1.* Negligence or failure to fulfill a duty or obligation. *2.* An offense, fault, misdemeanor, or misdeed; a tendency to commit such acts.

delinquent *1.* Characterized by neglect of duty or violation of law. *2.* Behavior characterized by persistent antisocial, illegal, violent, or criminal acts; a juvenile delinquent.

dependent nursing function A function the nurse performs, with another health care professional's written order, on the basis of that professional's judgment, and for which that professional is accountable.

deposition A sworn pretrial testimony given by a witness in response to oral or written questions and cross-examination. The deposition is transcribed and may be used for further pretrial investigation. It may also be presented at the trial if the witness can't be present or changes his testimony. Compare *discovery, interrogatories.*

directed verdict A verdict given by a jury at the direction of the trial judge.

direct examination The first examination of a witness called to the stand by the attorney for the party the witness is representing.

direct patient care Care of a patient provided in person by a member of the staff. Direct patient care may involve any aspect of the health care of a patient, including treatments, counseling, self-care, patient education, and administration of medication.

disclosure laws Legislation requiring that potentially confidential information be reported; for example, laws that mandate nurses report suspected child abuse or neglect.

discovery A pretrial procedure that allows the plaintiff's and defendant's attorneys to examine relevant materials and question all parties to the case. Compare *deposition, interrogatories, defense independent medical examination.*

discovery rule Rule stating that the statute of limitations begins to run when a patient discovers the injury. This may take place many years after the injury occurred and after the applicable statute of limitations has formally run out.

discretionary powers The freedom of a public officer to choose courses of action within the limits of his authority.

dismiss To discharge or dispose of an action, suit, or motion trial.

dispense To take a drug from the pharmacy and give or sell it to another person.

distributive justice The principle that advocates equal allocation of benefits and burdens to all members of society.

doctrine Rule, principle, or law that's established through repeated applications of legal precedents.

drug abuse The use of a drug for a nontherapeutic effect, especially one for which it wasn't prescribed or intended. See also *drug addiction.*

drug addiction A condition characterized by an overwhelming desire to continue taking a drug to which one has become habituated through repeated consumption because it produces a particular effect, usually an alteration of mental activity, attitude, or outlook. See also *drug abuse.*

dual agency doctrine A legal doctrine stating that both the agency and the "borrowing" party may be held liable for the actions of the agent. Under this doctrine, a nurse from a nurses' registry may be held to be the agent of both the registry and the hospital. Compare *borrowed-servant doctrine.*

due process rights Personal rights based on the principle that the government may not deprive an individual of life, liberty, or property unless certain rules and procedures required by law are followed.

durable power of attorney An instrument authorizing another person to act as one's agent or attorney, an "attorney-in-fact," if the principal person becomes incompetent. This power is revoked when the principal person dies. Compare *power of attorney*.

duty A legal obligation owed by one party to another. Duty may be established by statute or another legal process, such as by contract or oath supported by statute, or it may be voluntarily undertaken. Every person has a duty to avoid causing harm or injury to others by negligence.

E

emancipated minor A minor who is legally considered free from the custody, care, and control of his parents before the age of majority. Emancipated minors lose the right to parental support but may gain certain other rights, such as the right to consent to their own medical care and the right to enter into binding contracts.

ethics An area of philosophy that examines values, actions, and choices to determine right and wrong. The study of standards of conduct and moral judgments.

euthanasia Deliberately bringing about the death of a person who is suffering from an incurable disease or condition, either actively (for example, by administering a lethal drug) or passively (for example, by withholding treatment). Compare *right-to-die law*.

evidence Oral testimony, occurrences, or material objects that provide proof of facts.

excess judgment A judgment that exceeds the limit of a liability policy.

exclusionary rule A constitutional rule of law that states that otherwise admissible evidence may not be used in a criminal trial if it was obtained as a result of an illegal search and seizure.

executing a contract Carrying out all the terms of a contract.

exemplary damages See *punitive damages*.

expert witness A person who has special knowledge of a subject about which a court requests testimony. Special knowledge may be acquired by experience, education, observation, or study and isn't possessed by the average person. An expert witness gives expert testimony or expert evidence. This evidence usually serves to educate the court and the jury about the subject under consideration.

F

false imprisonment The act of confining or restraining a person without his consent for no clinical or legal reason.

fidelity Faithfulness to agreements that one has accepted.

fiduciary A person having a duty, created by his undertaking, to act primarily for the benefit of another in matters connected with that undertaking.

fiduciary relationship A legal relationship of trust and confidence that exists whenever one person relies on another such as a doctor-patient relationship.

floating Working in a unit other than one's regular unit.

forensic medicine A branch of medicine that deals with the legal aspects of health care. The application of medical knowledge to questions of law affecting life or property.

formulary A book that provides specifications for drugs.

fraud Intentional deception resulting in damage to another, whether to his person, rights, property, or reputation. Fraud usually consists of a misrepresentation, concealment, or nondisclosure of a material fact, or at

least misleading conduct, devices, or
contrivance.

G

general damages Compensation for
losses that are directly referable to a
legal wrong but that are abstract in
nature, such as pain and suffering or
a worsening change in lifestyle.
Compare *punitive damages, special
damages.*

good faith Total absence of intention
to seek unfair advantage or to de-
fraud another party; an intention to
fulfill one's obligations.

Good Samaritan acts State or provincial laws that provide civil immunity
from negligence lawsuits for individuals who stop and render care in an
emergency.

grandfather clause A provision permitting persons engaged in an activity before passage of a law affecting
that activity to receive a license
without having to meet the new requirements.

gross negligence The flagrant and in-
excusable failure to perform a legal
duty in reckless disregard of the consequences.

ground rules Rules governing a particular situation that describe legitimate behavior.

guardian ad litem A person appointed by the court to safeguard a minor's or other incompetent's legal interest during certain kinds of litigation.

H

homestead laws Laws protecting
any property designated as a homestead — any house, outbuildings, and
surrounding land owned and used as
a dwelling by the head of a family —
from seizure and sale by creditors.

hospice A system of family-centered
care designed to assist the chronical-
ly ill person to be comfortable and to
maintain a satisfactory lifestyle
through the terminal phases of dying. Hospice care is multidisciplinary and includes home visits, pro-

fessional medical help available on
call, teaching and emotional support
of the family, and physical care of
the client. Some hospice programs
provide care in a center as well as in
the home.

*human investigations committee (hu-
man subjects investigations committee)* A committee established in
a hospital, school, or university to review applications for research involving human subjects in order to
protect the rights of the people to be
studied. Also called human subjects
investigation committee.

I

immunity from suit Exemption of a
person or institution, by law, from
being sued.

impossibility defense A contract defense that says circumstances rendered the violation of a contract
(such as not showing up for work)
impossible to avoid. Compare *contract defense.*

incident An event that is inconsistent
with ordinary routine, regardless of
whether injury occurs.

incident report A formal, written report that informs hospital administration (and the hospital's insurance
company) about an incident and
serves as a contemporary, factual
statement of it in the event of a lawsuit.

incompetence The inability or lack of
legal qualification or fitness to discharge the required duty. Compare
*adjudicated incompetent, mental in-
competence.*

indemnification Repayment or compensation for a loss. A person who
has compensated another for injury,
loss, or damage caused by a third
party may file a suit seeking indemnification from the third party.

independent contractor A self-em-
ployed person who renders services
to clients and independently determines how the work will be done.

informed consent Permission obtained from a patient to perform a

specific test or procedure after the patient has been fully informed about the test or procedure.

injunction A court order restraining a person from committing a specific act or requiring the individual to do something.

in loco parentis Latin phrase meaning "in the place of the parent." The assumption by a person or institution of the parental obligations of caring for a child without adoption.

insurance adjuster One who determines the amount of an insurance claim and then makes an agreement with the insured as to a settlement.

intent A conscious desire and will to act in a particular way.

interrogatories A series of written questions submitted to a witness or other person having information of interest to the court. The answers are transcribed and are sworn to under oath. Compare *deposition, discovery.*

intervention 1. Any act performed to prevent harm from occurring to a patient or to improve the mental, emotional, or physical function of a patient. A physiologic process may be monitored or enhanced, or a pathologic process may be arrested or controlled. 2. The fourth step of the nursing process. This step includes nursing actions taken to meet patient needs as determined by nursing assessment and diagnosis.

JK

just cause A lawful, rightful, proper reason to act; a defendant establishes a cause for action in his favor.

L

law 1. In a field of study: a rule, standard, or principle that states a fact or a relationship between factors, such as Dalton's law regarding partial pressures of gas and Koch's law regarding the specificity of a pathogen. 2. *a.* A rule, principle, or regulation established and promulgated by a government to protect or to restrict

the people affected. *b.* The field of study concerned with such laws. *c.* The collected body of the laws of a people derived from custom or from legislation.

lay jury A jury made up of people who aren't from a particular profession. For example, a lay jury in a medical malpractice trial wouldn't contain any doctors, nurses, or other members of medical professions.

legal guardian An officer or agent of the court who is appointed to protect the interests of minors or incompetent persons and provide for their welfare, education, and support.

liable Legally bound or obligated to make good any loss or damage; responsible.

liability Legal responsibility for failure to act or for actions that fail to meet standards of care, which cause another person harm.

liability immunity Exemption of a person or institution, by law, from a legally imposed penalty.

libel A tort consisting of a false, malicious, or unprivileged publication aiming to defame a living person or to damage the memory of a dead person. Compare *defamation, slander.*

licensure The granting of permission by a competent authority (usually a governmental agency) to an organization or person to engage in a practice or activity that would otherwise be illegal. Kinds of licensure include the issuing of licenses for general hospitals or nursing homes; for health care professionals, such as doctors; and for the production or distribution of biologic products. Licensure is usually granted on the basis of education and examination rather than performance. It's usually permanent but a periodic fee, demonstration of competence, or continuing education may be required. Licensure may be revoked by the granting agency for incompetence, criminal acts, or other reasons stipulated in the rules governing the specific area of licensure.

licensure sanctions Actions taken against a practitioner's license as a result of some misconduct or malpractice. Sanctions may include revocation of the license or suspension.

litigant A party to a lawsuit. See also *defendant, plaintiff.*

litigate To carry on a suit or to contest a suit.

living will A witnessed document indicating a patient's desire to be allowed to die a natural death, rather than be kept alive by heroic, life-sustaining measures. The will applies to decisions that will be made after a terminally ill patient is incompetent and has no reasonable possibility of recovery. Compare *testamentary will.*

living will laws Laws that help to guarantee that a patient's documented wishes regarding terminal illness procedures will be carried out. Living will laws may set forth testator and witness requirements for executing a living will and medical requirements for terminating treatment. Living will laws may also address other issues, such as authorization of a proxy for health care decisions, immunity from liability for following a living will's directives, and the withholding or withdrawal of tube feedings. Also called natural death laws.

locality rule Allowance made when considering evidence in a trial for the type of community in which the defendant practices his profession and the standards of that community.

M

malfeasance Performance of an unlawful, wrongful act. Compare *misfeasance, nonfeasance.*

malpractice A professional person's wrongful conduct, improper discharge of professional duties, or failure to meet standards of care, which results in harm to another person. Also called professional negligence.

medical directive (physician's directive) A comprehensive advance care document that covers preferred treatment goals and specific scenarios of patient incompetence. It also includes the option to designate a proxy decision maker or power of attorney for the event of incompetence, the option to record a personal statement, and a place to designate wishes for organ donation.

medical record A written, legal record of every aspect of the patient's care. A record of a person's illnesses and their treatment.

medical release form The form an institution asks a patient to sign when he refuses a medical treatment. The form protects both the institution and the health care professional from liability if the patient's condition worsens because of his refusal.

medicolegal Of or pertaining to both medicine and law. Medicolegal considerations are a significant part of the process of making many patient care decisions and in setting policies regarding the treatment of mentally incompetent people and minors, the performance of sterilization or therapeutic abortion, and the care of terminally ill patients. Medicolegal considerations, decisions, definitions, and policies provide the framework for informed consent, professional liability, and many other aspects of health care practice.

mental competence The ability to understand information and act reasonably. A mentally competent person is capable of understanding explanations and is able to comprehend the results of his decisions.

mental incompetence The inability to understand the nature and effect of the action a person is engaged in. A mentally incompetent person is incapable of understanding explanations and is unable to comprehend the results of his decisions. Compare *adjudicated incompetent, incompetence.*

minor A person not of legal age; beneath the age of majority. Minors may not be able to consent to their own medical treatment unless they are legally emancipated. However, in many jurisdictions, parental consent is no longer necessary for certain types of medical and psychiatric treatment.

misdemeanor An offense that's considered less serious than a felony and carries with it a lesser penalty, usually a fine or imprisonment for less than 1 year.

misfeasance An improper performance of a lawful act, especially in a way that might cause damage or injury. Compare *malfeasance, nonfeasance.*

misrepresentation The statutory crime of giving false or misleading information, usually with the intent to deceive or be unfair.

mistreatment The use of medication, isolation technique, restraint, or related method that harms, or is likely to harm, a person. Compare *abuse, neglect.*

moral dilemma An ethical problem caused by conflicts of rights, responsibilities, and values.

N

natural death laws See *living will laws.*

neglect Refusal or failure to fulfill a health care provider's or health care facility's obligation to a patient; failure to provide treatment or services necessary to maintain the health or safety of a patient; may also include failure of a person who has financial responsibility to provide care. Compare *abuse, mistreatment.*

negligence Failure to act as an ordinary prudent person would under similar circumstances. Conduct that falls below the standard established by law for the protection of others under the same circumstances. Compare *comparative negligence.*

negligent nondisclosure The failure to completely inform a patient about his treatment.

next of kin One or more persons in

the nearest degree of relationship to another person.

non-delegable duty A duty that can't be delegated or assigned to another party.

nonfeasance Failure to perform a task, duty, or undertaking that one has agreed to perform or that one has a legal duty to perform. Compare *malfeasance, misfeasance.*

nonmaleficence An ethical principle based on the obligation to do no harm.

nurse practice act A law enacted by a state's legislature outlining the legal scope of nursing practice within that state.

O

occurrence policy A professional liability insurance policy that protects against an error of omission occurring during a policy period, regardless of when the claim is made.

occurrence rule Under this rule, the statute of limitations for filing a lawsuit starts running the day the incident occurred. The occurrence rule is generally the shortest period of time under which a lawsuit can be filed.

oral contract Any contract that isn't in writing or isn't signed by the parties involved.

ordinary negligence The inadvertent omission of the care that a reasonably prudent nurse would ordinarily provide under similar circumstances.

ostensible agent doctrine See *borrowed-servant doctrine.*

P

parens patriae A doctrine that appoints the state as the legal guardian of a child or incompetent adult when a person hasn't been appointed as guardian.

patient 1. A health care recipient who is ill or hospitalized. 2. A client in a health care service.

patient advocate A person (often a nurse) who seeks to protect a patient's rights from infringement by institutional policies.

patient antidumping laws Amendments to the Social Security Act intended to prevent hospitals from turning away patients who are uninsured or unable to pay. They require that hospitals participating in Medicare provide medical screening and stabilizing treatment for any patient who has an emergency condition or is in labor and provide guidelines and require documentation for transfers to other facilities or for hospital discharge.

patient classification systems Ways of grouping patients so that the size of the staff needed to care for them can be estimated accurately.

patient record A collection of documents that provides a record of each time a person visited or sought treatment and received care or a referral for care from a health care facility. This confidential record is usually held by the facility and the information in it's released only to the person or with the person's written permission, except in certain situations, such as when release is required by law. It contains the initial assessment, health history, laboratory reports, and notes by nurses, doctors, and consultants as well as order sheets, medication sheets, admission records, discharge summaries, and other pertinent data. A problem-oriented medical record also contains a master problem list. The patient record is usually a collection of papers held in a folder, but increasingly, hospitals are computerizing the records after every discharge, making the past record available on visual display terminals. Also called chart (informal).

patient's bill of rights Documents that define a person's rights while receiving health care. Bills of rights for patients are designed to protect such basic rights as human dignity, privacy, confidentiality, informed consent, and refusal of treatment. The American Hospital Association, the National League for Nursing, the American Civil Liberties Union, and other organizations and health care institutions have prepared patient's bill of rights. Concepts expressed in these documents may be incorporated into law. Although bills of rights issued by health care institutions and professional organizations don't have the force of law, nurses should regard them as professionally binding.

peremptory challenge A right given to attorneys at trial to dismiss a prospective juror for no particular reason; the number of times an attorney can invoke this right is usually limited.

persistent vegetative state A state of severe mental impairment in which only involuntary bodily functions are sustained.

physician's directive See *medical directive.*

plaintiff A person who files a civil lawsuit initiating a legal action. In criminal actions, the prosecution is the plaintiff, acting on behalf of the people in the jurisdiction.

policy A definite course or method of action selected from among alternatives and in the light of given conditions to guide, and usually determine, present and future decisions. Compare *rule.*

policy defense Rationale for denying coverage given by professional liability insurance carriers when a client submits a claim. Reasons for denial may include failure to pay a premium on time or failure to renew the policy.

power of attorney An instrument authorizing another person to act as one's agent or attorney; an "attorney-in-fact." Power of attorney continues to operate only with the continued consent of the person who granted it. If the grantor of the power should become incompetent, the power of attorney is automatically revoked. It's also revoked when the principal person dies. Compare *durable power of attorney.*

practicing medicine without a license Practicing activities defined under state or provincial law in the Medical Practice Act without medical supervision, direction, or control.

practicing pharmacy without a license Practicing activities defined under state or provincial law in the Pharmacy Practice Act without pharmacist supervision, direction, or control. These laws give pharmacists the sole legal authority to prepare, compound, preserve, and dispense drugs.

prescription drug Any drug restricted from regular commercial purchase and sale.

presumed consent A legal principle based upon the belief that a rational and prudent person would consent in the same situation, if able to. Applies primarily to emergency care of unconscious patients but may be expanded to cadaver organ donors.

prima facie A fact presumed to be true unless disproved by some evidence to the contrary.

privacy One's private life or personal affairs. The right to privacy refers to the right to be left alone and to be free from unwanted publicity.

privileged communication A conversation in which the speaker intends the information given to remain private between himself and the listener.

privilege doctrine A doctrine that protects the privacy of persons within a fiduciary relationship, such as a husband and wife, a doctor and patient, or a nurse and patient. During legal proceedings, a court can't force either party to reveal communications between them unless the party who would benefit from the protection agrees.

probation period A period of time during which an individual is observed and evaluated to ascertain fitness for a particular job or duty.

procedure Established guidelines for performing a task.

professional liability A legal concept describing the obligation of a professional person to pay a patient or client for damages caused by the professional's act of omission, commission, or negligence, after a court determines that the professional was negligent. Professional liability better describes the responsibility of all professionals to their clients than does the concept of malpractice, but the idea of professional liability is central to malpractice.

professional liability insurance A type of liability insurance that protects professional persons against malpractice claims.

professional negligence See *malpractice.*

protocol A code providing and prescribing strict adherence to guidelines for and authorization of particular practice activities.

proviso A condition or stipulation. Its general function is to except something from the basic provision, to qualify or restrain its general scope, or to prevent misinterpretation.

proximate cause A legal concept of cause and effect that says a sequence of natural and continuous events produces an injury that wouldn't have otherwise occurred.

proxy The recipient of a grant of authority to act or speak for another.

punitive damages Also called exemplary damages, punitive damages are compensation in excess of actual damages that are a form of punishment to the wrongdoer and reparation to the injured. These damages are awarded only in rare instances of malicious and willful misconduct. Compare *general damages, special damages.*

Q

qualified privilege A conditional right or immunity granted to the defendant because of the circumstances of a legal case.

quality of life A legal and ethical standard that's determined by relative suffering or pain, not by the degree of disability.

R

randomized-controlled study An experimental study to assess the effects of a drug or treatment in which the participants are randomly divided into two groups — one experimental (whose members are given the drug or treatment) and one control group (whose members might be given a placebo, or might not given any drug or treatment). Evaluations are then performed on both groups.

reasonably prudent nurse The standard a court uses to judge a nurse in a negligence suit. The court considers whether another nurse would have acted similarly to the defendant under similar circumstances.

rebuttable presumption A presumption that may be overcome or disputed by contrary evidence.

redefinition A rewriting of the fundamental provision of a nurse practice act. This changes the basic premise of the entire act without amending or repealing it.

refusal of treatment form A form provided by some facilities that a patient must sign to confirm that he has been fully informed of his medical condition and the likely consequences of his refusal of treatment, and to release the facility, including its employees and physicians, from liability for following his expressed wishes and directions.

registry 1. An office or agency in which lists of nurses and records pertaining to nurses seeking employment are maintained. 2. In epidemiology: a listing service for incidence data pertaining to the occurrence of specific diseases or disorders such as a tumor registry.

remand To send back. An appellate court may send a case back to the lower court that considered the case, ordering that further action be taken there.

reservation-of-rights letter A letter informing the insured and his employer that the insurer believes the case falls outside what is covered by the insurance policy.

res ipsa loquitur Latin phrase meaning "the thing speaks for itself." A legal doctrine that applies when the defendant was solely and exclusively in control at the time the plaintiff's injury occurred so that the injury wouldn't have occurred if the defendant had exercised due care. In addition, the injured party couldn't have contributed to his own injury. When a court applies this doctrine to a case, the defendant bears the burden of proving that he wasn't negligent.

respondeat superior Latin phrase meaning "let the master answer." A legal doctrine that makes an employer indirectly liable for the consequences of his employee's wrongful conduct while the employee is acting within the scope of his employment.

resuscitative life-support measures Actions taken to reverse an immediate, life-threatening situation (for example, cardiopulmonary resuscitation).

review committee A group of individuals delegated to inspect and report on the quality of health care in a given institution.

right-of-conscience laws Based on freedom of thought or of religion, these laws allow a health care provider to refuse to care for a patient when an objection to the care or non-care exists.

right-to-access laws Laws that grant a patient the right to see his medical records.

right-to-die law A law that upholds a patient's right to choose death by refusing extraordinary treatment. Also referred to as a natural death law or living will law. Compare *euthanasia.*

right to notice 1. A due process right requiring that the accused receive timely notice of both the pending charges and the hearing date. 2. An employee's right to receive sufficient notification or warning before termination. This allows the employee time to protest or appeal the termination and to seek employment elsewhere.

risk management The identification, analysis, evaluation, and elimination or reduction, to the extent possible, of risks to hospital patients, visitors, or employees. Risk management programs are involved with both loss prevention and loss control and handle all incidents, claims, and other insurance- and litigation-related tasks.

risk manager A person who identifies, analyzes, evaluates, and eliminates or reduces an organization's potential accidental losses. Almost always, a risk manager deals with situations in which the only possible outcome is a loss or no change in the status quo. Examples of the responsibilities of a risk manager include purchasing and managing insurance policies, inviting engineering professionals to examine the structural integrity of a building, or examining hospital policies and procedures to eliminate unnecessary risks.

rule A guide for conduct that describes the actions that should or shouldn't be taken in specific situations. Compare *policy.*

S

scope of practice In nursing, the professional nursing activities defined under state or provincial law in each state's (or Canadian province's) Nurse Practice Act.

service of process The delivery of a writ, summons, or complaint to a defendant. The original of the document is shown; a copy is served. Service of process gives reasonable notice to allow the person to appear, testify, and be heard in court. See also *summons.*

settlement An agreement made between parties to a suit before a judgment is rendered by a court.

slander Spoken words that may damage another person's reputation. Compare *defamation, libel.*

special damages Compensation for indirect loss or injury, such as present and future medical expenses, past and future loss of earnings, and decreased earning capacity. Also called consequential damages. Compare *general damages, punitive damages.*

specialty standard The standard of care that applies to a given nursing specialty.

staff 1. The people who work toward a common goal and are employed or supervised by someone of higher rank such as the nurses in a hospital. 2. A designation by which a staff nurse is distinguished from a head nurse or other nurse. 3. In nursing education: the nonprofessional employees of the institution, such as librarians, technicians, secretaries, and clerks. 4. In nursing service administration: the units of the organization that provide service to the "line," or administratively defined hierarchy, such as the personnel office is "staff" to the director of nursing and the nursing service administration.

standard 1. A criterion that serves as a basis for comparison for evaluating similar phenomena or substances such as a standard for the practice of a profession. 2. A pharmaceutical preparation or a chemical substance of known quantity, ingredients, and strength that is used to determine the constituents or the strength of another preparation. 3. Of known value, strength, quality, or ingredients.

standards of care Criteria that serve as a basis of comparison when evaluating the quality of nursing practice. In a malpractice lawsuit, a measure by which the defendant's alleged wrongful conduct is compared — acts performed or omitted that an ordinary, reasonably prudent nurse, in the defendant's position, would have done or not done.

standing orders A written document containing rules, policies, procedures, regulations, and orders for the conduct of patient care in various stipulated clinical situations.

statute of limitations Laws that set forth the length of time within which a person may file specific types of lawsuits.

statutory law A law passed by a federal or state legislature.

subpoena A writ issued under authority of a court to compel the appearance of a witness at a judicial proceeding; disobedience may be punishable as contempt of court.

substantive laws Laws that define and regulate a person's rights.

substitute consent Permission obtained from a parent or legal guardian of a patient who is a minor or who has been declared incompetent by the court.

substitute judgment A legal term indicating the court's substitution of its own judgment for that of a person the court considers unable to make an informed decision such as an incompetent adult.

sudden-emergency exception Defense used by hospitals in liability cases involving understaffing when staffing shortages couldn't have been anticipated, as opposed to chronic understaffing.

summary judgment A judgment requested by any party to a civil action to end the action when it's believed that there's no genuine issue or material fact in dispute.

summons A document issued by a clerk of the court upon the filing of a complaint. A sheriff, marshal, or other appointed person serves the summons, notifying a person that an action has been begun against him. See also *service of process.*

support group People whom a person confides in and draws on for support, either as individuals or in a group setting.

T

tampering To improperly or illegally interfere with or alter, such as altering a medical record with the intent to conceal an error.

temporary practice permit Permission granted by a state board of nursing to an out-of-state nurse enabling her to legally practice nursing until she can obtain a license from that state.

terminate 1. To end an employee's service. 2. In contract law: to fulfill all contractual obligations or to absolve oneself of the obligation to fulfill them.

termination The procedure an employer follows to fire an employee.

termination-of-treatment rule Under this rule, the statute of limitations begins on the last day of treatment. The termination-of-treatment rule is generally applied for instances in which treatment was given over an extended period of time. Compare *constructive-continuing-treatment rule.*

therapeutic privilege A legal doctrine that permits a doctor to withhold information from the patient if he can prove that disclosing it would adversely affect the patient's health.

toll A pause in the statute of limitations that occurs, for example, when a patient consults a lawyer who says he doesn't have a viable claim.

tort A civil wrong outside of a contractual relationship.

tortfeasor Wrongdoer, one who commits a trespass or is guilty of a tort.

traditional staffing patterns Work schedules that follow 8-hour shifts, 7 days per week, including evening and night shifts.

trial de novo A proceeding in which both issues of law and issues of fact are reconsidered as if the original trial had never taken place. New testimony may be introduced or the matter may be determined a second time on the basis of the evidence already produced.

U

unfair labor practices Actions taken by an employer that are prohibited by state and federal labor laws. This term commonly refers to tactics used by an employer to discourage employees from participating in union activities. For example, under the National Labor Relations Act, unfair labor practices include interfering with, restraining, or coercing employees who exercise their right to organize.

utilization management Evaluation of the necessity, appropriateness, and efficiency of the use of medical services, procedures, and facilities. This includes review of admissions, services ordered and provided, length of stay, and discharge practices on a concurrent and retrospective basis.

V

verbal order A spoken order given directly and in person by a doctor to a nurse.

WXYZ

willful conduct An intentional act as opposed to a mistake.

witness 1. One who gives evidence in a case before a court and who attests or swears to facts or gives testimony under oath. 2. To observe the execution of an act, such as the signing of a document, or to sign one's name to authenticate the observation.

workers' compensation Compensation to an employee for an injury or occupational disease suffered in connection with his employment, paid under a government-supervised insurance system contributed to by employers.

writ of habeas corpus Literally means "you have the body"; a process whereby an individual detained or imprisoned asks the court to rule on the validity of the detainment or imprisonment. If the person is granted the writ, he must be released immediately.

wrongful death statute A statute existing in all states that provides that the death of a person can give rise to a cause of legal action brought by the person's beneficiaries in a civil suit against the person whose willful or negligent acts caused the death. Prior to the existence of these statutes, a suit could be brought only if the injured person survived.

wrongful life action Also called wrongful birth. A civil suit usually brought against a doctor or health care facility on the basis of negligence that resulted in the wrongful birth or life of an infant. The parents of the unwanted child seek to obtain payment from the defendant for the medical expenses of pregnancy and delivery, for pain and suffering, and for the education and upbringing of the child. Wrongful life actions have been brought and won in several situations, including unsuccessful tubal ligations and vasectomies. Failure to diagnose pregnancy in time for abortion and incorrect medical advice leading to the birth of a defective child have also led to malpractice suits for a wrongful life.

Court case citation index

A

Alt v. John Umstead Hospital,
479 S.E.2d 800 (N.C. 1997),
pp. 117-118

Anderson v. Commission of Labor,
255 A.D.2d 678 (N.Y. Sup. Ct. 1998),
p. 43

Anderson v. Texas Health System,
d/b/a Presbyterian Hospital of
Kaufman and Presbyterian Health
Care System, and Jim Bryant, Jr.,
2000 WL 145082 (N.D. Tex. 2000),
pp. 142-143

B

**Battocchi v. Washington Hospital
Center,** 581 A.2d 759, 767 (1990),
p. 80

**Beaudoin v. Watertown Memorial
Hospital,** 32 Wis.2d 132, 145
N.W.2d 169 (Wis. 1966), *p. 11*

Busta v. Columbus Hospital Corp.,
916 P.2d 122 (Mont. 1996), *p. 118*

Byrne v. Boadle, Ct of Exchequer
(Eng. 1863), *pp. 10-11*

C

**Cannell v. Medical and Surgical
Clinic S.C.,** 21 Ill.App.3d 383, 315
N.E.2d 278 (1974), *pp. 148*

**Chin v. St. Barnabas Medical Cen-
ter, Immacula Louis-Charles,
Teresa Leib, Nancy Hosgesang,
Dr. Herbert Goldfarb, and C.R.
Bard, Inc.,** 711 A.2d. 352, cert.
granted, 719 A.2d 640 (N.J.) (No. C-
85 and C-86) (1998, September 11);
**Chin v. St. Barnabas Medical
Center,** 711 A.2d 352 (N.J. Supp.
1998), *p. 11*

Claypool v. Levin, 195 Wis.2d 535,
536 N.W.2d 206 (Wis. 1997), *p. 16*

Cline v. Lund, 31 Cal.App.3d 755,
107 Cal. Rptr. 629 (1973), *pp. 98-99,
189*

Commonwealth v. Anne Capute,
(Fall River, Mass., 1982), *p. 166*

Commonwealth v. Brandwein,
435 Mass. 623, 760 N.E.2d 724
(2002), *p. 146*

**Cooper v. National Motor Bearing
Co.,** 136 Cal.App.2d 229, 288 P.2d
581 (1955), *pp. 94, 109*

**Cooper v. Rehabilitation Facility
at Austin,** 962 S.W.2d 151 (Tex.
1998), *pp. 107-109*

Critchfield v. McNamara, 532
N.W.2d 287 (Neb. Sup. Ct. 1995),
pp. 80-81

Crowe v. Provost, 374 S.W.2d 645
(Tenn. 1963), *p. 10*

**Cruzan v. Director, Missouri De-
partment of Health,** 497 U.S. 261
(Mo. 1990), *p. 164*

DE

**Darling v. Charleston Community
Memorial Hospital,** 33 Ill.2d 326,
211 N.E.2d 253 (1965), *pp. 55-56,
188*

**Derry v. Edward Peskin, MD, Saint
Vincent Hospital, Arthur Curtis,
MD, Susan Palmer, RN, Ameri-
can Medical Response, Lisa
Lavoie, EMT, and David Wiggins,
EMT,** 97-1720-A, Mass. Super. Ct.
at Worcester (1999), *p. 78*

**Dessauer v. Memorial General
Hospital,** 96 N.M. 92, 628 P.2d 337
(N.M. Ct.App. 1981), *p. 37*

**Dimaranan v. Pomona Medical
Center, et al.,** 775 F.Supp. 338
(C.D. Cal. 1991), *pp. 62-64*

**Duling v. Bluefield Sanitarium,
Inc.,** 149 W.Va. 467, 142 N.E.2d 754
(1965), *p. 100*

F

Farrell v. Kramer, 193 A.2d 560 (Maine 1963), *pp. 59-60*

Flanagan v. John F. Kennedy Memorial Hospital, 446 Pa. Super. 107; 666 A.2d 333; 1995 Pa. Super. (1995), *pp. 78-79*

Fragante v. County of Honolulu, et al., 888 F.2d 591 (9th Cir. 1989), *p. 62*

Fraijo v. Hartland Hospital, 160 Cal.Rptr. 246 (1979), *p. 101*

Francis v. Memorial General Hospital, 104 N.M. 698, 726 P.2d 852 (N.Mex. 1986), *p. 193*

Freeman et al. v. Cresthaven Nursing Residence et al., Tex. Dist. Ct. Case No. B 0155491 (2001), *p. 22*

G

Gallimore v. Children's Memorial Hospital, 617 N.E.2d 1052 (Ohio 1993), *p. 37*

Garcia v. Presbyterian Hospital Center, 593 P.2d 487 (1979), *p. 16*

Gerard v. Sacred Heart Medical Center, 937 P.2d 1103 (Wash. 1997), *p. 118*

Glassman v. St. Joseph Hospital, 631 N.E.2d 1186 (Ill. 1994), *pp. 54-55*

Goff v. Physicians General Hospital of San Jose, 166 Cal.App.2d 314; 333 P.2d 29 (1958), *p. 89*

Grant, Administratrix of the Estate of Robert Burkhardt, Deceased v. Victory Park Nursing Home, CCP of Hamilton County, Ohio, No. A-9400115 (1994), *p. 114*

Guerra v. Diamond Central Nurses, Inc., Diamond Central Personnel Services, Inc., and Feeley Medical Services, Bexar County, Tex., District Court Case No. 98-PC-1630 (Tex. 2001), *pp. 133-134*

HI

Hammonds v. Aetna Casualty and Surety Co., 237 F.Supp. 96 (D.C. Ohio 1965), *pp. 143-144*

Harnish v. Lancaster General Hospital and Kurtis Jens, M.D., CCP of Lancaster County, No. 3549-1993 (Pa. 1999), *pp. 114-115*

Harrell v. Louis Smith Memorial Hospital, 397 S.E.2d 746 Georgia (1990), *p. 189*

Heinrich v. Conemaugh Valley Memorial Hospital, 648 A.2d 53 (Pa. Super. 1994), *p. 61*

Hicks v. State of Delaware, No. 93A-05-005, 1994 Del. Super. (April 1994), *p. 44*

Holton v. Memorial Hospital, 176 Ill.2d 95, 679 N.E.2d 1202 (Ill. 1997), pp. 49-51

Hunt v. Palm Springs General Hospital, 352 So.2d 582 (Fla. Dist. Ct.App. 1977), *p. 98*

J

Justice v. Natvig, 238 Va. 178, 381 S.E.2d 8 (Va. 1989), *p. 15*

K

Keene v. Brigham and Women's Hospital, Mass. Super. Ct. Case No. 95-01081 (2001), *p. 18*

Kempster v. Child Protective Services of the Department of Social Services of the County of Suffolk, 515 N.Y.S.2d 807 (N.Y. 1987), *p. 61*

Keyes v. Humana Hospital Alaska, Inc., 750 P.2d 343 (1988), *p. 30*

L

LaDuke v. Hepburn Medical Center, 239 A.D.2d 750 (App. Ct. N.Y. 1997), *pp. 160-161*

Lama v. Boras (P.R. 1994), *p. 75*

Lamarca v. United States, 31 F.Supp.2d 110 (N.Y. 1998), *pp. 108, 109*

Lester v. Southwest General Hospital, Cuyahoga County, Ohio, Court of Common Pleas Case No. 385668 (Ohio, 2001), *p. 124*

Long Term Care, Inc. v. Winifred W. Martin, Case No. 5D99-3540, Fla. Ct.App., 5th Dist., 778 So.2d 1100 (Fla. 2001), *p. 70-73*

Lopez v. Southwest Community Health Service, 833 P.2d 1183 (N.M. 1992), *p. 58*

Lopez v. Swyer, 115 N.J. Super. 237, 279 A.2d 116 (1971), *p. 17*

M

Manning v. Twin Falls Clinic & Hospital, Inc., 122 Idaho 47, 830 P.2d 1185 (1992), *p. 95*

McCrystal v. Trumbull Memorial Hospital, 684 N.E.2d 721 (Ohio App. 1996), *pp. 51-52*

McDonald v. Aliquippa Hospital 606 A.2d 1218 (Pa. Sup. Ct., 1992), *pp. 106-107, 109-110*

McIntosh v. Milano, 403 A.2d 500 (N.J. Sup. Ct. Law Div. 1979), *p. 157*

Merritt v. Karcioglu, 668 So.2d 469 (La.App. 1996), *pp. 188-190*

Methodist Hospital v. Ball, 50 Tenn.App. 460,362 S.W.2d 475 (1961), *p. 101*

Minster v. Pohl, 206 Ga.App. 617, 426 S.E.2d 204 (1992), *p. 94*

Misericordia Hospital Medical Center v. National Labor Relations Board, 623 F.2d 808 (2d Cir. 1980), *pp. 199-200*

Mutual Insurance Company of Arizona v. American Casualty Company of Reading, Pa., 189 Ariz. 22, 938 P.2d 71 (1997), *p. 27*

N

Nelson v. Trinity Medical Center, 419 N.W.2d 886 (N.D. 1988), *pp. 9-10*

Nolan vs. Jefferson Parish Hospital, Service District No. 2, State of Louisiana, d/b/a East Jefferson General Hospital, et al., 01-175 (La.App. 5 Cir. 6/27/01), 790 So.2d T25 (La. 2001), *pp. 141-142*

O

O'Neal v. Annapolis Hospital, 183 Mich.App. 281 (1990), *p. 100*

PQ

Palmer v. Clarksdale Hospital, 213 Miss. 601, 57 So.2d 473 (1952), *p. 94*

Parker v. Bullock County Hospital Authority, A 90A0 (Ala. 1990), *p. 58*

Pedersen v. Zielski, 822 P 2d 903 (Ala. 12/6/91), *p. 14*

People v. Doe, 410 N.Y.S.2d 233, 96 Misc.2d 975 (1978), *p. 145*

Prairie v. University of Chicago Hospitals, Ill.App.1 Dist.; 232, Ill. Dec. 520, 698 N.E.2d, 298 Ill.App.3d (1998), *p. 213*

R

Rampe v. Community General Hospital of Sullivan County, 241 A.D.2d 817, 660 N.Y.S.2d 206 (3d Dep't 1997), *p. 103*

Ramsey et al. v. Physicians Memorial Hospital, Inc., et al., 373 A.2d 76 (Md. 1977), *pp. 91-93*

Roach v. Springfield Clinic, 157 Ill.2d 29, 623 N.E.2d 246 (Ill. 1993), *p. 23*

Rounds v. Jackson Park Hospital and Medical Center, 319 Ill.App.3d 280 (First District, 2001), *p. 81*

S

Salter v. Deaconess Family Medical Center, 701 N.Y.S.2d 587 (1999), *p. 112*

Sanchez v. Bay General Hospital, 116 Cal.App.3d 776, 172 Cal. Rptr. 342 (1981), *p. 189*

Schessler v. Keck, 271 P.2d 588 (Cal.App. 1954), *p. 57*

Sweet v. Sisters of Providence, 881 P.2d 304 (Ala. 9/30/94), *p. 22*

T

Tarasoff v. Regents of the University of California, 17 Cal. 3d 425, 551 P.2d 334, 131 Cal. Rptr. 14 (1976), *p. 157*

Thomas et al. v. Corson et al., 265 Md. 84; 288 A.2d 379 (1972), *pp. 89-91*

Tuma v. Board of Nursing, 100 Idaho 74, 593 P.2d 711 (1979), *p. 180*

U

University of Texas Medical Branch v. Danesi, No. 01-96-01107-CV (Tex. 1999), *pp. 42-43*

V

Voorhees v. University of Pennsylvania, No.3558, 1997 Phila. Cty. Rptr. (June 1997), *pp. 34, 36-39*

WX

Walicez v. Dr. Gandhi Gutta, MD, and Alexian Brothers Hospital, Ill. Circ. Ct. Case No. 97L-8110 (2001), *p. 19*

Whalen v. Roe, 429 U.S. 589, 97 S.Ct. 869 (1977), *p. 153*

Widman v. Paoli Memorial Hospital, No. 85-1034 (Pa. 1989), *p. 119*

Wingo v. Rockford Memorial Hospital, 686 N.E.2d 722 (Ill.App. 1997), *p. 53*

Winkelman v. Beloit Memorial Hospital, 168 Wisc.2d 12, 484 N.W.2d211 (Wis. 1992), *p. 192*

Woodward v. Alan Myres, Karen Dean, RN, and Correctional Medical Services of Illinois, U.S. Dist. Ct. for the Northern Div. of Ill., No. 99 C 0290 (2001), *pp. 66-70, 71-72, 79, 85*

Wright v. Abbott Laboratories, Appeal from the U.S. Dist. Ct. for Dist. of Kansas (D.C. No. 97-CV-1333-JTM) (1999), *pp. 35, 39-42*

YZ

Young v. Board of Hospital Directors, Lee County, #82-429 (Fla. 1984), *p. 212*

General index

A

Abuse
  child, 61-62, 157
  elder, 63-64, 162
  emotional or psychological, 162
  patient, 162-164
  physical, 61-62, 157, 162
  reporting of, 61-62, 157
  sexual, 61-62, 157, 162
Accidents and injuries
  burns and, 112-113
  case studies of, 106-109
  equipment-related, 112-114, 120
  falls and, 107-111
  prevention of, 119-122
  risk assessment for, 119
  self-inflicted, 66-70, 71-72, 79, 85,
    114-115, 120, 121
  standard of care and, 119
Acquired immunodeficiency syndrome, privacy concerns in,
  153-155
Actual notice, 16, 110
Advance directives, 23, 163, 167
Advocacy, patient, 178-179, 180
Affirmative defense, 16
Agency nurses, standards of care
  for, 133-136
Alcohol abuse, by nurses, 184-187
American Nurses Association
  Code of Ethics of, 125
  staffing guidelines of, 190-191
  Standards of Nursing Practice of,
    77, 125, 126-130. *See also* Stan-
    dards of care.
Americans with Disabilities Act, 156
Analgesics
  abuse of by nurse, 174, 184-186
  documentation of, 171
  for dying patients, 165-166; 171.
    See also Terminal care.
Arbitration, 29-30
Assault, 5, 162
  restraints and, 117
  sexual, 167-169

Assessment, 88-105
  case studies of, 89-91
  communication findings from, 96
  components of, 91-95
  continuous, 96, 104
  data assessment in, 92
  documentation of, 96, 103, 104-105
  family interview in, 95
  guidelines for, 103-105
  history in, 93
  legal issues in, 95-101
  nurse-patient relationship and,
    95-96
  nursing actions and, 96-97
  nursing diagnoses and, 97
  as ongoing process, 94-95
  patient history in, 91-93
  physical examination in, 93-95
  review of prior medical records
    in, 95
  scope of, 94
  in special care units, 97-101, 98-100
  standards for, 94
  for suicide risk, documentation of,
    66-70, 71-72, 79, 85
  test results review in, 95
  thoroughness of, 94
  timely, 90
Assisted suicide, 166-167
Assumption of risk, 13
Attorney, selection of, 204, 206
Attorney-client privilege, 206
  incident reports and, 82-83
Authorization, under Privacy Rule,
  149-151
Autonomy, 177, 178

B

Battery, 5, 162
  restraints and, 117
Bed side rails
  falls and, 111-112
  as restraints, 117
Beneficence, 176, 177
Borrowed servant doctrine, 10, 98, 135
Boundary violations, 167-169
Breach of confidentiality, 141-158. *See
  also* Confidentiality.
  case studies of, 141-143, 146

Breach of contract
   by employee, 195
   by employer, 195-196
   insurance and, 31
Breach of duty, 6, 74-77, 102. *See also*
       Duty; Negligence.
   corporate liability and, 36-37, 109
   prima facie negligence and, 107
Burden of proof
   discovery and, 133
   res ipsa loquitur and, 11, 12
Burns, 112-113

C

Cancer, privacy concerns in, 153
Captain-of-the ship doctrine, 10
Causation, liability and, 10, 93,
       102-103, 110
Challenge
   for cause, 209
   peremptory, 209
Charge nurse, liability of, 196
Charting. *See also* Documentation;
       Medical records.
   subjective versus objective, 83, 86
Charting by exception, 74, 75
Child abuse and neglect, reporting of,
       61-62, 157
Circumstantial evidence, 113
Claims-made policy, 24-27
Client. *See* Patients.
Clinical trials, experimental drugs
       in, 40
Cloning, ethics of, 173-174
Code of Ethics, 125
Common law, 144
Communication. *See also* Reporting.
   ambiguous, 53
   of assessment findings, 96
   as duty, 51-52, 57
   with foreign language speakers, 64
   lack of, 49-51, 52-56, 80-81
   language barriers and, 62-64
   of medically significant informa-
      tion, 54-55, 80-81
   with patients, 20
   privileged, 61, 82-83, 143-144,
      145, 206
Comparative negligence, 13, 29
Compulsory nonsuit, 107
Computerized medical records, 87
   confidentiality of, 151-152

Confidentiality, 141-158. *See also un-*
      der Privacy.
   breach of, case studies of, 141-143,
      146
   for cancer patients, 153
   of computerized records, 151-152,
      153
   contact notification and, 154
   defamation and, 59
   disclosure requirements and,
      156-158
   of faxed records, 152
   fidelity and, 178
   guidelines for, 158
   for human immunodeficiency virus
      or acquired immunodeficiency
      syndrome patients, 153-155
   maintenance of, 156
   for patients with genetic disorders,
      155-156
   Privacy Rule and, 145-152. *See also*
      Privacy Rule.
   privilege and, 143-144
   public's right to know and, 156-158
Consent. *See* Informed consent.
Constructive continuing treatment
      rule, 15
Constructive notice, 16, 110-111
Contact notification, 154
Contract, breach of
   by employee, 195
   by employer, 195-196
   insurance and, 31
Contributory negligence, 13
Corporate liability, 36-37, 109
Counterclaims, 209
Court appearance. *See also* Litigation;
      Trial.
   preparation for, 207-208
Criminal liability, 6, 160-172
   for abuse, 162
   for assisted suicide, 166-167
   for boundary violations, 167-169
   definition of, 162
   disclosure rules for, 157
   documentation and, 171-172
   for euthanasia, 160-161, 164-166
   for mistreatment, 162
   for neglect, 163-164
   prevention of, 170-171
   for sexual misconduct, 167-169
   in terminal care, 164-167
Critical care nursing, liability in, 8

Cross-examination, 67, 213-214

D

Damage, from negligence, 103
Damages, 1
    apportionment of, 29
    general, 28
    limits on, 29
    property exemption for, 208
    punitive, 28
    refusal to pay, 31-32
    special, 28
Dangerous conditions, notice of,
        110-111
Death and dying. *See* Terminal care.
Defamation, 57-60
    by nurse, 57-59
    of nurse, 59-60
    qualified privilege and, 61
    whistle-blowing and, 183
Defective or dangerous equipment,
        23-24, 112-114, 120
Defense attorney
    attorney-client privilege and, 82-83
    selection of, 204, 206
Defenses
    affirmative, 16
    assumption of risk as, 13
    comparative negligence as, 13
    contributory negligence as, 13
    emergency, for understaffing,
        197-198
    false allegations as, 13
    statute of limitations as, 16
Delegation, 18-19
    respondeat superior and, 6-7. *See also*
        Respondeat superior.
Depositions, 67, 113, 206, 208-209
Descriptive ethics, 176
Diagnostic procedures
    assisting with, 22
    familiarity with, 22, 23
Direct examination, 213-214
Disciplinary action, for refusal to
        float, 193-195
Disclosure laws. *See* Reporting.
Discovery, 15-16, 113, 132-133,
        206-207
Dispensing, 45
Documentation, 20-22, 66-87, 140. *See
    also* Medical records.
    absent or inadequate, 73-74, 77-80

Documentation *(continued)*
    case studies of, 66-73
    of assessment, 96, 103, 104-105
    charting by exception and, 74, 75
    criminal liability and, 171-172
    electronic, 87
    FACT rule for, 21
    flow sheets in, 76
    guidelines for, 83-87
    incident reports and, 21-22, 81-83
    of informed consent, 86
    of medical condition, 70-73
    of pain management, 171
    policies and procedures for, 77,
        84, 87
    of refusal of treatment, 85
    of restraint, 22, 171
    standards for, 73-74, 77, 87
    subjective versus objective, 83, 86
    of suicide risk, 66-70, 71-72, 79, 85
    of verbal drug orders, 41-42
    in whistle-blowing, 183
Documents, signing as witness, 20
Double-effect doctrine, 165, 166
Double-limits policy, 24
Drug abuse, by nurses, 174, 184-187
Drug administration, 19. *See also* Drug
        orders; Medication errors.
    versus dispensing, 45
    five rights of, 44
    licensed practical nurse's responsi-
        bility in, 46
    nurse's responsibility in, 45-46
    policies and procedures for, 40
    refusal for, 39
    scope of practice and, 41, 44, 45
Drug control laws, 44-45
Drug dispensing, 45
Drug orders. *See also under* Medica-
        tion.
    questioning of, 38
    refusal to execute, 39
    verbal, documentation of, 41-42
Drugs. *See also under* Medication.
    failure to respond to, communica-
        tion of, 55-56
    falls and, 112
    government regulation of, 45
    legal definition of, 45
    prescription, 45
    tranquilizing, 117, 162, 163, 171
Drug trials, 40
Dual agency, 135

Due process, denial of, 71
Durable power of attorney, 23
Duty
    beneficence as, 176, 177
    breach of, 6, 102
    establishment of, 96
    legal definition of, 101-102
    nondelegatable, 36-37
    owed by hospital to patient, 37
Duty to warn, of threats of harm, 157
Dying patients. *See* Terminal care.

E

Elderly, mistreatment of, 63-64, 162,
        163-164, 170-171
Emergency defense, for understaffing,
        197-198
Emergency department nursing,
        8-9, 97
Emergency exception, for under-
        staffing, 198
Emotional abuse, 162
Employee termination, for refusal to
        float, 193-195
Employment contracts, breach of,
        195-196
Employment issues
    English-only requirements, 62-64
    staffing, 188-210. *See also* Staffing
        issues.
End-of-life issues. *See* Terminal care.
English-only requirements, 62-64
Equipment
    defective or dangerous, 112-114, 120
    safe use of, 23-24, 112-114, 120
Ethical dilemmas, 173-187
    case studies of, 173-174
    cloning, 173-174
    definition of, 176
    versus legal issues, 174-175
    patient advocacy and, 178-179
    whistle-blowing and, 179-184
Ethical principles, 176-178
Ethics
    confidentiality and, 146-147
    definition of, 176
    descriptive, 176
    normative, 176
Euthanasia, 160-161, 164-166
Evidence
    circumstantial, 113
    incident reports as, 81-83, 139
    medical records as. *See* Medical
        records.

Excess judgment, 27
Expert witness, 28
    nurse as, 212-213

F

FACT rule, 21
Failure to communicate information,
        49-57, 80-81. *See also* Commu-
        nication.
    case studies of, 49-57
Failure to document information,
        66-87. *See also* Documentation.
    case studies of, 66-73
Failure to perform proper assessment,
        88-105. *See also* Assessment.
    case studies of, 89-91
Failure to perform reasonable patient
        care, 123-140. *See also* Stan-
        dards of care.
    case studies of, 123-124
Failure to protect, 106-122. *See also* Ac-
        cidents and injuries.
    case studies of, 106-109
Falls, 107-111
    case study of, 107-109
    causation in, 110-111
    drugs and, 112
    prevention of, 22, 111-112
    risk assessment for, 109
    side rails and, 111-112
False allegations, 13
False imprisonment, 5
    restraints and, 117
Family, interviewing of, 95
Fidelity, 178
Firing, for refusal to float, 193-195
Five rights of medication administra-
        tion, 44
Floating, 192-195
Flow sheets, 76
Foreign language speakers
    interpreters for, 64
    nurses as, 62-64
Foreign-object cases, 11
Fraud
    in documentation, 74, 80
    statute of limitations and, 16

G

Gait, falls and, 112
General damages, 28
Genetic disorders
    insurance coverage and, 155-156
    privacy concerns for, 155-156

Good Samaritan laws, 32
Government requests, for medical
      information, 157-158

H

Health care facilities
   duties owed to patients by, 37
   liability of, 109-114
      for understaffing, 197-198
   neglect in, 163-164
   regulation of, 125, 163-164,
      170-171, 201
Health insurance, genetic disorders
      and, 155-156
Health Insurance Portability and Ac-
      countability Act, Privacy Rule
      and, 145-152
History, patient, 93
Homestead laws, 208
Hospice care. *See* Terminal care.
Hospitals. *See* Health care facilities.
Human immunodeficiency virus in-
      fection, privacy concerns in,
      153-155

I

Iatrogenic infections, 119
Immunity from liability, 61
Impaired providers, 174, 184-187
Incident reports, 21-22, 81-83, 136-139
   as evidence, 139
   in medical record, 137
Incompetence
   reporting of, 181
   statute of limitations and, 16
Indemnification, 29
Independent contractor, 10
Infection, hospital-caused, 119
Informed consent, 22
   documentation of, 86
   under Privacy Rule, 149, 151
   witnessing forms for, 20
Injury. *See also* Accidents and in-
      juries.
   from negligence, 103
Insurance
   health, genetic disorders and,
      155-156
   liability. *See* Liability insurance.
Insurance adjustor, 83
Intensive care unit, legal issues for,
      97-101

Intentional tort, 4, 5
Internet, Privacy Rule and, 151-152
Interpreters, 64
Interrogatories, 206
Interview
   family, 93
   patient, 93
Invasion of privacy, 5. *See also* Confi-
      dentiality; Privacy rights.
Isolation techniques, 162, 163, 171

JK

Joint Commission on Accreditation of
      Healthcare Organizations, 77
   privacy rights and, 125
   staffing levels and, 201
   standards of care of, 125
Jury, lay, 29
Justice, 176

L

Language barriers, interpreters
      and, 62
Late entries, in medical record, 73, 83
Law
   common versus statutory, 144
   definition of, 176
Lawsuits. *See* Litigation.
Lawyer, selection of, 204, 206
Lawyer-client privilege, 206
   incident reports and, 82-83
Lay juries, 29
Legal consultant, versus expert
      witness, 212-213
Legal doctrines, 6
Legal issues, versus ethical dilemmas,
      174-175
Legal proceedings. *See* Litigation.
Liability. *See also* Malpractice; Negli-
      gence.
   of agency nurses, 134-135
   avoidance of, 18-24
   of charge nurse, 196
   corporate, 36-37, 109
   criminal, 160-172. *See also under*
      Criminal.
   in critical care nursing, 8
   defenses against. *See* Defenses.
   in emergency department nursing,
      8-9
   immunity from, 61
   for medication errors, 36-48
   in obstetric nursing, 7-8

Liability *(continued)*
  premises, 109-114
  in psychiatric nursing, 9
  understaffing and, 198-201
  vicarious, 9
Liability insurance, 24-32
  claims-made policy and, 24-27
  cost of, 27
  coverage under, 24, 25, 31-32
  damages and, 1, 28, 29
  deductibles for, 30
  defensive provisions of, 31
  denial of coverage and, 31-32
  duration of coverage and, 25-26, 31
  employer's, 30-32
  excess judgment and, 27
  exclusions in, 26
  indemnification and, 29
  insurer's participation in lawsuit
      and, 27, 28, 31, 205-206
  limits of, 25, 26, 31-32
  with multiple insurers, 28-29
  need for, 24
  occurrence policy and, 24
  out-of-court settlements and, 28
  overview of, 24, 25-26
  policy clauses in, 25, 26
  policy defense and, 29
  selection of, 25-26
  single- versus double-limits policy
      and, 24
  subrogation and, 27
  threshold limit for, 30-31
Libel, 57-60
  qualified privilege and, 61
  whistle-blowing and, 183
Licensed practical nurse, role of in
      drug administration, 46
Licensure, medication errors and, 41,
      43-44
Litigation
  versus arbitration, 29-30
  causes of, 4-6
  damages in. *See* Damages.
  defense attorney in, 204, 206
  defense independent medical ex-
      amination in, 207
  deposition in, 208-209
  discovery in, 15-16, 113, 132-133,
      206-207
  indemnification in, 29
  insurer's participation in, 27, 28, 31,
      205-206

Litigation *(continued)*
  Nurses Claims Data Bank and, 205
  nurse's involvement in, 203-214
  out-of-court settlement and, 28, 208
  peremptory challenges in, 209
  preliminary action in, 203-205
  preparing defense in, 206-207
  preparing for court appearance
      in, 207-209
  prevention of, 18-24
  response to summons in, 203-204
  restrictions on, 29-30
  screening panels for, 29-30
  trial in, 209-214. *See also* Trial.
Litigation-prone patients, characteris-
      tics of, 21
Living wills, 23, 163, 167
Long-term care facilities
  neglect in, 163-164
  regulation of, 163-164, 170-171

M

Malpractice
  breach of duty and, 102
  causation and, 10, 93, 102-103, 110
  defenses against. *See* Defenses.
  definition of, 4
  elements of, 101
  incident reports and, 81-83
  injury from, 103
  liability for. *See* Liability.
  versus negligence, 6. *See also* Negli-
      gence.
  reporting of, 2-3
  understaffing and, 198-201
Malpractice insurance. *See* Liability
      insurance.
Malpractice litigation. *See also* Litiga-
      tion.
  causes of, 4-6
  prevention of, 18-24
Maltreatment. *See* Abuse; Neglect.
Manager incompetence or miscon-
      duct, reporting of, 179-184
Mandatory overtime, 196-197
Manuals, nursing department,
      131-132, 139. *See also* Policies
      and procedures.
Medical incompetence or miscon-
      duct, reporting of, 181

Medical records. *See also* Documenta-
     tion.
  attorney-client privilege and, 82-83
  charting by exception in, 74, 75
  computerized, 87
    confidentiality of, 151-152, 153
  confidentiality of, 141-158. *See also*
    Confidentiality.
  consent forms in, 86
  contents of, 74, 84
  correction or alteration of, 22, 74,
    80, 83, 85
  disclosure rules for, 156-158
  failure to properly maintain, 74
  faxed, 152
  flow sheets in, 76
  guidelines for, 83-87
  incident reports in, 137. *See also* In-
    cident reports.
  late entries in, 73, 83
  legal significance of, 73-74
  loss of, 74, 80
  omissions in, 77-80, 83, 85
    case studies of, 66-73
  patient access to, 148
  personal opinions in, 83
  prior, review of, 95
  retention of, 17-18
  review of, for litigation, 207
  tampering with, 74, 80
  unauthorized entries in, 85-87
  vague entries in, 83
Medicare or Medicaid, 163-164
Medication errors, 23, 34-48, 37-38.
    See also Drugs.
  case studies of, 34-46
  legal consequences of, 43-44
  liability for, 36-43
  loss of benefits and, 43-44
  loss of licensure and, 43-44
  mental anguish and, 42-43
  prevention of, 19-20, 44-48
  questioning drug orders and, 38, 39
  right-of-conscience laws and, 39
  scope of practice and, 41
  types of, 36-43
Mental incompetence, statute of limi-
    tations and, 16
Minors, statute of limitations and, 16
Mistreatment. *See* Abuse; Neglect.
Moral dilemmas. *See* Ethical dilem-
    mas.

Moral distress, 176
Morals, definition of, 176

N
Narcotic analgesics
  abuse of by nurse, 174, 184-186
  documentation of, 171
  for dying patients, 165-166. *See also*
    Terminal care.
National Labor Relations Board, 200
National League for Nursing, 179
National Practitioner Data Bank, 2-3
Neglect
  child, 61-62, 157
  elder, 63-64
  patient, 163-164, 179-184
  reporting of, 61-62, 157, 179-184
Negligence, 5
  breach of duty and, 74-77, 102
  causation and, 10, 93, 102-103, 110
  comparative, 13, 29
  contributory, 13
  criminal, 6, 160-172. *See also*
    Criminal liability.
  defenses against. *See* Defenses.
  elements of, 101
  incident reports and, 81-83
  injury from, 103
  liability for. *See* Liability.
  versus malpractice, 6. *See also*
    Malpractice.
  prima facie, 107
  rebuttable presumption of, 22, 74
  reporting of, 55-56, 181
  standard of care and, 74
  understaffing and, 198-201
Non-English speakers
  interpreters for, 64
  nurses as, 62-64
Nonmaleficence, 176-178
Non-suit, compulsory, 107
Normative ethics, 176
Notice
  actual, 16, 110
  constructive, 16, 110-111
Nurse
  agency, standards of care for,
    133-136
  as expert witness, 212-213
  incompetence or misconduct of,
    179-184
    reporting of, 181, 185-186

Nurse *(continued)*
  independent actions of, 96-97
  inexperienced, 23
  litigation-prone, 21
  reasonably prudent, 18, 98-100,
    130-131
  responsibilities of in drug adminis-
    tration, 45-46
  substance abuse by, 174, 184-187
  as witness. *See* Witness; Witnessing.
Nurse-patient ratio, 190. *See also*
    Staffing issues.
Nurse-patient relationship
  duty to provide care and, 95-96
  as privileged relationship, 143-144
Nurse practice acts, 88
Nurses Claims Data Bank, 205
Nurse's notes, 80
Nursing actions, independent, 96-97
Nursing department manual, 131-132,
    139. *See also* Policies and pro-
    cedures.
Nursing diagnoses, 97
Nursing Home Reform Amendments,
    170
Nursing homes
  neglect in, 163-164
  regulation of, 163-164, 170-171
Nursing orders, standing, 132
Nursing shortage, 190. *See also*
    Staffing issues.
Nursing standards. *See* Standards of
    care.

O
Obstetric nursing, liability in, 7-8
Occurrence policy, 24
Occurrence rule, 14
Omnibus Budget Reconciliation Act,
    Nursing Home Reform
    Amendments of, 170
Opioid analgesics
  abuse of by nurse, 174, 184-186
  for dying patients, 165-166. *See also*
    Terminal care.
  documentation of, 171
Orders. *See* Drug orders; Nursing or-
    ders; Physician orders.
Out-of-court settlement, 28, 208
Overtime, mandatory, 196-197

PQ
Pain management. *See* Analgesics.
Palliative care. *See* Terminal care.
Partial summary judgment, 113
Patient
  boundary violations with, 167-169
  litigation-prone, 21
  mistreatment of, 162-164
  neglect of, 163-164
  personal relationships with,
    167-169
Patient advocacy, 178-179, 180
Patient history, 93
Patient incidents, reporting of. *See*
    Incident reports.
Patient rapport, 20
Patient records. *See* Medical records.
Patient rights
  interpretation of, 180
  statement of, 179
Patient's Self-Determination Act, 23
Peremptory challenges, 209
Personal notes, 80
Personal relationships, with patients,
    167-169
Physical examination, 93-95
  documentation of, 96
Physician misconduct, reporting of,
    181-183
Physician orders. *See also* Drug orders.
  changes in, 19
  clarification of, 19
  implementation of, 19, 104, 105
  independent nursing actions and,
    96-97
  modification of, 96-97
Plaintiff, 203
Policies and procedures
  compliance with, 23
  deviation from, 132-133
  for documentation, 77, 84, 87
  for drug administration, 40
  keeping current with, 139
  manuals of, 131-132, 139
  standards of care and, 131-133. *See*
    also Standards of care.
  updating of, 23
Policy defense, 29
Postanesthesia care unit, legal issues
    for, 97-101
Practicing medicine without a license,
    20, 45, 101. *See also* Scope of
    practice.

Premises liability, 109-114
Prescription drug, legal definition of, 45
Pretrial detainees, legal rights of, 66-70, 71-72
Prima facie negligence, 107
Privacy Act of 1974, 144-145
Privacy rights, 5, 141-158. *See also* Confidentiality.
  defamation and, 59
  Health Insurance Portability and Accountability Act and, 145-152
  protection of, 156
  state law and, 144
Privacy Rule, 145-152
  authorization under, 149-151
  consent under, 149, 151
  Internet and, 151-152
  minimum necessary disclosures under, 151
  notice under, 151
  persons subject to, 150
  purpose of, 150
Privileged communication, 61
  attorney-client, 206
    incident reports and, 82-83
  nurse-patient, 143-144
  physician-patient, 145
Procedures
  administrative. *See* Policies and procedures.
  therapeutic or diagnostic
    assisting with, 22
    familiarity with, 22, 23
Professional boundaries, 167-169
Professional misconduct, 167-169
  reporting of, 181-184
Proximate cause, 10, 93, 102-103, 110
Psychiatric nursing, liability in, 9
Psychological abuse, 162
Public's right to know, privacy rights and, 158
Punitive damages, 28

R

Reasonably prudent nurse standard, 18, 98-100, 130-131. *See also* Standards of care.
Rebuttable presumption of negligence, 22, 74
Records. *See* Medical records.

Refusal of treatment, documentation of, 85
Rehabilitation Act of 1973, 156
Reporting
  of abuse and neglect, 61-62, 157
  contact notification and, 154
  of human immunodeficiency virus or acquired immunodeficiency syndrome, 153
  incident reports and, 81-83, 136-139
  of medically significant information, 54-55, 80-81
  of negligence, 55-56
  of nurse misconduct, 181, 185-186, 187
  privacy rights and, 156-158
  qualified privilege and, 61
  requirements for, 157-158
    for National Practitioner Data Bank, 2-3
  of staff incompetence or misconduct, 181-182
  of substance abuse, 174, 185-186, 187
  of understaffing, 201
Reservation-of-rights letter, 31-32
Res ipsa loquitur, 10-12, 113
Respondeat superior, 6-7, 109
  agency nurses and, 134-135
  delegation and, 18-19
  insurance coverage and, 30-32
  medication errors and, 37
Restraint, 115-119, 120-121, 162, 163, 170-171
  documentation of, 22, 171
  in nursing homes, 170-171
Right-of-conscience laws, 39
Rights, definition of, 176
Right-to-die laws, 164-165
Right-to-know laws, privacy rights and, 156-158
Risk, assumption of, 13
Risk managers, incident reports for, 21-22

S

Safety precautions, 23-24
  actual or constructive notice and, 110-111
  for disease transmission, 119
  for equipment, 23-24, 112-114, 120
  for falls, 111-112
  for restraints, 115-119, 120-121

Scope of practice
  for agency nurses, 135-136
  floating and, 192-195
  medication administration and, 41,
      44, 45
  practicing medicine without a
      license and, 20, 45, 101
  in special care units, 98, 99, 100-101
Screening panels, malpractice, 29-30
Seclusion, 162, 163, 171
Settlement, out-of-court, 28, 208
Sexual abuse, 61-62, 157, 162
Sexual misconduct, 162, 167-169
Short staffing. *See* Understaffing.
Side rails
  falls and, 111-112
  as restraints, 117
Single-limits policy, 24
Slander, 5, 57-60
  qualified privilege and, 61
  whistle-blowing and, 183
Special care units, legal issues for,
      97-101
Special damages, 28
Specialty standards, 125
Staff incompetence or misconduct,
      reporting of, 179-184
Staffing issues, 188-201
  agency nurses and, 133-136
  breach of contract as, 195-196
  case studies of, 188-201
  examples of, 191-192
  floating as, 192-195
  mandatory overtime as, 196-197
  nurse-patient ratio as, 190
  nursing shortage and, 190
  understaffing as, 190-201. *See also*
      Understaffing.
Standards of care, 6, 124-140
  for accident prevention, 119
  adherence to, 139-140
  for agency nurses, 133-136
  of American Nurses Association,
      125, 126-130
  for assessment, 88
  case studies involving, 123-124
  deviation from, 132-133
  documentation and, 73-74, 77, 87
  evolution of, 88, 125
  of Joint Commission on Accredita-
      tion of Healthcare Organiza-
      tions, 125
  legal significance of, 130-131

Standards of care *(continued)*
  local versus national, 125-130, 131
  minimal, 125
  negligence and, 74
  policies and procedures and,
      131-133. *See also* Policies and
      procedures.
  reasonably prudent nurse standard
      and, 18, 98-100, 130-131
  sources of, 102
  in special care units, 98
  specialty, 125
Standards of Nursing Practice, 77
Standing orders
  nursing, 132
  physician. *See* Physician orders.
Statute of limitations, 6, 12-17
  actual or constructive notice
      and, 16
  application of, 14-16
  constructive continuing treatment
      rule and, 15
  controlling, 12-14
  as defense, 16
  definition of, 12
  discovery rule and, 15
  extension of, 17
  for mentally incompetent patients,
      16
  for minors, 16
  proof of fraud and, 16
  purpose of, 12
  termination-of-treatment rule and,
      14-15
  tolling of, 16
Statutory law, 144
Stress management, 169-170
Subjective versus objective charting,
      86
Subpoena, 148
Subrogation, 27
Substance abuse, by nurses, 174,
      184-187
Sudden emergency exception, 198
Suicide
  assisted, 166-167
  prevention of, 114-115, 120, 121
  risk assessment for, documentation
      of, 66-70, 71-72, 79, 85
Summary judgment, 67
  partial, 113

T

Temporary staff. *See* Agency nurses; Staffing issues.
Terminal care
  advance directives in, 23, 163, 167
  assisted suicide in, 166-167
  criminal liability in, 164-167
    prevention of, 170-171
  documentation of, 171
  double-effect doctrine in, 165, 166
  euthanasia in, 160-161
  living wills and, 167
  standing orders in, 167
  wills and, 167
Termination, for refusal to float, 193-195
Termination-of-treatment rule, 14-15
Test results, review of, 95
Therapy. *See* Treatment.
Threats, duty to warn of, 157
Tort, 4
  definition of, 4
  intentional, 4, 5
  unintentional, 4, 5. *See also* Negligence.
Tranquilizers, 117, 162, 163, 171
Treatment
  assisting with, 22
  failure of, communication of, 54-55
  familiarity with, 22, 23
  inadequate, reporting of, 55-56
  termination of, 14-15, 160-161, 164-167
Triage, 97
Trial. *See also* Litigation.
  cross-examination in, 213-214
  direct examination in, 213-214
  expert witnesses in, 28, 212-213
  proper demeanor in, 209-213
  steps in, 210-211
  testimony in, 209-213
  timeline for, 209-213

U

Understaffing, 190-192. *See also* Staffing issues.
  agency nurses and, 133-136
  chronic, 198-201
  collective action against, 199-201
  coping with, 198-201
  defenses for, 197-198
  floating and, 192-195

Understaffing *(continued)*
  Joint Commission on Accreditation of Healthcare Organizations rules for, 201
  liability for, 197-198
  mandatory overtime and, 196-197
  reporting of, 201
Unemployment compensation, 43
Unfair labor practice, 201
Uniform Business Records Act, 17-18
Unintentional tort, 4, 5. *See also* Negligence.
Unions, understaffing and, 199-201
Unsafe conditions, notice of, 110-111

V

Values, definition of, 176
Verbal drug orders, documentation of, 41-42
Vicarious liability, 9
Violence, duty to warn and, 157

WXYZ

Whistle-blowing, 179-184, 187
Willful conduct, 43
Wills
  advice on, 167
  living, 23, 163, 167
Witness
  cross-examination of, 67, 213-214
  deposition of, 67, 113, 206, 208-209
  direct examination of, 213-214
  expert, 28
    nurse as, 212-213
Witnessing
  of advance directives, 23
  of documents, 20
Workers' compensation, privilege doctrine and, 145